Interpreting Convergence in the European Union

Interpreting Convergence in the European Union

Patterns of Collective Action, Social Learning and Europeanization

Christos J. Paraskevopoulos

Foreword by Robert Leonardi

First published 2001 by
PALGRAVE
Houndmills, Basingstoke, Hampshire RG21 6XS and
175 Fifth Avenue, New York, N. Y. 10010
Companies and representatives throughout the world

PALGRAVE is the new global academic imprint of
St. Martin's Press LLC Scholarly and Reference Division and
Palgrave Publishers Ltd (formerly Macmillan Press Ltd).

ISBN 0–333–92188–7

This book is printed on paper suitable for recycling and
made from fully managed and sustained forest sources.

A catalogue record for this book is available
from the British Library.

Library of Congress Cataloging-in-Publication Data
Paraskevopoulos, Christos J., 1958–
    Interpreting convergence in the European Union : patterns
    of collective action, social learning and Europeanization /
    Christos J. Paraskevopoulos.
        p. cm.
    Includes bibliographical references and index.
    ISBN 0–333–92188–7
    1. Aegean Islands (Greece and Turkey)—Politics and government.
    2. European Union countries—Politics and government. 3. Regional
    planning—European Union countries. I. Title.
    JN5016 .P38 2000
    341.242'2—dc21
                                                                00-055674

10 9 8 7 6 5 4 3 2 1
10 09 08 07 06 05 04 03 02 01

Printed and bound in Great Britain by
Antony Rowe Ltd, Chippenham, Wiltshire

To Christina

Contents

List of Tables and Figures   x
Preface   xiv
Foreword   xvi
Abbreviations   xviii
Introduction   xx

1   SOCIAL CAPITAL, INSTITUTIONAL NETWORKS
    AND LEARNING: CONCEPTUALIZING
    GOVERNANCE IN THE ERA OF GLOBALIZATION   1

    1.1 Global challenge and local response   1
    1.2 'Paradigm shift' in regional development:
         re-conceptualizing regional governance   5
    1.3 Social capital, institutional networks and
         learning: the debate   8
    Conclusions   29

2   SOCIAL LEARNING AND ADAPTATION WITHIN
    EUROPEAN REGIONAL POLICY   31

    2.1 European regional policy and Europeanization
         of local systems of governance   31
    2.2 European regional policy and 'traditional'
         integration theory   44
    2.3 Social capital, institutional networks and
         learning in EU regional policy: 'socializing'
         rational choice new institutionalism in
         integration theory   48
    2.4 The structure of the state and local capacity
         for learning   56
    2.5 Social capital, institutional learning and
         European regional policy: the methodology   58
    Conclusions   63

3   GREECE: RESTRUCTURING UNDER PRESSURE OR
    THE RESPONSE TO AN EXTERNAL SHOCK   64

    3.1 State structure and intergovernmental
         relations: from local clientelism to clientelist
         corporatism   64
    3.2 Regional policy in Greece: national and
         European contexts   84
    3.3 Civil society and the cultural schism   90
    Conclusions   93

4   INSTITUTIONAL CAPACITY AND POLICY
    ENVIRONMENT IN THE SOUTHERN AEGEAN
    ISLANDS   95

    4.1 Local characteristics and political climate   95
    4.2 Economic structure, boundedness and
         adaptation   99
    4.3 Local institutional networks and their
         learning capacity   108
    4.4 Social capital and civic culture in the
         Southern Aegean Islands   121
    Conclusions   124

5   INSTITUTIONAL CAPACITY AND POLICY
    ENVIRONMENT IN THE NORTHERN AEGEAN
    ISLANDS   126

    5.1 Local factors and political climate   126
    5.2 Economic structure, boundedness and
         adaptation   130
    5.3 Local institutional networks and their
         learning capacity   135
    5.4 Social capital and civil society in Northern
         Aegean islands   150
    Conclusions   154

6   CATCHING UP BY LEARNING IN EUROPEAN
    STRUCTURAL POLICY: POLICY NETWORKS AND
    ADAPTATION IN THE SOUTHERN AEGEAN ISLANDS   156

    6.1 From the IMP to the MOPs   156
    6.2 Planning and implementing the CSF (MOP 1989–93)   159

    6.3 Institution-building, policy networks and
         adaptation   171
    Conclusions   186

7   NEITHER LEARNING NOR LEADERSHIP: POLICY
    NETWORKS AND STATE-DRIVEN ADAPTATION IN
    THE NORTHERN AEGEAN ISLANDS   **188**

    7.1 Planning and implementing the IMP in the
         Northern Aegean   188
    7.2 The effectiveness gap in implementing the
         first CSF (MOP 1989–93)   190
    7.3 Institution-building, policy networks and
         adaptation   199
    Conclusions   215

8   CONCLUSIONS: SOCIAL CAPITAL, INSTITUTIONAL
    LEARNING AND ADAPTATION WITHIN EUROPEAN
    REGIONAL POLICY. IMPLICATIONS FOR
    INTEGRATION THEORY   **218**

    8.1 National structures, local institutional
         capacity and the European challenge   219
    8.2 Social capital, learning and adaptation: an agenda
         for Europe in the twenty-first century?   224
    8.3 Implications for policy and integration
         theory   234

Notes   238

Appendix: Descriptive Graphs   255

Bibliography   258

Index   273

List of Tables and Figures

Tables

1.1 Networks by Territorial Scope and Dominant Actor   23
2.1 Average Contribution of the Private Sector to the
     CSFs by Country and Objective (1989–93)   43
3.1 Distribution of Functions by Level of Government in
     Greece   73
4.1 Principal Indicators per Region (NUTS II)   99
4.2 Centrality Measures of General Exchange Network in
     the SAI   109
4.3 Centrality Measures of General Exchange Network in
     the Dodecanese Prefecture   114
4.4 Centrality Measures of General Exchange Network in
     the Cyclades Prefecture   119
4.5 SAI Membership of Voluntary Organizations, 1996   123
5.1 NAI Permanent Inhabitants per Foreign Tourist
     Boarding   137
5.2 Centrality Measures of General Exchange Network in
     Northern Aegean Islands   138
5.3 Centrality Measures of General Exchange Network in
     the Lesbos Prefecture   142
5.4 Centrality Measures of General Exchange Network in
     the Chios Prefecture   146
5.5 Centrality Measures of General Exchange Network in
     the Samos Prefecture   149
5.6 NAI Membership of Voluntary Organizations, 1996   153
6.1 Funding of the First CSF (1989–93) MOPs in Greek
     Regions   163
6.2 SAI: Groups of Islands According to Level of
     Development   164
6.3 Southern Aegean Regional Partnership for Monitoring
     the MOP (1989–93)   172
6.4 SAI: Centrality Measures of General Exchange and
     Policy Networks   174
6.5 Community Initiatives and Transnational Networks
     in Dodecanese   178

6.6 Dodecanese Prefecture: Centrality Measures of General
Exchange and Policy Networks   179
6.7 Cyclades Prefecture: Centrality Measures of General
Exchange and Policy Networks   184
7.1 Northern Aegean Regional Partnership for Monitoring
the MOP (1989–93)   201
7.2 NAI: Centrality Measures of General Exchange and
Policy Networks   202
7.3 Lesbos Prefecture: Centrality Measures of General
Exchange and Policy Networks   205
7.4 Chios Prefecture: Centrality Measures of General
Exchange and Policy Networks   210
7.5 Samos Prefecture: Centrality Measures of General
Exchange and Policy Networks   214
8.1 Indicators of Learning Capacity in SAI and NAI   226
8.2 Institutional Networks by Type in SAI and NAI
regions   233

Figures

2.1 Learning and Adaptation in Multi-Level Governance
Networks   54
3.1 Intergovernmental Relations in Greece Prior to the
Last (1994) Reform   72
3.2 Intergovernmental Relations in Greece after the 1994
Reform   75
3.3 Regional Planning and Centre–Periphery Relations in
Greece   88
4.1 Average Annual Change of GDP in Greece, Southern
Aegean and Northern Aegean, 1970-91   100
4.2 Per Capita GDP Index for Greece, Southern Aegean
and Northern Aegean, 1970, 1981 and 1991   101
4.3 Welfare Indicators for Greece, Southern Aegean and
Northern Aegean   102
4.4 Regional Distribution of Foreign Tourist B & B in Hotel
Units (1991)   103
4.5 SAI Regional GDP by Sector of Production (1994)   104
4.6 Employment by Sector of Production in Dodecanese   105
4.7 Cyclades Prefecture: Agriculture and Tourism in the
GDP   107
4.8 Institutional Networks in SAI Region   110

4.9   Structural Equivalence of Network Actors in
      Dodecanese   115
4.10 Institutional Networks in Dodecanese   116
4.11 Structural Equivalence of Network Actors in
      Cyclades   120
4.12 Institutional Networks in Cyclades   121
4.13 Membership of Voluntary Organizations by Category:
      Southern and Northern Aegean   122
5.1   NAI Regional GDP by Sector of Production (1994)   132
5.2   Defence Dependence of Greek Regions (NUTS II)   133
5.3   Lesbos Prefecture: Share of Agriculture in GDP   134
5.4   Samos Prefecture: Employment by Sector of
      Production   135
5.5   Chios GDP by Sector of Production (1994)   136
5.6   Institutional Networks in the NAI Region   139
5.7   Structural Equivalence of Network Actors in Lesbos   143
5.8   Institutional Network in Lesbos   144
5.9   Structural Equivalence of Network Actors in Chios   147
5.10 Institutional Network in Chios   148
5.11 Structural Equivalence of Network Actors in Samos   151
5.12 Institutional Network in Samos   151
6.1   Aegean Islands IMP: Degree of Completion
      (31 December 1993)   157
6.2   Structure of the Aegean Islands MOPs (1989–93)
      per sub-programme   160
6.3   SAI MOP (1989–93): Distribution of Funds per Sector
      of Infrastructure   161
6.4   Aegean Islands Regions: Absorption Coefficients
      (CSF 1989–93)   162
6.5   SAI: Absorption Capacity per Group of Islands   165
6.6   SAI MOP (1989–93): Share of Prefectures in the
      Sub-programmes   166
6.7   SAI MOP (1989–93): Absorption/Commitments
      Coefficients   167
6.8   SAI MOP (1989–93): ERDF Sub-programme Absorption
      Rates   168
6.9   SAI MOP (1989–93): Local Government Sub-
      programme Absorption Rates   169
6.10 Policy Network in SAI   175
6.11 Structural Equivalence of Policy Network Actors in
      Dodecanese   180

6.12   Policy Network in Dodecanese   181
6.13   Structural Equivalence of Policy Network Actors in
       Cyclades   185
6.14   Policy Network in Cyclades   186
7.1   NAI MOP (1989–93): Distribution of Funds per Sector
       of Infrastructure   191
7.2   NAI MOP (1989–93): Structure per Sub-programme   192
7.3   NAI MOP (1989–93): Absorption Rate per Sub-
       programme   193
7.4   NAI MOP (1989–93): Share of the Prefectures in Sub-
       programmes   195
7.5   NAI MOP (1989–93): ERDF Sub-programme
       Absorption Rates   196
7.6   NAI MOP (1989–93): Local Government Sub-
       programme Absorption Rates   197
7.7   Policy Network in the NAI   203
7.8   Structural Equivalence of Policy Network Actors in
       Lesbos   207
7.9   Policy Network in Lesbos   208
7.10   Structural Equivalence of Policy Network Actors in
       Chios   212
7.11   Policy Network in Chios   213
7.12   Structural Equivalence of Policy Network Actors in
       Samos   216
7.13   Policy Network in Samos   216

Descriptive Graphs

A.1   Social Capital and Exchange Networks   255
A.2   Exchange Networks and Economic Performance   255
A.3   Social Capital and Policy Networks   256
A.4   Policy Networks and Economic Performance   256
A.5   Social Capital and Economic Performance   257
A.6   Policy Networks and Absorption Capacity   257

Preface

This book draws on my Ph.D thesis completed in the Government Department at the London School of Economics and Political Science (LSE). The book introduces the notion of collective action as a prerequisite for achieving convergence and cohesion, and hence for facilitating the processes of social learning and integration in the European Union (EU). Within this framework, institutional networks and social capital play a crucial role, by influencing actors' preferences and shaping institutional (inter-organizational) interactions through the processes of political exchange and socialization, and thus constituting crucial conceptual tools that determine the learning capacity of the national and subnational systems of governance. Although the main focus of the book is on the policy-making process and governance structures in the EU regional policy environment, both its core theoretical hypotheses and the conclusions drawn from empirical research may be applicable to almost all areas of public policy-making in the European Union. The most important attribute of this book is that it adopts a political science approach to the study of European integration, using the relevant theoretical and analytical tools of public policy-making and politics rather than those of international relations.

This idea about the necessity for a shift in EU studies from IR great theories to political science conceptual tools first came to me in 1994. Then, while I was studying for an M.Sc. in European Studies at the LSE, I began to realize the limits of the 'dominant' theories of integration, namely 'Neo-functionalism' and 'Intergovernmentalism', to capture the complexities of an emerging political system such as that of the EU. My intuition was leading me to the assumption that it would be extremely difficult to approach the day-to-day policy-making functions of a political system without the analytical tools of government and political science, namely without shedding light on crucial questions such as: how are actors' preferences formed and shaped; what is the role of institutions in the process; and how and under what conditions do preferences and institutions lead to specific policy outcomes? It was this theoretical 'vacuum' that led me gradually to approach – in a parallel way with other scholars as I realized later (S. Bulmer, 1994) – the new institutionalist school of thought in political science, which gave me the conceptual tools to investigate my theoretical hypotheses about the role of 'collective action problems' in public policy-making and subsequently in the integration process in the European Union. This book is my answer to the question of how these 'collective action problems' could be resolved.

I hope that this book may be useful to both academics and policy-makers. First, it can be used as a teaching tool on EU policy-making in general and EU regional policy in particular. Second, it may be of interest for those involved in political science research on the EU, particularly in the field of comparative public policy. Finally, this book may be a source of new ideas for policy-makers at both the national and subnational levels of government.

This book would not have been possible without the encouragement and support of friends and colleagues. I would like to express my gratitude to all those who have helped and supported me during this long journey. I am indebted to my supervisor, Dr. Robert Leonardi. He has supported me both morally and technically, by providing me with all the necessary infrastructure in research facilities, by encouraging me to continue when things felt bleak, and, finally, by urging me on when routine threatened to weaken my interest. I am also indebted to my advisor, Professor G. W. Jones, who has patiently read and reread numerous chapters and was always keen to discuss any subject, to encourage me to develop my ideas and to build up a real thesis on which this book is based.

I owe a special thanks to: Shari Garmise, whose suggestions and assistance with networks and information technology have been invaluable; Charlie Jeffery for all his help and encouragement; D. N. Chryssochoou, who, beyond being a close friend, has been a provider of enduring support at very crucial moments of this odyssey; Achilleas Mitsos for all his support during the fieldwork in Brussels; and Professor N. Mouzelis, who has always been available to read my work and answer questions.

Finally, I thank wholeheartedly the numerous people who have helped me in a wide variety of ways: Professor Michael Keating and all the participants of the Oslo ECPR-Workshop (1996) for their useful comments and suggestions on parts of my work; Professor Paul Whiteley and all the participants of the Bern ECPR-Workshop (1997); Susanne Schmidt, Mark Aspinwall and the participants of the Warwick ECPR-Workshop (1998); Professors P. Getimis, N. Konsolas and P. Kazakos, Dr E. Plaskovitis, and in the European Commission Dr M. Camchis and P. Spyrou (DG XVI).

Christos J. Paraskevopoulos

Foreword

This volume by Christos Paraskevopoulos represents a considerable innovation in the literature on the socio-economic convergence of underdeveloped regions in the European Union by demonstrating that difficult concepts can be operationalized in an interesting way in order to shed light on the impact of European policies in concrete cases. He takes two geographically similar regions in the same country receiving approximately the same amount in Structural Funds and operating under the same rules but where – since the beginning of the European Union's cohesion policy in 1989 – the two regions have converged toward the European mean at different speeds. The central hypothesis of the volume is that their difference in speed is attributable to the two regions' different patrimony in terms of the thickness of their institutional networks and the strength of social capital in facilitating the collective action of individuals located within the networks. The importance of the book is that it provides evidence of the interplay between social capital and prospects for economic development in a context that is relatively new. No one else has tried to experiment with the notion of social capital in the context of Greece, a country where it is commonly assumed that the civil society is weak and local governing institutions are fragmented and intermediate levels of government are in their infancy and thus are no match for the dominant hierarchical clienteles. Previous research on political interactions in Greece has pointed out the role played by clienteles in managing links between the national and peripheral areas in the country.

In operating a cohesion policy under such conditions one would expect to find that the primary links between the local communities and the European and national levels to be overwhelmingly influenced by clienteles and vertical interactions governed by formal institutions. This is not what Paraskevopoulos has found in the two island groups. One set of islands in the southern Aegean is characterized by: a quick adoption to the rules and procedures of the Structural Funds, an improvement of the structure of policy networks for purposes of extracting the full growth potential from the investments provided by the Funds, and an ability to overcome the self-imposed restrictions of the formal Greek state apparatus. The other set of islands in the northern Aegean does not demonstrate these same abilities due to, as Paraskevopoulos argues, the thinner and more vertically oriented nature of the network structure and the presence of lower levels of social capital.

Such a finding is of importance to both the conceptualization and implementation of cohesion policies within the European Union. What it suggests is that the European Union in pursuing its cohesion policies should focus not only on the provision of the 'harder' economic components of development strategies – such as capital for the start-up and expansion of firms, vocational education to raise the skill levels of workers, infrastructure to facilitate the circulation of goods, the opening up of markets and reducing the costs of transactions – but it must also concentrate on those 'softer' social components which help to determine whether the initial investment provided by the Structural Funds will, in fact, be put to full use in the local context. The evidence provided by Paraskevopoulos in Greece and Putnam, Leonardi and Nanetti in Italy suggests that the presence of social capital and thick interpersonal networks helps to favour a better and quicker response on the part of local communities to the opportunities for development presented by the EU's cohesion policies.

The study conducted by Paraskevopoulos also speaks to the broader concern associated with investment policies to spur socio-economic development in less developed areas inside and outside of the European Union. The provision of investments is by itself a necessary but not sufficient condition for the promotion of robust and rapid development. A necessary condition for such an outcome is the presence of social capital and thick associational networks capable of organizing collective action for the achievement of common goods for all of society. Development can be construed as a common good. And this is especially the case in locations where the major form of economic activity is tied to mass tourism managed on a diffused basis. The tourism industry that has developed in the southern Aegean is not tied to large, capital intensive enterprises that exclude the local inhabitants from becoming stake holders and active participants in the service activities – bars, restaurants, hotels, room rentals, camping facilities, etc. – which abound in Greek tourist areas. But what happens in other contexts where the local social capital endowments are not so favourable and where access to an engine for diffused socio-economic growth is not present?

ROBERT LEONARDI

Abbreviations

ASCAME	Union of Mediterranean Chambers of Commerce
CAP	Common Agricultural Policy
CEC	Commission of the European Communities
CI	Community Initiative
CIP	Community Interest Programmes
CoR	Committee of Regions
CSF	Community Support Framework
DG	Directorates-General
DG V	Directorate-General for Employment, Industrial Relations and Social Affairs
DG XVI	Directorate-General for Regional Policies and Cohesion
DG XXIII	Directorate-General for Enterprise Policy, Distributive Trade, Tourism and Cooperatives
EAGGF	European Agricultural Guidance and Guarantee Fund
EC	European Community
ECJ	European Court of Justice
ECOFIN	Council of Economic and Financial Ministers
ECU	European Currency Unit
EEA	European Economic Area
EEC	European Economic Community
EIB	European Investment Bank
EMU	Economic and Monetary Union
EP	European Parliament
ERDF	European Regional Development Fund
ESC	Economic and Social Committee
ESF	European Social Fund
EU	European Union
EURISLES	European Islands System of Links and Exchanges
EUROCHAMBRES	European Chambers of Commerce and Industry
EUROSTAT	Statistical Service of the EU
FIFG	Financial Instrument for Fisheries Guidance
GDP	Gross Domestic Product
GFCF	Gross Fixed Capital Formation
GNP	Gross National Product

IMP	Integrated Mediterranean Programme
KEPE	National Centre for Planning and Economic Research
KKE	Communist Party of Greece
KKEes	Communist Party of the Interior
MOP	Multi-fund Operational Programme
NAI	North Aegean Islands
ND	New Democracy Party
NPCI	National Programmes for Community Interest
NSSG	National Statistical Service of Greece
NUTS	Nomenclature of Statistical Territorial Units
OP	Operational Programme
PASOK	Panhellenic Socialist Movement
PPS	Purchasing Power Standard
RDA	Regional Development Agency
RDP	Regional Development Plan
ROP	Regional Operational Programme
SAI	South Aegean Islands
SEA	Single European Act
SEM	Single European Market
SMEs	Small and Medium-size Enterprises
SNA	Social Network Analysis
TEU	Treaty on European Union
VAT	Value Added Tax

Introduction

The technological, economic and political changes that have led to the great transformations we have experienced since the 1970s, marked by the emergence of globalized information and economic activities, have emphasized the role of the learning institutional infrastructure at each level of governance, as a prerequisite for managing uncertainty and risk inherent in modern institutional settings. Thus, notions of learning and adaptation are being increasingly debated in a wide range of social sciences, from international relations and political science to regional development. In all these contexts learning implies the process by which actors acquire new interests and identities and form their preferences through 'structure–actor' interactions, thus adapting their behaviour to the changing environment. Subsequently, the variables that may determine the capacity for learning and adaptation to the EU have emerged as a crucial issue in a wide range of social sciences as well.

This book contributes to this debate by introducing new ideas about learning and adaptation in the European policy-making environment in general and in European regional policy in particular. It demonstrates that, notwithstanding the crucial role of national or international factors in facilitating or inhibiting the potential of regional systems of governance within the European environment, the processes of adaptation, adjustment and hence convergence and socio-economic cohesion within the EU depend crucially on the learning capacity of the local institutional infrastructure, whereby institutional relationships and policies adapt to meet changing conditions.

The central hypothesis is that the capacity of the local institutional infrastructure for learning and adaptation to the European environment depends on the presence both of thick institutional networks that cross the public–private divide, combining multiple resources, and social capital that facilitates collective action among the actors within the networks. Thus social capital and institutional networks constitute key components of learning and adaptation processes, by facilitating collective action among actors and shaping local interactions through political exchange and socialization. Since, however, the Europeanization of public policy in general and of regional policy in particular constitutes a longstanding challenge to the administrative structures of centralized member-states, it is viewed as a positive external shock for promoting institution-building, learning and policy-making innovation at regional and local levels. Furthermore, given that the structure of a state plays an important role in determining the learning and adaptation capacity of the local institutional infrastructure, it should be taken into account in evaluating that capacity.

The research compares the response of two regions of Greece (Southern and Northern Aegean Islands) – similar in physical resources and financial support provided by the national and European regional policy – to the challenges of Europeanization.

The book comprises eight chapters. Chapter 1 establishes the general theoretical framework of the book, linking social capital, institutional networks and learning within the new conception of governance in the era of globalization. Chapter 2 discusses the theoretical aspects of European regional policy and integration theory, defines learning, adaptation and Europeanization of regional systems of governance and subsequently establishes the hypothesis that social capital and a specific type of institutional network are prerequisites for learning and adaptation in the field of European regional policy. Finally, it outlines the methodology of the research study and identifies specific criteria for measuring the learning capacity. Chapter 3 presents the structural and cultural characteristics of the Greek socio-political system, as well as the main aspects of the transformation of national regional policy within the European context. Chapters 4 and 5 map the institutional infrastructure in both regions, distinguishing their political, economic, institutional and cultural features. Chapters 6 and 7 examine the processes of institutional and policy adaptation to the European policy-making environment in structural policy in both regions and evaluate their learning capacity. Finally, chapter 8 compares the two cases and draws general conclusions regarding the role of social capital and institutional networks in facilitating the processes of learning, adaptation and Europeanization, and extracts the implications for European regional policy and integration theory.

C. J. P.

1
Social Capital, Institutional Networks and Learning: Conceptualizing Governance in the Era of Globalization

Introduction

This chapter establishes the general theoretical framework of the book. The first section discusses the implications of the technological, economic and political changes that led to globalization for the transformation of production, the redefinition of the notion of 'local', and, subsequently, for the reformulation of regional policies. The second section explores the impact of these changes on the conceptualization of local governance, emphasizing the role of endogenous social, political and economic resources. Finally, the third section establishes the linkages between the main theoretical concepts of the book, that is social capital, institutional networks and learning.

Global challenge and local response

There is a close relationship between the theories of regional development elaborated in the last thirty years, the phases in the development process of European countries, and the strategies that have been adopted in policies aimed at reducing regional disparities (Molle and Cappellin 1988). Traditional regional development theories and policies were consistent with the characteristics of the post-war period until the early 1970s: these included the predominance of the Fordist model of production,[1] the rapid expansion of European economies and the strategic role of investment in capital-intensive sectors (Cappellin, 1992). One of the key issues in understanding the basic arguments of these theories is overcoming the basic assumptions of neoclassical economic models (perfect competition, full employment, constant returns to scale and perfect mobility of factors of production), and concentrating on various forms of market failure (Tsoukalis, 1993: 229). Therefore, the approaches that have been advanced to explain the process of economic convergence in nation-state systems point to state intervention, whether more or less, as a countervailing factor to market failures, that stimulate growth over time. Within this framework, the role of the state is crucial in formulating regional development strategies, which therefore tend to have a top-down structure. Thus, by the 1960s the region had become a secondary locus of economic activity, while regional and local governments were subordinate agencies in national social welfare administrations (Sabel, 1994a: 102).

The main theoretical framework used in the development of regional policies within nation-states and at European level (see Chapter 2) is *cumulative causation* theory (Myrdal, 1957), based on a criticism of the comparative advantage model in international trade (Holland, 1976; Robson, 1987). The major argument is that market forces cannot bring about an equal redistribution of factors of production or income and consequently there are no strong reasons to expect the elimination of regional problems through the free interplay of market forces. Therefore, initial differences in productivity and economic development can lead to circular and cumulative causation and thus growing polarization between different regions. The logic of *backwash* effects implies that the production factors – capital, skilled labour, entrepreneurship, technology – move towards the core areas. On the other hand, *spread* effects may arise from an increased demand for imports and from diseconomies of location associated with over-congestion in the rapidly growing centres. The relative importance of *backwash* and *spread* effects determines the evolution of regional disparities. A similar, rather pessimistic, view has been adopted by the Marxist and neo-Marxist schools of thought, emphasizing the systemic logic of regional disparities (Holland, 1976; 1980).

Under these conditions, the emphasis on economies of scale and the creation of large industrial enterprises as a means to promote growth (Hamilton, 1986; Apter, 1987) has constituted an intrinsic element of regional development policies adopted by most European countries during the post-Second World War period. In the same vein, other countries, adopting the *growth-pole* approach[2] (Perroux, 1955), emphasized the role of planned and concentrated growth of specific development poles (urbanized, metropolitan areas), in reducing centre–periphery disparities.

Taken as a whole, these theoretical approaches are mainly focused on economic factors as the determinants of regional disparities and have underestimated the role of the endogenous dynamics in the development process. Along with the *core–periphery* theories (Tarrow, 1977; Rokkan and Urwin, 1983), they view the periphery as characterized by a) physical distance from the centre; b) dependence on the centre for its livelihood and well-being; and c) an inferior allocation of economic, political and cultural resources (Tarrow, 1977: 15–38). The variation, however, in the geography of regional disparities (that is regions of Third Italy and Spain) raises the issue of the role played by crucial non-economic factors, such as social, cultural and political (institutional infrastructure) resources, in the development process.

Indeed, the economic, technological and political changes that have occurred since the early 1970s led to the transformation of production, and particularly the move from mass production towards the 'flexible specialization' paradigm,[3] which marked the emergence of the subnational institutional infrastructure as a crucial parameter in the development process. This trend, which has been favoured by increased international competition, and the internationalization, fragmentation and volatility of the markets is seen as a key factor encouraging the emergence of the region as an integrated unit of production and as a key locus of socio-economic governance. Additionally, the increasing importance of quick adaptation to changing market demand and subsequently the need for promoting viable small-scale production (economies of scope instead of economies of scale) have emphasized the role of intra-regional institutional interactions and socio-cultural factors in the development process (Sabel, 1994a, b; Hirst and Zeitlin, 1992; Storper, 1995; Piore and Sabel, 1984). Two major types of institutional framework have been identified for achieving flexibility: either industrial districts of horizontally integrated and spatially concentrated small and medium-sized firms, or large decentralized companies. This *'double convergence'* (Sabel, 1994a) of small and large structures, however, is not associated exclusively with the industrial districts-related pattern of regional development, but rather it should be seen as an indication of a more general trend, involving decentralized organizational structures and horizontal cooperative networks that characterize regional economic and political systems in a wide range of development sectors, such as tourism (Stokowski, 1994). Thus, the emergence of regions should be seen as a response to the economic and technological changes of the 1970s, intrinsic characteristics of which are, on the one hand, the progressive crisis of the Fordist pattern of production and the Keynesian welfare state and, on the other, the increasing role of flexible production methods.

Yet, the emergence of regions and localities should be understood within the context of a changing, globalizing political economy, which implies:

i)   the global centralization of the financial system and the resulting dominance of finance over production;

ii)   the transnationalization of technology and the increasing speed of redundancy of new technology;

iii) the importance of knowledge and expertise as factors of production;

iv)   the rise of global oligopolies;

v)   the rise of transnational economic diplomacy;

vi)   the globalization of communication and immigration flows leading to the rise of global culture and the delinking of identities and symbols from territory; and

vii) as a result of all the above, the development of global geographies (Amin and Thrift, 1994: 2–4).

The increasing intensity of the globalization of economic activities and information, however, does not necessarily imply a homogeneity of preferences in the framework of a global village, but rather stresses the existence of local specificities. Thus, the processes of globalization and localization coexist in the so-called *'global–local interplay'* (Dunford and Kafkalas, 1992: 3–38). The local is embedded in the global and, hence, the degree to which it can mediate this relationship shapes its ability to define its economic development trajectory. These seemingly contradictory movements are seen as having led to the weakening of traditional nation-states and the erosion of their autonomy. Thus, the *'hollowing out'* of the state may be interpreted as a result of its weakened ability to regulate effectively the economy within its own borders because of the internationalization of economic processes: 'this loss of autonomy creates in turn both the need for supranational coordination and the space for subnational resurgence' (Jessop, 1994: 264). Consequently, the response of most of the traditional European nation-states, which, overwhelmed by the globalization of economic relationships as well as of the risks of financing the welfare state, have adopted strategies of devolution and decentralization, should be attributed to this trend (Leonardi and Garmise, 1993).

Furthermore, greater decentralization and deconcentration may be interpreted as an adaptation to the increased importance of the local sphere in everyday life. R. Watts notes:

> 'what we are witnessing today is a twofold process in which, on the one hand, there is a pressure throughout the world for larger political units capable of promoting economic development, improved security, rising standards of living, influence in an era of ever-growing world-wide interdependence; on the other hand, there is the search for identity which arises from the desire for smaller, self-governing political units, more responsive to the individual citizen and the desire to give expression to primary group attachments ... which provide the distinctive basis for a community's sense of identity and yearning for self-determination' (1981: 3–4).

Therefore, regionalization[4] and regionalism should be seen as two interdependent and interrelated concepts, given that, while the former is interpreted as a mainly *from above* process, the latter constitutes a movement *from below*.[5] As Harvie has argued, 'regionalization, the chopping-up of problems into manageable areas, has now given way to a subjective and aggressive regionalism' (1994: 4).

'Paradigm shift' in regional development: re-conceptualizing regional governance

The emergence of new patterns of regional development has very often been considered as linked to changes in the mode of organization of production. The shift in the pattern of production, marked by the gradual change of the *'technological trajectory'*[6] from the Fordist model to the flexible specialization paradigm and the re-consolidation of the region as a fundamental basis of economic and social life, has promoted a new approach to regional development, which emphasizes the role of endogenous resources in the development process (Cappellin, 1992: 2). This theoretical interpretation of regional development is based on the assumption that the major factors affecting regional development, such as physical infrastructure, labour, capital and technology are rather immobile. Therefore, regional policy should not aim at the mobility of factors of production, as suggested by traditional theories, but at: a) full employment and b) greater productivity of local resources (Cappellin, 1992: 3). In achieving these goals the endogenous approach emphasizes the role played by small firms, as well as interactive relationships between grassroots groups in the social system and local or regional political institutions. In that sense, it can be seen as a reaction against the Perrouxian growth-pole theory and other theories that have emphasized the role of capital-intensive investments and state institutions in determining development (Leonardi, 1995a: 39).

The endogenous approach has been elaborated by various scholars, and the different contributions emphasize different aspects. Some underline the self-centred characteristics of regional development and the need for regional autonomy. Others emphasize the role of cooperative relations among local actors in the regional economy, to counterbalance the negative impact of automatic market mechanisms. Other contributions analyse the effects of changes in production and transportation technologies on the spatial diffusion of industrial and service activities. Finally, others focus on the role of local factors in the process of innovation–diffusion and on the spatial concentration of high-tech activities (Cappellin, 1992). The end result of these reformulations of the problem of development has been above all a different conceptualization of space and territory. In contrast with the assumptions of the functionalist paradigm, which considered space as simply the place where the effects of the process of development occurred, the endogenous approach pays attention to the territorial dimension of development and to the categories of environment *(milieu)*. Thus, territory is seen as 'the sedimentation of specific and interrelated historical, social and cultural factors in local areas which generate significantly different processes of development due to local specifications' (Garofoli, 1992: 4). Under these considerations the concept of space cannot be interpreted only as the distance between different places and a source of costs for economic agents, but instead as 'the distinguishing feature of territory, that is a strategic factor of development opportunities, a clustering of social relations and the place where local culture and other non-transferable local features are superimposed' (Garofoli, 1992: 4). Moreover, it represents the meeting place of market relationships and social regulation forms, which determine different forms of organization of production and different innovative capacities.

Based on this reformulation of the concepts of territory and space the process of endogenous development underlines the grassroots character and a high degree of autonomy of local development. Thus development should not be seen as a consequence of decentralization processes or processes of industrial relocation, but rather as the outcome of the sprouting of new entrepreneurship and the presence of social, cultural and economic variables that favour the starting up of new economic activities. In that sense development is viewed as a bottom-up process rather than as an outcome of a top-down redistributive function of national government (Cappellin, 1992: 3; Garofoli, 1992: 13). *Development from below* concentrates on factors which influence the adoption of new production processes and product innovation rather than on prices of various production inputs. As Garofoli notes, endogenous development means in effect:

a) the capacity to transform the socio-economic system;
b) the ability to react to external challenges;
c) the promotion of social learning;
d) the ability to introduce specific forms of social regulation at local level which favour the above mentioned points.

Endogenous development is, in other words, the ability to innovate at local level (1992: 7).

As has already been pointed out, the endogenous development approach differentiates itself from traditional theories by emphasizing the importance of the presence of a well-developed institutional infrastructure at regional and local levels, that is 'a series of interlocking institutions, ad hoc structures, relationships and agreements for collective action' (Leonardi, 1995a: 222). One of the main prerequisites of the scheme is the existence of effective regional and local governments. While the role of the private sector is to concentrate on the productive and distribution phases of the economic process, the role of public subnational institutions is to provide the collective goods, such as social services, investment projects and policy planning. Therefore, regional government plays a crucial role in identifying the types or sectors of production where the regional economy has a comparative advantage, in providing the appropriate incentive structure, and in stimulating synergistic[7] effects between the participant actors to maximize effectiveness in the use of resources (Cappellin, 1992: 7; Leonardi, 1995a: 40). On the other hand, the role of local government is to create a social and physical infrastructure (research, vocational training, marketing) that will maximize the external economies of scale for the firms. Thus, regional and local governments become moderators of regional development, within the concept of the region as an institutional or political entrepreneur (Leonardi, 1995a), which implies the region is not only the mediator for the payment of governmental subsidies and transfer payments, but also the initiator of development strategies and participant in the development process.

Thus, through redefinition of the roles of state, civic society and market, governance in the endogenous approach is envisaged as the process by which the national or global environment is mediated by the subnational institutional infrastructure in ways that affect the locality's development potential. Hence, notwithstanding the role of national and international actors, the local institutional infrastructure capacity for learning and adaptation is raised as a crucial parameter of the way in which local economies and societies are embedded in the global environment.

Social capital, institutional networks and learning: the debate

The bottom-up or endogenous approach to regional development has raised the issue of crucial non-economic factors[8] as determinants of the outcome of development policies, emphasizing the impact of territory and local *milieu* (institutional, social, cultural and historical features) on the process of economic development. By providing stable rules and procedures that facilitate the exchange and flow of information, institutions[9] reduce uncertainty and provide the framework for individuals and organizations to achieve and benefit from collective action, thus facilitating economic governance. Economic dynamism or backwardness, on the other hand, is seen as a function of the way in which institutions develop and change, and, implicitly, of the way in which resources and power are distributed both locally and between the local, the national and the global. Therefore, focus on institutional networks alone is insufficient for understanding the complexities of the development process. What is required is institutional networks with learning capacity, that is networks capable of adapting to the changing environment (Garmise, 1995a). In that sense, the learning capacity of the subnational institutional infrastructure constitutes a prerequisite for the formulation of coherent and viable regional development strategies (M. Rhodes, 1995).

The notion of learning has emerged in a wide range of social sciences – from evolutionary economics[10] to political science – as a crucial conceptual tool for explaining adaptation and change of system parameters at both micro and macro levels. In political science, learning as an explanatory variable for major changes (paradigm shifts) in the policy-making process has become a crucial concept for analysing state–society relations and hence for contemporary theories of the state (Hall, 1993). This book focuses on institutional learning as an intermediate-explanatory variable of the successful adaptation of local political and economic systems to the global and European environment through the processes of *political exchange* and *socialization*. The academic debate on the prerequisites for institutional learning and successful adaptation concentrates on a wide range of variables that may affect the learning capacity of the local institutional infrastructure.

The first obvious observation is that learning is crucially influenced by previous policy attempts (Hall, 1993) and dependent on the way in which the system of intra-regional interactions is shaped on a bottom-up basis, that is the way in which the local institutions are networked. However, since institutional learning is a predominantly interactive process, which cannot be simply reduced to a function by which 'the less proactive regions ... learn from the activities of their more dynamic counterparts' (M. Rhodes, 1995: 329), the adequacy of information flows and communication as well as the presence of fora for dialogue among the actors is seen as the second most important factor affecting the learning capacity of the local institutional infrastructure (M. Rhodes, 1995). Thus, by the joint involvement of institutional actors in the processes of *'learning by doing'* and *'learning by past successes and failures'*, institutions can become adaptable for the long term rather than adapted to the specific, current conditions (Garmise, 1995a). Learning in this environment is a function of past policy attempts (and the involved actors' interpretation of their successes and failures), of the capacities of institutions to design new activities, and of the changing ideas and shifting alliances and balance of power among the actors.

Additionally, when multiple organizations (subnational authorities, business and trade associations, universities and other research-related agencies) are involved in combined learning, the ability to share knowledge[11] and understanding requires that the interpretation is mutually consistent. In other words, knowledge is relational and understanding cannot be seen as completely disassociated from the relationships through which it is shared. Hence, 'learning is ... a socially embedded process which cannot be understood without taking into consideration the institutional and cultural context' (Lundvall, 1992: 1). Thus, dialogue and communication – key components of learning – are empowered or inhibited by the socio-political processes that conceptualize human behaviour. Through this process of actor–structure interaction, information exchange and communication, actors interpret knowledge and acquire new knowledge, shape their identities and interests and form their preferences. Finally, since learning is a process of 'waking up and catching up' (Sabel, 1994b:

137) and therefore usually undermines the stability of relations between the transacting actors, institutions (norms, conventions) provide the glue that cements and re-stabilizes the relations among the involved actors.

Moreover, the learning process has implications for the organizational structure of the regional politico-economic system. On the one hand it requires that the organizations involved are flexible enough to make the appropriate structural adjustments for exploiting the benefits of learning. On the other, the learning process is crucially dependent on experts who specialize in specific policy areas (Hall, 1993; Checkel, 1998). Because this combination of flexibility and specialization is best achieved in networked organizations, the network paradigm constitutes the appropriate organizational form for the learning process (Storper, 1995).

In this context, if institutional networks are to promote self-sustaining development, they must be able continually to revise their activities according to both the changing circumstances and the understanding that evolves from shared experiences. Thus dialogue, as an intrinsic element of the learning process, constitutes the framework for defining and redefining common goals and objectives. Networks, on the other hand, as conduits of regional/local rules and practices, must build a consensus on development goals.

Furthermore, since endogenous decision-making requires the presence of sufficient institutional and financial resources at subnational level, the degree of decentralization of the state administrative structure plays an important role in the learning process (Garmise, 1995b; M. Rhodes, 1995). However, existing evidence on intra- and interstate differentiation in the level of institutional learning and adaptation points to the dynamic character of intergovernmental relations, which cannot be simply reduced to a symptom of the state structure (Klausen and Goldsmith, 1997). Hence, the crucial prerequisite for institutional learning and adaptation is certain capacities for collective action at regional and local levels which facilitates the shaping of the system for interaction and coalition-building among key social and economic actors (Garmise, 1995b; Jeffery, 1997; Paraskevopoulos, 1997; 1998b,c). In that sense, both formal and crucial informal institutional arrangements play a decisive role in determining the learning capacity of local systems of governance and their capacity for adapting to changing conditions. The increasing importance of certain capacities for collective action as the crucial prerequisite for institutional learning and adaptation is underlined by the emergence of the network paradigm as an operational element of the institutional infrastructure at all stages of policy-making.

The crucial question, however, refers to the old problem of the origins of structure or culture. Are formal institutions the means to achieve collective action and economic performance, or is their success dependent on the existence of important informal norms that evolve from culture, traditions and social behavioural codes? Empirical evidence suggests the differentiation of social norms is highly correlated with varying levels of institutional and economic performance at any level of governance (Putnam, 1993; Whiteley, 1997). A lively, multi-disciplinary literature has examined, in various ways, the linkages between socio-political structure, institutional learning, and economic performance at the regional level.

Rational actors and dilemmas of collective action

How and why dilemmas of collective action arise within contemporary economic and social structures, and the way in which they could be resolved, constitute the crucial parameters upon which the creation of effective local synergies is dependent and, subsequently, the main issue for modern development strategies based on the bottom-up approach to regional development. The conceptualization of the role of institutions and socio-cultural factors in resolving collective action problems and thus determining the outcome of development policies should be seen as one of its key contributions.

Contemporary research in political science, economic history and economics focuses on the way in which individual rationality could be reconciled with society rationality: that is the reason for the creation of dilemmas of collective action. 'Collective dilemmas arise when choices made by rational individuals lead to outcomes that no one prefers' (Bates, 1988: 387). Game theory has illustrated the essential property of collective dilemmas and the conditions under which rational self-interested individuals can arrive at a Pareto-inferior solution: that is, one that leaves both parties worse off than they would have been had they cooperated (Scharpf, 1991; 1993).

The *tragedy of the commons*, ever since Hardin's challenging article,[12] has been considered classically symbolic of the way in which rationally acting individuals, who use a scarce resource in common, can degrade the environment and eventually destroy the collective resource on which the livelihood of all depends.

In the *prisoner's dilemma* game, the lack of communication between two prisoners makes defection a dominant strategy. Each is told if he alone implicates his partner he will not be punished, but if he remains silent, while his partner confesses, he will be punished severely. If both remained silent, both would be let off lightly, but being unable to communicate, each is better off squealing, no matter what the other does.

Public goods also constitute prisoners' dilemmas. A public good (namely security) can be enjoyed by everyone, regardless of whether he or she contributes to its provision. Under ordinary circumstances, therefore, no one has an incentive to contribute to the public good, causing all to suffer.

In the *logic of collective action* the presumption that the possibility of a benefit for a group would be sufficient to generate collective action to achieve that benefit is challenged: 'unless the number of individuals is quite small, or unless there is coercion or some other special device to make individuals act in their common interest, rational, self-interested individuals will not act to achieve their common or group interests' (Olson, 1971: 2). Olson's argument is based on the assumption that one has little incentive to contribute voluntarily to the provision of a collective good, unless he could be excluded from the benefits of that good, once it is produced.

All these concepts are extremely useful for explaining 'how perfectly rational individuals can produce, under some circumstances, outcomes that are not "rational" when viewed from the perspective of all those involved' (Ostrom, 1990: 6). This does not arise from misanthropy. Even if neither party wishes harm to the other, and even if both are conditionally predisposed to cooperate, they can have no guarantee against reneging, when verifiable and enforceable commitments are absent. As D. Gambetta has pointed out, 'it is necessary not only to trust others before acting cooperatively, but also to believe that one is trusted by others' (1988: 216). The performance of all social institutions from international credit markets to modern national and regional governments, depends on the way in which those dilemmas of collective action can be resolved (Putnam, 1993: 164).

One of the most classic solutions in confronting the dilemmas of collective action is the Hobbesian one of third-party enforcement: that is the imposition of a coercive power to create cooperative solutions. It implies the state should enable its subjects to do what both parties cannot do on their own: trust one another. Such a solution, however, is seen as too expensive. The third-party enforcement 'would involve a neutral party with the ability, costlessly, to be able to measure the attributes of a contract and, costlessly, to enforce agreements ... These are strong conditions that are seldom, if ever, met in the real world'

(North, 1990: 58). On the other hand, impartial enforcement being itself a public good is subject to the basic dilemma of collective action. To solve the problem, the third party must itself be trustworthy, but there is no power to ensure it would not defect: 'put simply, if the state has coercive force, then those who run the state will use that force in their own interest at the expense of the rest of the society' (North, 1990: 59). Therefore, game theory suggests that third-party enforcement does not constitute a stable equilibrium, that is one in which no player has an incentive to change his behaviour.

The crucial question, however, is 'why uncooperative behaviour does not emerge as often as game theory predicts' (Gambetta, 1988: 217). Game theorists generally agree that cooperation is difficult to sustain when the game is not repeated, so the defector cannot be punished in successive rounds, when information on the other players is lacking and there are large numbers of players. When the prisoner's dilemma game is played only once, the dominant strategy for players is to defect. In an iterated prisoner's dilemma game, however, there is no dominant strategy. Axelrod's (1984; 1997) optimistic view about the ability of actors to devise cooperative solutions to problems without the intervention of a coercive power is based on the assumption that the winning strategy under these conditions of repeated play is the strategy of *tit-for-tat*, that is one in which the player responds in kind to the action of other players.[13] Although each of these factors is important, they seem to imply that impersonal cooperation should be rare. Nevertheless, it seems to be common in much of the modern world.

The new institutionalists

From the old debate between the *substantivist* and the *formalist* schools in anthropology[14] flow two broad intellectual streams in the description and explanation of social action in general and of economic action in particular. The first, characteristic of the work of most sociologists, views the actor as socialized and the action as governed by social norms, rules and obligations. Its principal virtues lie in its ability to describe action and institutions in a social context and to explain the way action is shaped, constrained and redirected by the social context. The second intellectual stream, characteristic of the work of most economists, sees the actor as acting independently and wholly out of self-interest, while the basic principle of action is that of maximizing utility. This principle of action has generated the extensive growth of the political philosophy theories of utilitarianism and contractarianism, upon which the rational-choice models in neoclassical economic theory and political science are based (Coleman, 1988: 95–6; Green and Shapiro, 1994). This intellectual divide in the social sciences constitutes the main source for the new institutionalist school of thought in political science, comprising three main analytical approaches: rational choice, historical and sociological (Hall and Taylor, 1996).

Rational-choice new institutionalism in political science, economic history and economics attempts to show 'the conditions under which particular institutions arise and the effects of these institutions on the functioning of the system' (Coleman, 1988: 97) and exhibits a renewed concern with institutions as a means for resolving collective dilemmas (North, 1990; Shepsle, 1989; Scharpf, 1989; Moe, 1990; Williamson, 1975). In particular, rational-choice new institutionalists see in collective dilemmas reasons for the existence of institutions, that is 'forms of hierarchy in which sanctions are employed to make self-interested choices consistent with the social good' (Bates, 1988: 387), or 'the rules of the game in the society – the humanly devised constraints – that shape human interaction' (North, 1990: 3). They seek to conceptualize institutions as external constraints to personal freedom of choice which shape actors' preferences and optimize their behaviour, thus facilitating collective action[15] (Ostrom, 1986; Moe, 1990; Shepsle, 1989). Through this process, the individual actors' rationality-based preferences are structured and equilibrated by institutions. This idea of '*structure-induced equilibrium*', developed by K. Shepsle, points to the direction of 'incorporating institutional features into rational choice approaches' (1989: 137) and views institutions as an intervening variable between actors' preferences and policy outcomes. Thus, institutions are considered as the appropriate tools for structuring the interactions and the exchange relations among the actors, which are based on methodological, individualist calculations of utility maximization.

New institutional economics, in particular, has emphasized the impact of formal institutions (hierarchical firms) on the reduction of transaction costs,[16] on thus enabling agents to overcome problems of opportunism and hence on performing economic functions (Williamson, 1975; North, 1990). Thus, new institutional economics focuses on the origins of efficient institutions that promote the making of contracts, the enforcement of property rights, the removal of production externalities and the provision of public goods, that is mechanisms for reconciling the gap between individual and collective interests. Given, however, that both production externalities and public goods constitute prisoner's dilemmas, rational-choice new institutionalists' basic argument is contractarian in spirit: 'persons facing collective dilemmas might prefer to live in a world in which the freedom to choose is constrained' (Bates, 1988: 397).

Yet, rational-choice new institutionalism leaves open a crucial question: how and why are formal institutions provided? The problem seems to be similar to the solution of the third-party enforcement in the sense that the institutional solution itself constitutes a collective dilemma and, hence, it seems to be subject to the very incentive problems it is supposed to resolve: the demanders of institutions may be unable to secure their supply. To resolve the problem an alternative soft approach to the origins of institutions has been developed: 'rather than being founded on notions of contracting, coercion, and sanctions, [... institutions should be] based on concepts such as community and trust', or, 'in a world in which there are prisoner's dilemmas, cooperative communities will enable rational individuals to transcend collective dilemmas' (Bates, 1988: 398–9).

Thus, economic sociology's criticism of the undersocialized character of new institutional economics focuses on its attempt to explain social institutions from a functional-neoclassical point of view (Granovetter, 1985). Granovetter's *embeddedness argument* stresses the role of networks of relations in generating trust and in establishing expectations and norms: 'social relations, rather than institutional arrangements or generalized morality, are responsible for the production of trust in economic life' (1985: 491). The embeddedness approach emphasizes the social character of economic action, the role of networks as a function between markets and hierarchies, and the process of institution-building (Granovetter, 1985). In that sense, it points to the influence of social and cultural contexts upon the rational or purposive action and sees social structure, learning and adaptation as interrelated concepts.

Granovetter's embeddedness thesis, Coleman's theory of collective action, and R. Burt's *structural*[17] approach to action constitute an integral part of the behavioural revolution in political science (Shepsle, 1989), focusing on the development of a new theoretical orientation, that emphasizes the role of social and cultural contexts in affecting rational or purposive action, and views social structure, institutional and economic performance as interdependent concepts upon which the development of social organization depends. In that sense, they may be seen as attempts to bridge the gap between the rational choice approach on one hand and the historical/sociological institutionalist approaches on the other. The last, without denying the rational and purposive character of human behaviour, emphasize path dependence and unintended consequences as features of institutional development

(Thelen and Steinmo, 1992; Pierson, 1997), and the role of cultural norms and social appropriateness in affecting individual action (March and Olsen, 1989; DiMaggio and Powell, 1991). Thus, they adopt a rather 'thick' interpretation of institutions, which are defined as: 'the formal and informal procedures, routines, norms and conventions embedded in the organizational structure of the polity or political economy' (Hall and Taylor, 1996: 938), and viewed as an independent variable, which affects actors' perceptions about their interests and identities. Social capital has emerged as the appropriate conceptual tool for this theoretical enterprise: to '*socialize*' rational-choice institutionalism (Coleman, 1988: 96).

Social capital: enhancing civicness and building civil society

Social capital has emerged as the crucial conceptual tool that, by facilitating 'certain actions of actors within the structure' (Coleman, 1988: 98), leads to the crossing of the old schism between structure and culture. As an available resource for action it is one way of introducing social structure into the rational choice paradigm (ibid., 1995; Ostrom, 1992; 1995a; 1995b; 1998). Although Coleman's (1990: 300–2) definition of social capital[18] as 'a set of social-structural resources, inherent in the social organization, that constitute capital assets for the individual' implies it refers to individual actors (persons), it has been acknowledged as a crucial factor for facilitating collective action among corporate actors as well: 'because purposive organizations can be actors just as persons can, relations among corporate actors can constitute social capital for them as well' (Coleman, 1988: 98). Thus, social capital refers 'to features of social organization, such as trust, norms, and networks that can improve the efficiency of society by facilitating coordinated action' (Putnam, 1993: 167) or, 'to internalized norms which stress the acceptance on the part of citizens of the positive role played by collective action in pursuing collective goods related to economic growth and social protection' (Leonardi, 1995b: 169). Therefore, voluntary cooperation is easier in a community[19] that has inherited a substantial stock of social capital, and the pursuit of collective goods is not seen as in contradiction with the pursuit of maximizing individual wealth. J. Coleman notes:

> Social capital is defined by its function. It is not a single entity but a variety of entities, with two elements in common: they all consist of some aspect of social structures, and they facilitate certain actions of actors – whether persons or corporate actors – within the structure. Like other forms of capital, social capital is productive, making pos-

sible the achievement of certain ends that in its absence would not be possible. For example, a group whose members manifest trustworthiness and place trust in one another will be able to accomplish much more than a comparable group lacking that trustworthiness and trust ... Like physical capital and human capital, social capital is not completely fungible but may be specific to certain activities ... Unlike other forms of capital, social capital inheres in the structure of relations between actors and among actors. It is not lodged either in the actors themselves or in physical implements of production. (1988: 98; 1990: 302–4).

Another main feature of social capital is that it is ordinarily a public good, whereas conventional capital is considered to be a private good. Therefore, like all public goods, it tends to be undervalued and undersupplied by private agents, which means that social capital, unlike other forms of capital, must often be produced as a by-product of other social activities (Coleman, 1990: 317).

Trust constitutes the most important form of social capital. It is linked to the volatility and hence uncertainty of modern economic and institutional settings and is seen as the crucial conceptual mechanism to resolve this uncertainty by shaping the relations between partners and facilitating collective action: 'trust, the mutual confidence that no party to an exchange will exploit the others' vulnerability, is today widely regarded as a precondition for competitive success' (Sabel, 1993b: 104). This is the main reason for the increasing attention many scholars have paid to the crucial role played by trust in the emergence of flexible regional systems of political and economic governance since the 1970s (Sabel, 1994a: 131–2; Lorenz, 1992).

A case that illustrates the role of trustworthiness in facilitating cooperation is that of rotating credit associations, which are informal savings institutions. In a typical rotating credit association each member contributes a monthly sum and each month a different member receives this month's pot to be used as he or she wishes. But without a high degree of trustworthiness among the members, the institution could not exist. Thus, the reputation for honesty and reliability is an important asset for any would-be participant. In a small, highly personalized community the threat of ostracism is a powerful, credible sanction. In more diffuse, impersonal societies, by contrast, more complex networks of mutual trust must be woven together to support the rotating credit associations (Putnam, 1993: 168). In many cases members must trust in the trust of others to complete their obligations and hence social networks allow trust to become transitive and spread. Rotating credit associations illustrate the way in which external sources of social capital – pre-existing social relations between individuals – help to overcome problems of imperfect information and enforceability, facilitating the solution of problems of collective action. Given, however, that in modern economies and societies, what is required is the impersonal form of trust, a problem arises about how personal trust can become social trust.

Social trust in modern complex settings can arise from two related forms of social capital: norms of reciprocity and networks of civic engagement. Social norms transfer the right to control an action from an actor to others because that action has externalities, that is consequences (positive or negative) for others. Norms arise when 'an action has similar externalities for a set of others, yet markets in the rights of control of the action cannot easily be established, and no single actor can profitably engage in an exchange to gain rights of control' (Coleman, 1990: 251). The most important norm is reciprocity (Ostrom, 1998: 10). It is of two sorts: balanced and generalized (Putnam, 1993: 172). Balanced reciprocity means a simultaneous exchange of equivalent values, while generalized reciprocity is based on a continuing relationship of exchange, which involves mutual expectations that a benefit granted now should be repaid in the future: 'if A does something for B and trusts B to reciprocate in the future, this establishes an expectation in A and an obligation on the part of B, which can be conceived as a credit slip held by A for performance by B' (Coleman, 1990: 102).

The norm of generalized reciprocity constitutes a highly productive component of social capital. Communities in which this norm is followed can more efficiently restrain opportunism and resolve problems of collective action by reconciling solidarity and self-interest. Generalized reciprocity is associated with dense networks of social exchange, through which the core relationships between reciprocity, reputation and trust are developed in a mutually reinforcing way (Ostrom, 1998). Thus norms, and hence social capital, are sustained by socialization and by sanctions, and in that sense the theory of social capital may be seen as compatible with the 'limited rationality' model of promoting norms, upon which Axelrod's evolutionary approach to norms is based (Axelrod, 1997: 40–68). These norms (Storper 1995: 'untraded interdependencies') facilitate the stability of intra-network relations and hence the inbuilt capacity of institutional networks to learn and adapt to changing circumstances.

The crucial question, however, is whether or not trust and subsequently social capital can be created where it is in demand. Renewed concern about the role of the state in promoting collective action and building social capital through successful state/society synergies has emerged recently.[20] The basic argument in the *problematique* of 'crossing the great divide' derives from the debate between the endowments and constructability approaches to state/society synergies. The former emphasizes the dependence of successful state/society synergies on a pre-existing strong civil society and the presence of a substantial stock of social capital and therefore points to a long-run process for success, while the latter stresses the possibility of short-run institution-building through synergistic relations.

According to the latter, the joint involvement of state, market and civil society (voluntary) institutions in development projects and the thus created synergistic relationships are viewed as key factors for enhancing collective action and enabling actors to be involved in the production of public goods. The evidence of successful synergies with a key role attributed to the state comes from areas of the globe (that is Third World countries) where the presence of social capital is in demand. Moreover, this 'constructability' effect, as regards social capital, of the state's involvement in synergistic relations with society seems to be particularly relevant to success stories of development, such as those of the 'East Asian Miracle' countries. In analysing East Asian countries the argument points to the complementary and mutually supportive relations between public and private actors that are substantiated by the development of dense networks crossing the two spheres and to the crucial role played by the presence of Weberian qualitative features in the public bureaucracy structure which add to its efficacy and facilitate the process of successful public/private synergies (Evans, 1996b).

The existing evidence from countries of southern Europe (Grote, 1997; Putnam, 1993), however, seems to point in the opposite direction: that the combination of a centralized state structure and a weak civil society creates conditions favourable for hierarchical, clientelistic intergovernmental relations and networks that inhibit rather than encourage the long-standing process of successful synergies and social capital-building. Moreover, even though the role of the state in particular cases such as those of East Asian countries, or even in some that are traditionally rich in cooperative and coherent relations between public and private actors, for instance Germany and the Nordic countries, cannot be overlooked, the crucial question arises about whether these successful synergistic relations have been facilitated by traditions of civic and asso-ciational life. In that sense, the existing evidence on the interregional (actually inter-Länder) differentiation in terms of synergistic networks and subsequently successful or unsuccessful adaptation in Germany – that is Baden-Württemberg as against Nordrhein–Westfalen (Grabher, 1993) – as well as the strong associational tradition in the Nordic coun-tries should be stressed.

In general, what the European experience seems to suggest is that issues, such as the structure and the degree of centralization of the state and the strength of civil society, constitute the crucial parameters that determine the administrative capacity of the state and shape public–private relations. Thus the main features of the state structure in degrees of bureaucratization, centralization and clientelism can account for the way in which local problems are regulated and state/society relations are shaped. Top-down initiatives based on hier-archical (clientelistic), intergovernmental networks cannot constitute a viable basis for the long-standing processes of social capital-building and crossing the public–private divide (Paraskevopoulos, 1998a).

Sabel's optimistic view, based on the notion of 'studied trust' seems to be more relevant. Studied trust refers to a 'kind of consensus and the associated forms of economic transactions' that result from associative, or cooperative, or autopoietic – that is self-creating – reflexive systems.[21] These are systems in which 'the logic governing the develop-ment of each of the elements is constantly reshaped by the develop-ment of all the others: the parts reflect the whole and vice versa' (Sabel, 1993b: 125–30). Sabel's optimism on the creation of trust is based on the hypothesis that 'trust is a constitutive – hence in principle ex-tensive – feature of social life' (1993b: 140).

Both the paradigm of rotating credit associations and Sabel's argu-ment of studied trust underline the cumulative character of social capital. Success in starting small-scale institutions enables individuals to build on the thus-created social capital to solve larger problems with more complex institutional arrangements. Trust and other forms of social capital, such as norms and networks, constitute 'moral resources', that is 'resources whose supply increases rather than decreases through use and which become depleted if not used' (Gambetta, 1988: 56). For these reasons the creation and destruction of social capital are marked by virtuous and vicious circles[22] (Putnam, 1993: 170; 1995a, b). This presumption has engendered criticisms, focusing on its historicism and 'path dependence' logic (Goldberg, 1996; Sabetti, 1996; Levi, 1996; Tarrow, 1996). The inherent-in-

institutional-learning evolutionist approach does not contradict the path-dependence analysis, in the sense that the function of 'learning to cooperate' should be considered as a rather slow and evolutionary process. This approach, however, should be distinguished from the deterministic interpretations of history, since it relies on actor-based models of cooperation for promoting norms and for the creation of social capital through the 'structure–actors' interactions and hence redefines the role of public policy in encouraging initiatives, rather than imposing collective action and coordination. It is in that sense that institutional learning and adaptation can be pursued.

Trust and inter-organizational networks have been extensively used as factors that underpin the industrial districts of SMEs and the restructuring process in areas of industrial decline. However, although the research in tourist development so far is mainly focused on the micro-level of inter-personal networks among tourist activity participants, the study of inter-organizational networks in tourism is seen as 'the next type of structural analysis to develop in leisure research' (Stokowski, 1994: 86). In that respect, this study may be seen as a novel approach to the role of institutions and institutional networks in the process of local development. Furthermore, there are some similarities in institutional and policy adaptation between the productive systems based on the tourist industry and those undergoing industrial restructuring (namely the shift from massive to flexible forms of tourism).

Institutional networks and learning

To understand the distinctive theoretical underpinnings of the network approach one needs to go beyond the individualistic interpretations of rational action, based on calculations of utility maximization and ignorance of the social context within which the actor is embedded (Knoke and Kuklinski, 1982: 9). Networks, in general, are based on relations or linkages and therefore they cannot be dissociated from the social or organizational system, which involves many other actors. Thus institutional networks can be defined as systems of interactions involving both public and private institutional actors (individuals, groups, organizations), which are linked around a certain policy domain or territory and hence bounded by it.[23] By definition, a network should not be seen merely as a corporate body, but instead as a new quality completely different from the total of the features of the involved organizations. In that sense, the nature of the linkages and interactions among the actors may affect the pattern of behaviour of any particular actor: 'the patterning of linkages can be used to account for some aspects of behaviour of those involved' (Mitchell, 1969,[24] cited in Knoke and Kuklinski, 1982: 13). Hence, network analysis assumes the structure of the relations and interactions can either facilitate or constrain the actions of the involved organizations. Since structure is interpreted as the 'regular and persistent pattern in the behaviour of the elementary parts of the system' (Berkowitz, 1982: 1), what distinguishes one network from another is the differentiation of its inter-organizational structure (Knoke, 1990). Thus different networks demonstrate different structures, and hence network analysis focuses on the mapping of structures (Dowding, 1994b: 73). The main structural features to categorize networks are: territorial scope, dominant actors, and density or thickness.

Three types of territorial network have been identified (Leonardi, 1995a): 1) intra-regional, which are those within one region or locality; 2) interregional, which are networks between regional actors within a national territory; and 3) transregional, which are networks between actors in different countries. Intra-regional networks constitute the common type of network within which the system of interactions among the actors is shaped at the regional or local levels. The presence of this type of network constitutes a prerequisite if the learning and institution-building processes are to be pursued because they integrate all the area resources, and particularly information and knowledge with regard to the specificities of the region concerned. Regions, which possess this first level of institutional infrastructure, can develop linkages on the interregional or transregional level to achieve access to other sources (national, European), or to pursue joint lobbying strategies. The ideal qualitative features of this type of network would involve crossing the public–private divide, by the participation of both public and private actors in joint initiatives, and the formulation of a proactive development strategy. Interregional networks, on the other hand, are less spread, given that in most nation-states in Europe the state–region relationships are traditionally more dominant than that of region to region. Finally, transregional networks constitute a relatively new phenomenon in Europe, since the main motivation for the creation of this type of network derives from the emergence of regionalism in the late 1970s.

With regard to the dominant actors, Garmise (1995a) distinguishes governmental, sectoral and functional networks. Governmental networks are characterized by the predominance of central government agencies and, therefore, these networks usually demonstrate a vertical structure, which has particular consequences for network relations. Sectoral networks emerge around specific sectors of the local economy, such as an industry, a service or a sphere of voluntary activity. Finally, functional networks consist of both governmental and sectoral actors. The main feature of the sectoral and functional networks is that they tend to have a horizontal rather than vertical structure. Functional networks are considered as providing the nucleus support structure for the learning process, since they tend to shape public–private relations at the local level, thus incorporating multiple types of resources required for the development process. Table 1.1 provides an illustration of these two categories of network.

Thus, the most effective institutional networks are those which are based on intra-regional functional networks. These networks, by enabling public and private actors to be actively involved in the provision of public goods, and by integrating most of the region's resources, constitute the foundation of and the appropriate regulatory framework for development strategies that reflect the local identity and the local demands.

Institutional thickness is the last and most important structural feature of networks. This is the combination of structural and cultural qualitative elements that determine the level of local institutional capacity. In other words, institutional thickness means 'the combination of factors including inter-institutional interaction and synergy, collective representation by many bodies, ... and shared cultural norms and values' (Amin and Thrift, 1994: 15). In structural characteristics, thickness means the density of inter-institutional interactions, which, however, are conditioned by the way in which the resources are distributed among the actors and the strength of the system of cultural norms in which they are embedded, that is social capital. The distribution and integration of resources points to the fact that thickness cannot be sustained without intra-regional functional networks. The role of social capital, on the other hand, is to facilitate communication among the

Table 1.1   Networks by Territorial Scope and Dominant Actor

Territorial Scope Dominant Actor	Intra-regional	Interregional	Transregional
Governmental	Intra-regional Governmental	Interregional Governmental	Transregional Governmental
Sectoral	Intra-regional Sectoral	Interregional Sectoral	Transregional Sectoral
Functional	Intra-regional Functional	Interregional Functional	Transregional Functional

Source: Garmise, 1995a: 63

actors and thus the diffusion of information and knowledge, which are the most important resources for learning.

Relevant but not synonymous to thickness is the debate on the strength or weakness of the linkages between institutions within networks. The strength of the linkages and the number of ties any institutions share are closely linked to crucial issues such as the flow of information and the diffusion of knowledge among the actors, the prevention of opportunism, and the danger of *institutional lock-in*. Strong ties are viewed as encouraging malfeasance, preventing the flow and diffusion of information and knowledge, thus undermining the learning process and increasing the danger of institutional lock-in. G. Grabher's work on the Ruhr region has shown how networks that were perfectly dense and adapted produced cognitive and institutional lock-in when the strong ties among the core actors undermined the adaptability of the region to the necessity of structural adjustment and led it into the trap of rigid specialization (1993: 275). Conversely, weak ties facilitate the learning process, by functioning as bridges between strongly tied network subgroups, thus providing pathways for the diffusion of information: 'weak ties are more likely to link members of different small groups than are strong ones, which tend to be concentrated within particular groups' (Granovetter, 1973: 1376).

Although Granovetter's analysis of the advantages of weak ties can perfectly account for a wide range of issues, such as the role of institutions (i.e. family) in the semi-periphery, illustrated by Banfield's (1958) *amoral familism*, learning institutional networks should constitute a combination of strong and weak ties. This combination can counterbalance the positive and negative characteristics of each type of tie, providing trust and access to new knowledge and information, and preventing institutional lock-in. Hence, learning institutional networks should combine a core of actors (that is an intra-regional functional network) linked with strong ties, and a range of other local actors connected through looser ties to the core network.

The role of power and exchange in networks

The concept of power is a crucial and extensively debated issue in political science. Dowding distinguishes between 'outcome power': 'the ability of an actor to bring about or help to bring about outcomes'; and 'social power': 'the ability of an actor deliberately to change the incentive structure of another actor or actors to bring about or help to bring about outcomes' (1996: 5). However, this thesis has adopted Metcalfe's definition of power, that is 'the ability to attain higher levels of collective performance' (1981: 504), which seems to be more suitable because it conceives of power as the outcome of collective action among the actors.

Within the inherent in networks bargaining and negotiation contexts there are four ways for actors to achieve collective performance by exercising power: persuasion, threats, reward, or a 'throffer', which is a combination of threats and offers[25] (Dowding, 1991: 68). To make all these instruments of power operational within the bargaining process an actor needs to have a number of potential resources. Harsanyi has identified four categories of important resource in this respect: information or knowledge, legitimate authority, unconditional incentives (where an actor must pay the price or reap the benefit whether or not he/she does what the other wants, namely the law), conditional incentives (either reward or punishment conditional on the behaviour the powerful wants to impose) (1969, discussed in Dowding, 1991: 70–2).[26] Additionally, stubbornness and reputation have also been identified as important resources for bargaining and overcoming problems of collective action where a group cannot mobilize itself to act (ibid.: 145–6).

Knowledge and information are considered as the most important resources of power for facilitating the learning process within networks and subsequently their capacity for adapting to changing conditions. On the one hand, since learning, adaptation, institutional and economic performance constitute public goods and are of general interest to most participants, persuasion is the most effective political tool because it implies the voluntary involvement of actors in achieving collective performance. On the other, because information and knowledge are perceived as crucial resources within an inter-organizational environment dominated by uncertainty and interdependence, they provide actors with the potential to influence the policy-making process, by imposing their interpretation of common problems and solutions on others (Haas, 1992). Thus, actors have an incentive to increase their access to these resources, since this can lead to changes of attitudes and patterns of behaviour of the other actors. Hence, the role of knowledge and information as resources of power is crucial in two respects: first for persuasing actors to be involved in collective action, and second, for influencing policy-making through the processes of problem-identification and solution-provision.

Given that inter-organizational networks are characterized by a significant amount of expertise and specialization and hence resource interdependencies among the actors (Kenis and Schneider, 1991), power relations within networks are based mainly on the process of exchange (Marin, 1990). Exchange relations involve a variety of resources: money, information, authority. Exchange is seen as one way to achieve collective action. This is the process by which 'possibilities for action, linked to the possession of mutually valued resources, are exchanged between complex organizations' (Parri, 1989: 200). Exchange, like power, presupposes a bargaining and negotiation framework within which actors are offering something of value to achieve their own objectives. Thus it can take place at a functional or territorial level and involves both public and private actors. For example, a state organization may allow the influence of a private organization on the policy process in exchange for that organization's resources. In that sense, bargaining and negotiation are considered as intrinsic elements of the cooperation and institution-building processes: 'the process of negotiation is itself a vital part of the institution-building process' (Amin and Thrift, 1994: 15). Moreover, negotiation constitutes an integral part of the process of coalition–building, which plays an important role in the way in which both institutional- and policy-learning are pursued (Sabatier, 1993). The crucial question, however, is how external shocks influence the coalition blocks and subsequently how these changes affect the relations among the actors.

Stability and change in networks

What the discussion so far suggests is that inherent resource interdependencies and the process of exchange determine, to a significant degree, the distribution of power within the network. Thus, the system of exchange constitutes a power dependence framework, within which corporate actors spend resources to achieve objectives (Rhodes and Marsh, 1992). In this framework, however, it is implicitly acknowledged that no actor is completely autonomous but depends, to varying degrees, on the resources exchanged with other organizations. This restricted autonomy points to the fact that political exchange should be distinguished from exchange within the free market model, because its fundamental bases are the notions of self-organization and antagonistic cooperation that help competitive, functionally interdependent actors manage the uncertainties of complex strategic interactions and be collectively involved in the provision of public goods in multiple policy areas (Marin and Mayntz, 1991). Resource interdependency alone, however, does not determine the structure of the network. Since actors' social positions, strategies and objectives vary, the exchange of resources and the subsequent formation of the system of interactions may lead to asymmetrical interdependencies amongst the involved organizations, hence the differentiation of network structures across sectors and localities.

Furthermore, although within the power-dependence framework networks, especially in neo-corporatist systems of governance,[27] are considered as the appropriate institutional systems to accomplish the interest intermediation function (Rhodes and Marsh, 1992), in the context of the learning process a much broader interpretation of their role should be applied. Even though the interest intermediation function cannot be overlooked, the main role of the networks as actors in a learning environment is to shape the interactions among the public and private actors and to coordinate resources and initiatives for the general interest of the community. Under these considerations, the revolutionary contribution of the network paradigm is the redefinition of the notion of the public sphere by combining governmental, private and voluntary actors.

The process of exchange, however, is crucially influenced by the local context. Although it is based on rational choices of the actors, the impact of historical and cultural factors cannot be ignored. While history and geography determine to a significant degree the way resources have been distributed, actors' choices with regard to the exchangeable resources are conditioned by norms, values, conventions and rules of behaviour. In fact, mutually reinforcing self-perceptions may distort actors' collective judgements concerning the value of certain resources. Thus, exchange relations do not depend on the availability of resources, but on actors' perceptions about their value and usefulness. In that sense, even in the process of exchange between actors within networks, collective action is facilitated or inhibited by the presence or lack of social capital (Marin, 1990: 14).

Under these considerations, the multiplicity and differentiation of network structures between policy areas within a region or between regions in the same policy area is explained by the differentiation in the distribution of resources and the variety of socially constructed exchange choices. The distribution of resources among and within the public and private sectors and the way in which these resources are distributed territorially determine the territorial scope and the dominant actors within a network. Thus within centralized states, because central-state actors hold most of the public-sector resources, several local agents tend to exchange more with these central-state organizations than with their local counterparts. On the other hand, network density is shaped by the degree of concentration or dispersion of resources among the actors and by the value attributed to these resources for the day-to-day function of the network. Hence network thickness depends, to a significant degree, on the multiplicity, the variety and the regularity of the exchanges. Thus, the process of exchange is considered the most important component for maintaining network continuity over a long period of time (Garmise, 1995a). Networks based on the process of exchange constitute long-term events and not opportunistic, short-term institutional actors which focus merely on reaping quick gains by exploiting temporary chances.

However, three categories of factor have been identified that can cause networks to change. The first source of change derives from the transformation of the external parameters, that can subsequently result in redistribution of resources and power within the network. These transformations may include shifts in the socio-economic conditions, technological changes, shift in governing coalitions, initiation of new policy and funding decisions, and finally influence by other subsystems. With regard to the last parameter, there are cases in which the success of specific networks encourages the creation of collective action subsystems or groups which in turn at a later stage cause network change from the outside (Dowding, 1994b: 73). The second category of factor that causes networks to change is the deliberate or accidental restructuring of internal power relations. This can be the outcome of changes in the strategy of a group of actors within the network. Finally, the third important source of change derives from the learning process. Since new ideas and approaches may be adopted as a result of the learning process, changes may be required in the use of resources and therefore a new shift in the balance of power within the network. What needs to be stressed is that in all these cases change constitutes a shock to network structure, which is followed by a renewed balance among winners and losers. The latter are expected to resist change and fight to maintain their influence within the network.

To sum up, intra-regional functional networks, by integrating most of the region's resources and overcoming the public–private divide, provide the appropriate organizational structure for an institutional environment favourable for learning. However, although the way resources, and particularly knowledge and information, are distributed plays an important role in shaping the intra-regional institutional interactions and achieving collective action through the process of exchange, the broad social context and the socialization function determine the value of the resources and hence the way in which the exchange process is shaped. Therefore, since learning is crucially influenced by the level of collective action among the actors, exchange and socialization constitute procedural components of the learning process. Hence social capital, as the conceptual tool of the socialization function, constitutes a prerequisite for the learning process within networks.

Conclusions

This chapter has demonstrated that the technological, economic and political changes that have underpinned the emergence of globalization emphasize the role of the endogenous political and socio-cultural resources in the development process. Thus, in the era of globalization the way in which the local is embedded into the global depends crucially on the presence of a learning institutional infrastructure at the local level rather than on the protective role of the state.

Learning is a function of past policy attempts, their interpretation and experience obtained by the local institutional infrastructure, which, in this way, becomes capable of adapting to changing conditions. Therefore, the presence of fora for dialogue and communication that facilitate the flow, diffusion and exchange of information and knowledge among the actors constitute preconditions for a policy environment favourable for learning. Thus, the process of exchange and hence the distribution of resources and power among the actors constitute an important component of the learning process. The process of exchange, however, is crucially influenced by the socio-cultural context within which the valuation of the exchangeable resources takes place. Thus social norms and conventions constitute crucial parameters for the exchange process and subsequently for learning, which is viewed as a function depending crucially on both the exchange and socialization processes.

Within this framework, institutions and institutional networks provide the appropriate organizational structure for collective action and learning, by shaping intra-regional institutional interactions and overcoming the public–private divide. In that sense, social capital and institutional networks are considered prerequisites for the learning process and subsequently for adaptable institutional infrastructure at both regional and local levels: by facilitating collective action among the actors, the former, and integration of resources through the process of exchange, the latter.

Finally, the concept of learning discussed in this book implies the process of both structural and policy adaptation, whereby institutional networks and policy choices are changed to suit changing conditions. What is considered its key contribution, however, is its attempt to capture the system of interactions between culture and structure, that is the causal nexus between cultural norms and attitudes and the institutional structure (institutional networks) that make up the civic community. In that sense, learning may be seen as a concept developed to bridge the gap between the rational and historical/sociological new institutionalist approaches in political science: on the one hand, by taking into account the role of the contextual factors (historical and cultural parameters of institutional evolution) and on the other, by refusing the pure path-dependence and teleological assumptions of historical new institutionalism.

2
Social Learning and Adaptation within European Regional Policy

Introduction

In chapter one social capital and institutional networks were identified as key components of the learning institutional infrastructure and hence of dynamic economic governance at the regional level, facilitating coordination of resources and collective action among the actors through the processes of political exchange and socialization.

This chapter introduces the same concepts – social capital and institutional networks – in the field of European regional policy as prerequisites for learning, adaptation and Europeanization of regional systems of governance. The first section explores the evolutionary process of building a European regional policy and identifies the impact of Europeanization on local systems of governance, establishing specific criteria for measuring it. The second and third sections examine the theoretical justification of European regional policy within the framework of Integration theory and set out the main theoretical hypotheses. The fourth section discusses the constraints on the local capacity for learning that emerge from the structure of the state. Finally, the fifth section presents the methodological approach for investigating the relationship between local institutional capacity and European regional policy.

European regional policy and Europeanization of local systems of governance

Structural policy is considered the most important redistributive instrument at EU level. It represents approximately 35 per cent of the budget and most of that money goes to the less-developed countries and regions. Net annual transfers to Greece, Ireland and Portugal usually exceed 3 per cent of their respective GDP (Tsoukalis, 1998). After the coming into force of the Maastricht Treaty in particular, the goal of economic and social cohesion is linked to the steps towards further economic integration, namely to the process for the creation of EMU.

The theoretical justification for fostering economic and social cohesion at the EU level has constituted a key element of both academic debate and everyday policy-making at European level, since the establishment of the EEC in 1957. Four main arguments have been developed for this justification (Armstrong, 1989). First, EU regional policy can improve efficiency in the use of funds, by targeting spending and by imposing discipline on the policies of member-states. Second, the coordination of member-states' regional policies can reduce the scope for costly and inefficient competition for mobile investments between nations and regions. Third, the 'vested interest' argument points to the unacceptability of major regional disparities on grounds of social equity. Finally, there is an argument that regional disparities may be a barrier to further integration.

The evolutionary process of building a coherent and effective European regional policy has more or less followed the gradual path of the integration process. In general, three main phases have been identified in the evolution of European regional policy since the establishment of the EEC in 1957 (Tsoukalis, 1993). The first phase, which lasted until 1975, was characterized by the lack of any well-structured and coherent regional policy and by the predominance of the sectoral, rather than the integrated approach to regional development. The second phase, which lasted until the 1988 reform of the Structural Funds, was marked by the strengthening of the regional policy dimension of the existing institutions, the creation of new instruments and the steady increase of allocated funds. The third phase is closely linked to the 1988 reform of the Structural Funds, which has constituted a turning-point in the search for greater effectiveness and efficiency of common instruments and the further increase in funds for regional policy. This evolutionary process is seen as 'attempts to improve the adaptive capacity of regional economies adversely affected by processes of economic transformation or to increase the growth potential of backward economies' (Chesire *et al.*, 1991: 169).

The emergence of European regional policy on the EC policy-making agenda: from the treaty of Rome to the 1988 reform of the Structural Funds

Although the original six members of the European Community, with the exception of Italy which was the only country with serious regional problems, constituted a relatively homogeneous economic group, the Treaty of Rome did indicate a general goal to reduce regional disparities,[1] while the European Investment Bank (EIB), the European Social Fund (ESF) – established in 1957 – and, to a lesser extent, the European Agricultural Guidance and Guarantee Fund (EAGGF) – established in 1964 – provided loans and development assistance to depressed regions. A major report on regional problems, submitted by the European Commission to the Council in 1965 signalled the start-up of the process for the creation of the Directorate-General for Regional Policy (DG XVI) by the 1967 Merger Treaty.

With the first enlargement of the EC in 1973 – to include Britain, Ireland and Denmark – and the subsequent change in the political balance within the EC, regional policy issues moved to the centre stage of policy-making, since two of the new member-states (Ireland and Britain) had strong reasons for backing such a policy (Chesire, *et al.*, 1991). Ireland viewed regional policy as a way of overcoming its poor, peripheral position, while Britain, with a small, highly efficient and modern agrarian sector but severely hit by problems of industrial decline, viewed regional policy as: 1) a way to cope with de-industrialization, which had a strong spatial dimension; and 2) a way of counterbalancing the costs of the Common Agricultural Policy (CAP) to which Britain would be a net contributor (Garmise, 1995a).

The creation of the European Regional Development Fund (ERDF) in 1975, which gave the EU 'a financial instrument for explicit regional intervention' (Croxford, *et al.*, 1987: 25), has been seen as the result of this new political balance. However, although the creation of this new institution was considered as the first step towards the establishment of European regional policy, the principles that governed its activity during its first years were based on the notion that regional development policy was predominantly a national rather than a Community concern, in the sense that both the decision-making and implementation processes of regional policy constituted exclusive competences of the national governments (Nanetti, 1990). Thus, the Community's role was limited in providing financial resources, which, primarily, were in the form of grants for infrastructure investments, in accordance with national quotas whereby each member-state received a guaranteed level of support. Nonetheless, a major part of this financial assistance was directed to member states with GDP per capita below the Community average.

The increasing importance of regional policy issues at European level was the driving force of a series of step-by-step reforms of the ERDF, which gradually transformed it into a real planning instrument for development strategy (Nanetti, 1990). The first (1979) reform brought about the following important changes in the function of the Fund. First, a five per cent non-quota element was established, that could be used at the discretion of the Commission to finance development projects, focusing on regions with development problems emerged as a by-product of the implementation of other Community policies.[2] Second, within this non-quota section, financial assistance was provided for multi-annual, rather than yearly programmes. Third, there had been a shift regarding the qualitative characteristics of the supported projects, in the sense that not only infrastructure-related, but a broader range of projects and initiatives (that is support to SMEs) could get financial assistance. Finally, the funds could be allocated to areas and regions, not necessarily designated by the national governments. In that sense, by enhancing the discretionary competences of the EC Commission, these changes have been interpreted as early steps towards the 'Europeanization' of European regional policy (Cheshire *et al.*, 1991).

After a 1981 proposal presented to the Council by the Commission, in 1984 the Council adopted a regulation[3] which introduced the second major reform of the Fund. The 1984 reform of the ERDF replaced the system of fixed national quotas with a system of indicative ranges (minimum and maximum) for the allocation of the funds to each member-state. Within the new system, the minimum limit represented the guaranteed level of each country's allocated funds. This part of the national allocations amounted to 88.6 per cent of the funds, while the remaining amount was left to be allocated at the Commission's (ERDF) discretion. To receive funds above the minimum range of national allocations, member-state governments had to submit proposals fulfilling the priority and eligibility criteria established by the Commission. Given that in Regulation 1787 there was a provision for replacement of the individual project approach by the 'integrated-programme approach', this latest reform, by increasing the Commission's room for manoeuvre in monitoring and managing the allocation of the funds, may be seen as another step towards the Europeanization of both the functional level and the scope of the Community's regional policy. Moreover, the management of the 'notorious' additionality principle was gradually moved from the hands of member-state governments towards the supranational level (EU Commission).

This gradual shift from the 'individual project' towards the 'programming' approach had been formulated within two types of programming: the National Programmes of Community Interest (NPCI) and the Community Interest Programmes (CIP) which constitute the first version of what since has become known as Community Initiatives. Whereas the former were based on the national governments' programming initiatives, the latter, which constituted the formulation of the non-quota section of ERDF, were originated in initiatives taken by the Commission, which usually referred to regions of more than one member-state. The major innovation brought about by the programming approach is the initiation of the principle of the 'contractual partnership' within the framework of European regional policy. What this principle implies is the partnership between supranational (EU Commission), national (national governments) and subnational (regional or local) authorities on a contractual basis in the planning, implementation and monitoring processes of European regional policy (Nanetti, 1990). This innovation may be seen as the departure point for the Europeanization function of subnational elites on a bottom-up basis.

The catalytic political and economic changes of the early 1980s in Europe and the subsequent enlargement of the EC with the accession of Greece (1981), and Spain and Portugal (1986), signalled a new shift of European regional policy towards the integrated approach to development. The integrated approach has been interpreted as the move from the independent and uncoordinated actions of each particular Fund, to coordinated structural interventions. Therefore, it should involve: first a restructuring of the three Funds responsible for the development policy (ERDF, ESF and EAGGF-Guidance section); and second, coordinated structural interventions in the economic and social spheres of areas with regional problems. Although the integrated approach had been adopted in two pilot projects in Naples (1979) and in Belfast (1981) with poor results, its first ambitious test was the introduction of the Integrated Mediterranean Programmes (IMPs) in 1985. They constituted the most numerous integrated actions undertaken by the Community (29) in three countries (France, Italy and Greece), accompanied by significant resources (6.6 billion ECUs) and their introduction was linked to the need of the most vulnerable economic sectors of the member-states, and most notably agriculture, to be prepared for increased competition arising from the imminent entry into the Community of Spain and Portugal.

The creation of the IMPs signalled a radical departure for European regional policy, by introducing the following major innovations in planning, implementation and monitoring processes. First, they were the implementation instruments of strategic coordinated actions in almost every economic sector, involving infrastructure, industry, agriculture and vocational training. The main goal was Community investment to provide additional resources, which could enhance the potential for endogenous local development in the areas concerned (as discussed in chapter one). The second radical aspect of the IMPs was the central role attributed to the subnational level of government through partnership institutional arrangements at all stages of policymaking: planning specific programmes, implementing individual 'measures' or actions, monitoring their progress, and evaluating the overall impact. Thus, the committees responsible for the overall implementation of the programmes were made up of regional governments, national and Commission representatives. A third major change introduced by the IMPs was the requirement for both *ex ante* and *ex post* evaluation of the programmes. The former involved the projected impact of the investment on crucial regional indicators, such as the level of employment and regional GDP, while the latter concerned the qualitative and quantitative evaluation of the results achieved after implementation of the programmes. Codification of the contractual approach, through the requirement for a legally binding contract signed by the Commission, regional and member-state authorities, constituted the final and most important innovation introduced by the IMPs, since the principle of partnership, reinforced during the 1988 reforms of the Structural Funds, was to become the revolutionary feature of European regional policy (Nanetti, 1996).

The financial outcome of all these changes was that funds available through the ERDF grew steadily over the years. Thus, the initial allocation of 257.6 million ECUs increased tenfold in the period 1975–87 and before the scheduled doubling of the Fund for the period 1989–93 its allocation reached 3.3 billion ECUs in 1987, accounting for almost 10 per cent of the EC annual budget, while the total of structural actions in the same year accounted for 19 per cent of the budget, or 7 billion ECUs. However, the total amount of money remained small when compared with the expenditures for regional policy at the national level (Tsoukalis, 1993). In 1988, before the implementation of the reform, ERDF assistance amounted to only 0.09 per cent of EC GDP and 0.46 per cent of Gross Fixed Capital Formation (GFCF) (CEC, 1990b).

From the single European act (SEA) to the treaty on European union (TEU) and beyond

The programme for the completion of the Single Market, initiated by the 1985 White Paper, and its liberalization effect on the function of European markets has coincided, as it should be expected, with an increased concern with the tackling of the problems of social and economic cohesion to enable all regions to exploit the opportunities presented by the single market (Nanetti, 1996). Thus the goal of economic and social cohesion was eminent in the Single Act Treaty[4] (Art. 130 a–e). The doubling in real terms of the resources available to the Funds responsible for regional policy – the ERDF, the ESF and the EAGGF (Guidance section), all three referred to as Structural Funds – was agreed by the Brussels European Council in February 1988, accompanied by a major qualitative change in the principles of the structural policy.

Two major qualitative features have been identified in the reform of the Structural Funds:[5] first, the generalized adoption of the integrated approach and, second, the further enforcement of the Commission's discretionary power to prioritize the region-objectives and to concentrate structural interventions on a limited number of clearly defined goals, thus signalling the move towards further Europeanization of regional policy.

In particular, the first policy principle, which characterizes the reform of the Funds, is the geographical targeting of their resources, transforming regional policy into an instrument with real economic impact by focusing on the greatest concentration of structural interventions. Five priority objectives[6] were assigned to the Funds upon which the EIB was also expected to redefine its contributions.[7] It is worth noting that the major concentration of resources (80 per cent of the three Funds between 1989 and 1993) was focused on the objectives with real 'regional' dimension (1, 2 and 5b).[8] The second major innovation brought about by the reform was the institutionalization of the integrated approach, by combining the interventions in financial commitments running over larger periods of time (multi-year, multifaceted programmes, the so-called Community Support Frameworks or CSFs), instead of financing individual projects proposed by the member-states. This development reflects the lessons learned from the implementation of the IMPs. The third and arguably most important innovation is the institutionalization of the principle of partnership. At all stages (planning, implementing and monitoring) of the CSFs, the EU Commission, national and regional authorities are engaged in formal negotiations which lead to close cooperation and coordination. Whereas the Commission used to deal exclusively with national governments, which articulated their own regional plans, since 1988 the process has been open to subnational governments to be involved in the planning and implementation of Operational Programmes (OPs). The reinforcement of the principle of *additionality*, which requires that the financial contribution by the Structural Funds should be in addition to the funds that would have been given by national governments in its absence, was the fourth important characteristic of the reform. Finally, the reformulation and expansion of the former (under the 1984 Regulation of the Funds) Community Interest Programmes (CIPs) into what has become known as Community Initiatives (CIs)[9] has constituted a major motivation for regional mobilization at European level. The Community Initiatives are subject-oriented Community-wide projects focusing on a particular problem or type of region, designed by the Commission and usually involving the transregional cooperation of regions in more than one member-state. In that sense, because of the upgraded role attributed to the Commission and the subnational authorities vis-à-vis the national governments, they are seen as reliable instruments for enhancing the adaptation and Europeanization processes at regional level. For the period of the first CSFs (1989–93) there were twelve Community Initiatives,[10] representing a financial commitment of 3800 million ECUs from which 2100 million were focused on objective 1 regions.

The coming into force of the Treaty on European Union (TEU) paved the way for the 1994–99 second phase of the CSFs. In the Maastricht Treaty cohesion is mentioned as a central concern linked to the goal of achieving economic and monetary union (EMU). To meet the convergence criteria laid down by the Treaty the weaker national economies have focused on the adjustment of their macro-economic policies (reduction of budgetary deficits) by reducing the funding of extensive development projects at national, regional or local levels. Under these considerations, pursuit of the goal of cohesion at EU level is viewed as facilitating the structural adjustment of the member-states.

The doubling, once again, of the resources available to the Structural Funds for the period 1994–99 (27.4 billion ECUs by 1999), agreed at the Edinburgh Summit of December 1992, and the two new additions to the institutional set-up of the EU, namely the Cohesion Fund and the Committee of Regions (CoR), brought about by the TEU, have extended the scope and contributed to the further institutionalization of EU regional policy. The Cohesion Fund makes financial contributions to projects in the fields of transport infrastructure and environment and is targeted at those member-states with a per capita Gross National Product (GNP) below 90 per cent of the EU average, that is Spain, Portugal, Ireland and Greece. However, the creation of the Cohesion Fund has coincided with the establishment of a direct link between structural and macro-economic policies at national level. According to the new, and much criticized, *conditionality* principle introduced to the Cohesion Fund, any financial assistance provided by the Fund is governed by the existence of a programme of economic convergence approved by the Council (ECOFIN).

The creation of the CoR, even though it has not been given decision-making powers by both Maastricht and Amsterdam Treaties, is considered an important institutional innovation, contributing to the recognition of the role of subnational (regional, local) levels of government in the EU policy-making process, along with other interest groups (Economic and Social Committee). However, the limited role of the Committee within the EU system of governance is partly attributed to the multiplicity and differentiation of regional interests at European level, such as existing antithesis within the Committee between regional and local-level representatives (Jeffery, 1995: 256; Hooghe, 1995: 181).

With regard to the content of the 1993 reforms, although it has been argued their main feature was orientation towards reinforcing the role of the member-states *vis-à-vis* the Commission and the subnational governments (Mitsos, 1995; Hooghe, 1996), they have largely continued the thrust of the 1988 reforms by improving the efficiency of management and monitoring procedures. The first important change is the strengthening of monitoring and assessment provisions by laying down explicit requirements for *ex ante* and *ex post* evaluation of the programmes. These procedures will be under the supervision of the Commission. The second change is the wording of provisions on the *additionality* principle. The change involves widening the parameters for evaluating the member-states' consistency in coping with the principle. Thus, while the main criterion for this evaluation was the level of expenditure during the previous programming period, the new wording suggests other factors such as privatization programmes and business cycles in the national economy should count as well. The third and most important change is financing and managing Community Initiatives for the period 1994–99.[11] The amount to be devoted to the CIs was reduced from 10 per cent to 9 per cent of the total Structural Funds budget, leaving the remaining 1 per cent to be spent in so-called Pilot projects (Art. 10). More importantly, to improve the coordination function of the CIs, a management committee[12] was created to approve or reject by qualified majority the proposals for CIs submitted by the Commission. Finally, the list of the regions eligible under Objective 1 was substantially amended by the inclusion of the new German Länder and the reclassification of other regions (Hainault in Belgium, Flevoland in the Netherlands, certain districts in northern France, Merseyside and the Highlands and Islands in the UK, and Cantabria in Spain), while a new instrument – the Financial Instrument for Fisheries Guidance (FIFG) – was established to provide support for the fisheries sector.

Facing the challenge of enlargement in the dawn of the twenty-first century, the Commission's proposals on structural policy, included in the *Agenda 2000*, are aimed at reconciling the interests of major net contributors to the EU budget, namely the northern European countries and most notably Germany, with those of present beneficiaries (southern European countries and Ireland) and of prospective members, that is the countries of eastern Europe (Tsoukalis, 1998). Thus, keeping unchanged the upper ceilings of own resources and structural interventions, at 1.27 per cent and 0.47 per cent of the EU GNP respectively, the Commission has estimated that a total amount of ECU 275 billion (at 1997 prices) will be allocated to structural policies for the period 2000–6, as compared with ECU 200 billion for the period 1994–99. Within this budget framework, 210 billion are to be spent for existing members through the Structural Funds, while 45 billion are to be earmarked for new members, including 7 billion in the form of pre-accession aid for all candidates, and the remaining amount to be spent through the Cohesion Fund (CEC, 1997).

The financial framework, involving the level of both the revenue and the expenditure within which structural policy is the second biggest expenditure after the CAP, will be the subject of long and difficult negotiations. However, the whole process will be crucially affected by the viability of the EMU and single currency projects, which during the same period are expected to be facing the repercussions of the inherent deficiencies in experiment, such as the asymmetry between centralized monetary and decentralized fiscal policies, the rigidities of labour markets and the mosaic of diversified structures of welfare and social security provisions among member-states across Europe (McKay, 1999).

Nonetheless, the evolutionary process of building a European regional policy has constituted a challenge for well-established structures within the systems of governance at both national and subnational levels and played a decisive role both in the administrative restructuring process within the member-states and in enhancing the institutional capacity of subnational systems of governance. Let us examine the changes in the system parameters that the Europeanization process has engendered for the local systems of governance across Europe.

Europeanization of subnational governments: definition and identification

The Europeanization function is the process by which governance structures at national and subnational levels adapt both their institutional and policy components to meet the requirements of the rapidly changing European environment. Given the Europeanization of the structures, cultures and processes of public policy-making accompanied by the emergence of a more pluralistic policy environment at European level, it is difficult to identify any field of public policy which is not subject to some degree of EU influence (Mazey and Richardson, 1993; Scharpf, 1994; Goldsmith, 1993). On the other hand, the size of the Commission's 'adolescent bureaucracy' (Mazey and Richardson, 1993: 10) is considered to be relatively small, with regard to EU policy objectives (Goldsmith, 1993). Thus, the Europeanization of public policy constitutes a rather enduring and longstanding challenge to the administrative structures of member-states, and it is viewed as a positive external shock for promoting institution-building, learning and policy-making innovation at national and subnational levels, even if the pre-existing institutional infrastructure was poor.

In the field of regional policy, Europeanization has played a decisive role in administrative restructuring within member-states and in enhancing the institutional capacity of subnational systems of governance. In particular, changes in the system parameters that the Europeanization process has engendered for local systems of governance across Europe have become evident through the involvement of subnational authorities in actions and programmes related to the EU policy-making process. In that sense, it is almost synonymous with the 'subnational mobilization' (Hooghe, 1995) at European level.

The objectives of subnational authorities for developing linkages with the Commission are to enhance their resource base in information, finance and knowledge, and to influence the EU policy process in order to circumvent or roll back central government or European policies that undermine or constrain local government activities. On the other hand, the EU Commission has two reasons for deepening its relationship with subnational governments: first, subnational authorities can provide the Commission with first-hand information on both the policy objectives and the success (or lack of success) of policies which are already implemented, thus counterbalancing the inherent expediencies in information provided by national government; second, subnational authorities can provide the Commission with the institutional capacity it lacks to implement and monitor EU policies, especially in federal or regionalized countries, where policies and regulations have a direct impact on both federal/national and regional institutional structures (Marks, 1996; Goldsmith, 1993). Moreover, by participating in transregional networks, subnational governments may derive benefits from the lack of congruence between the definition of eligibility for funding territorial units used by the Commission, the well-known NUTS (Nomenclature of Statistical Territorial Units), and the designations within each member-state (Goldsmith, 1993). This differentiation has been seen as a factor that encourages the cooperation of regional authorities on a transnational basis to exploit EU funding opportunities.

Four stages have been identified in the Europeanization process of subnational governments (John, 1994). The first stage could be characterized as minimal Europeanization, where subnational authorities simply implement EU directives and regulations, manage European information and communicate this information to the whole range (public and private) of local actors. This activity depends crucially on the state structure, on local institutional capacity and on the intensity of the identity or interest-related national/regional conflicts (Marks, 1996; Marks *et al.*, 1996a). As a 1992 survey conducted in Britain reveals, almost 60 per cent of English and Welsh local authorities had specialized staff working on EU matters, whereas the equivalent proportion in Denmark does not exceed 8 per cent (Goldsmith, 1993).

The second stage, financial Europeanization, is reached by those subnational governments who are able to gain access to more EU funding and use these resources to promote local economic development. Subnational governments in Objective 1, 2 and 5b regions are considered as most mobilized in this area. The development of network linkages with other local organizations through their joint involvement in EU programmes or initiatives – local networking – is seen as the third stage of the Europeanization process. The Structural Funds programmes constitute a strong incentive for private sector involvement in development projects to be shared with public agencies and institutions, thus overcoming the public–private divide (Benington and Harvey, 1994).

Finally, the full Europeanization stage involves a shift from the reactive to the proactive policy approach towards the EU, which is substantiated by the participation of subnational institutions in trans-European collaborative networks, the creation, through these networks, of advisory channels linked to the Commission to influence the policy-making process, and the launching of European-style policy initiatives at local level.

What is required to identify the degree of Europeanization is in-depth case study analysis. However, the degree of private sector financial contribution to the CSFs has been used as an indicator of local actors' participation in the European development process on a transnational basis (Garmise, 1995a). Table 2.1 below presents data on the average contribution of the private sector to the CSFs for the period 1989–93, based on the statistical bulletins 'The Community's Structural Interventions' (CEC, 1992a; 1992b).

In general, the private sector was found to participate financially to some extent in most (91.3 per cent) of all CSFs. Comparing this result with the data available on the IMPs – the first major implementation of the integrated approach – an important finding emerges: that private sector participation in EU projects has substantially increased in terms

Table 2.1 Average (%) Contribution of the Private Sector to the CSFs by Country and Objective (1989–93)

Private Sector Contrib. (%)	Total	Object. 1	Object. 2	Objects 3/4	Object. 5b
Country					
Belgium	17.06	–	25.44	0.13	24.85
Denmark	20.89	–	45.84	0	30.2
France	19.14	9.17	26.06	0	29.3
Germany	39.51	47.48*	5.3	0.47	47.9
Greece	7.5	7.5	–	–	–
Ireland	25.22	25.22	–	–	–
Italy	12.6	7.05	49.8	0	49.62
Luxembourg	35.32	–	43.84	0	21.5
Netherlands	12.5	–	22.13	2.7	17.6
Portugal	7.8	7.8	–	–	–
Spain	15.01	16.30	13.78	0	14.13
UK	12.27	24.47	14.77	0	6.8
EU 12	17.48	18.52	19.68	0.24	33.29

Note: This represents contributions to the CSF for the New German Länder (Council Regulation EEC 35.75/1990), which was approved in March 1991 (CEC, 1992a).
Source: adapted from CEC (1992a; 1992b)

of both the number of projects and initiatives and the percentage of overall funding. In particular, the private sector was involved in 28 per cent (around 46 per cent in France, 28 per cent in Italy and 10 per cent in Greece) of individual interventions by the IMPs (Bianchi, 1993: 61), while the overall financial participation of the private sector in the IMPs was 11.7 per cent,[13] compared to 17.48 per cent in the Structural Funds. What these data suggest is the longer a country is involved in EU Structural Funds programmes, the greater its ability to mobilize private funds in development-related objectives.

To sum up, the process of Europeanization of regional and local systems of governance plays a crucial role in shaping public–private relations and promoting networking at regional and local levels. Hence, its impact on endogenous local development capacity is twofold: a direct one, by providing increased resources, and an indirect one, by shaping intra-regional cooperation and thus promoting the creation of intra-, inter- and transregional networks that support local development initiatives. However, since the degree of Europeanization of local governance systems varies significantly across Europe, the pre-requisites for successful adaptation and Europeanization of local insti-tutional infrastructure need to be identified. This is the task of the next two sections, which deal with the establishment of linkages between European regional policy, integration theory, and the main theoretical concepts of this book: that is social capital, institutional networks and learning.

European regional policy and 'traditional' integration theory

The gradual Europeanization of regional policy since the introduction of IMPs in 1985 and in particular the operationalization of the princi-ples of partnership and subsidiarity, as the main components of European structural policy after the 1988 reform of the Structural Funds the former and of the emerging Euro-polity the latter, are seen as having far-reaching repercussions for the EU system of governance. First, although the formal incorporation of subsidiarity in the TEU (Art. 3B) poses it as a mainly procedural criterion for delineating compe-tences between EU Commission and member-state governments, its substantive meaning – the need for policy to be made at the closest possible level to the citizen (Art. A) – plays a key role in promoting accountability and transparency in the policy-making process. Hence it is seen as a recognition of the necessity for flexibility in EU decision-taking processes. Second, this flexibility implies the need for flexibility within member-states, that is the need for devolution and deconcentration of their administrative and economic structures. Third, the operationalization of partnership promotes cooperation between supranational, national and regional elites and, at a second stage, encourages the creation of synergistic networks between public, private and voluntary-community actors at local level. Finally, encouragement of synergies among the actors and formation of a system of intra-regional cooperation is linked to the outward-looking orientation of local governments, namely their capacity for developing linkages and participating in transnational networks (Paraskevopoulos, 1997; 1998). In that sense the degree of partnership and synergy creation at regional and local levels has been adopted as a criterion for the degree of Europeanization of local governments (John, 1994; Benington and Harvey 1994: Goldsmith, 1993).

Thus the institutionalization of subnational governments has substantiated their chance of bypassing central governments in the policy-making process, challenging the latter's traditional role as 'gatekeepers', in S. Hoffmann's (1966: 862–915) terms, between subnational and supranational levels of government, which subsequently opens up possibilities for coalition between these two against the centre (member-states). The emergence of regionalism and the concept of 'Europe of Regions', however, should be seen as linked to the increasing intensity of change and globalization in the political economy (discussed in chapter one) and, therefore, the response of most of the traditional European states, which have adopted strategies of devolution and decentralization, should be attributed to this trend[14] (Leonardi and Garmise, 1993). Thus, academic debate on the impact of the Single European Market (SEM) on regional disparities and role of state and regional institutions in the integration process has influenced integration theory.

In particular, the 'side payment' argument (Marks, 1992: 194–206) is linked, on the one hand, to the impact of the SEM on regional disparities and, on the other, to the intergovernmentalist approach to regional integration in Europe. Thus, in terms of the formal policy-making process at EU level, it has been, almost generally, accepted as providing a powerful explanation for the growth of the Structural Funds' budget over a long period of time.

The predominance of the supply-side/neo-liberal orientation in the programme for completion of the SEM is viewed as leading to an inevitable process of Myrdalian 'circular and cumulative causation' and 'backwash effects' (discussed in chapter one). In a similar vein, the new theories of international trade place emphasis on the role of economies of scale, imperfect competition, differentiated products and innovation (Krugman and Venables, 1990; Tsoukalis, 1993; 1998). According to this core-dominance hypothesis, the core of the EU is viewed as centred on the famous *golden banana*, which runs from south-east England to northern Italy, while the periphery is represented by the whole or some parts of southern and western Europe (Amin and Tomaney, 1995a; Hadjimichalis, 1994). Subsequently, the SEM and the programme for EMU provide benefits to the rich regions, who are the only real enthusiasts of regionalism. The most relevant case used to underline the argument is the *Four Motors of Europe* project, which is a cooperative network between four of Europe's economically strongest regions: Baden–Württemberg, Rhone Alpes, Lombardia and Catalunya (Amin and Tomaney, 1995a; Hadjimichalis, 1994). By contrast, Europe's less-favoured regions are viewed as trying to survive within a global environment dominated by multinational corporations and transnational banks without having any chance of sustainable development (Amin/Tomaney, 1995a; 1995b; Hadjimichalis, 1994; Amin/Malmberg, 1994).

Based on this analysis the intergovernmentalist and 'side payment' approaches view the development of European structural policy as a process of successive side-payment rounds in large intergovernmental bargains aimed at buying off the agreement of weaker member-states in other policy areas, such as market integration or enlargement. Thus, the creation of the ERDF in 1975 is seen as the outcome of pressures imposed by the 1973 enlargement by the entry of the UK, Denmark and Ireland, the introduction of IMPs as the result of the threat by Greece, Italy and France to veto the 1986 enlargement to include the Iberian peninsula, and the 1988 and 1992 decisions for doubling the Funds' budget as buying off the agreement of the weaker European economies for the programme of market liberalization and the creation of the SEM (Taylor, 1991; Pollack, 1995). Additionally, the orientation of the Cohesion Fund in providing support for the poorest member-states, rather than the poorest regions, is viewed as a clear reaffirmation of the intergovernmental nature of the EU policy-making structure and of the dominant role of national sovereignty in economic policy. Hence, the nation-state is viewed, on the one hand, as a gatekeeper balancing domestic demands and international pressures (Moravcsik, 1991; Taylor, 1991; 1993; Anderson, 1990) and on the other as a key actor in formulating regional development strategies (Amin and Tomaney, 1995a; 1995b; Teague, 1995; Pollack, 1995). The involvement of the German federal government in structural policy through the joint task mechanism (*Gemeinschaftsaufgabe*) and in supporting national cohesion through operation of the *Länderfinanzausgleich* mechanism has been normally used as the most relevant example.

Nevertheless, there is little evidence on the contribution of economic integration to the widening of regional disparities (Barro and Sala-i-Martin, 1991). Conversely, theoretical approaches to and empirical evidence on the effects of integration have created an unclear landscape (Hooghe and Keating, 1994). What the evidence from the interregional rankings clearly indicates is that some regions are more capable than others of adjusting to the rapidly changing economic and social environment. Successful regional development strategies in regions across Europe, such as the regions of 'third' Italy, southern Germany (Bavaria, Baden-Württemberg) and Spain (Catalunya, Madrid, Murcia) can be used as the most prominent examples. Moreover, it is doubtful whether successful regional development strategies in southern Germany should be attributed to the support provided by a powerful nation-state, given that, despite the interlocking character of the federal system, development strategies are usually the outcome of bottom-up initiatives (Morgan, 1992). Thus, as Marks has argued, the uncertain effect of market and monetary integration on the less favoured regions weakens the side payments hypothesis, because would-be recipients cannot demonstrate the certainty of losses as a result of these processes. Therefore, the increase in Structural Funds spending may be driven by new conceptions of equality and fairness within the EU (Marks, 1992: 202–4).

On the other hand, the 'unintended consequences'[15] of intergovernmental redistributive decisions in the EU policy-making process should not be overlooked. Even though most of these decisions may be formally attributed to classical intergovernmental bargains, the dynamics of the system cannot be confined within the limits of the intergovernmentalists' reductionism. Hence, although intergovernmentalism describes adequately the formalities of the decision-making process in the EU, it is incapable of capturing the dynamics of the system,[16] within which, at least after the completion of the internal market (SEA), the role of nation-state has, to a significant degree, been replaced by the 'voluntarism of the market and civil society' (Streeck and Schmitter, 1991: 157). Moreover, although neofunctionalism's emphasis on the role of interactions between supranational institutions and domestic non-state actors within the 'spillover' process implicitly acknowledges a role of learning in the transformation of loyalties and identities on a top-down basis (Haas, 1958; Lindberg and Scheingold, 1970; 1971), it seems to be incapable of capturing the complexities of the *domestic preference formation function* and the bottom-up dynamics of the system, within which the multiplicity of interests has emerged as its main feature (Marks *et al.*, 1996b; Schmidt, 1996).

All these considerations have constituted the theoretical and empirical underpinnings of the system of 'multilevel governance' (Marks, 1993: 392; Scharpf, 1994) or 'co-operative regionalism' (Scott, *et al.*, 1994: 47–67) in the EU, involving the 'outflanking' (Marks, 1992: 212) of the states, on the one hand by the transfer of authority to EU supranational institutions and on the other by the emergence of powerful regional bodies. Additionally, there is evidence of a shift in the pattern of regional interests representation at European level (namely the limited role of the Committee of Regions within the EU system of governance) from the well-known, specific nation-states, neo-corporatist system, to a rather pluralistic and more competitive paradigm, which is conceptualized as a system of 'competitive federalism' or 'disjointed pluralism' (Streeck and Schmitter, 1991: 159). Within this multi-layered policy-making environment, characterized by a high degree of interaction between actors, regional and local systems of governance are increasingly affected by linkages with the supranational level and by their capacity to exploit the challenges those linkages present. Subsequently, the learning capacity of the institutional infrastructure at any level of governance is viewed as a crucial parameter that can improve levels of effectiveness and efficiency of policy-making, by facilitating the adaptation process. Since, however, actors' preferences and institutions are seen as important determinants of the outcome of the learning process, the role and specific weight of institutions constitute a crucial issue for both learning and integration processes.

Social capital, institutional networks and learning in EU regional policy: 'socializing' rational choice new institutionalism in integration theory

While new institutionalism (with its three main strands – rational choice, historical, sociological – depending on the specific weight attributed to the institutional function *vis-à-vis* actors' preferences within the framework of the fundamental equation of political science[17]), 'borrowed' from political science, has relatively recently emerged within EU studies as a new and perhaps dominant theoretical framework, few scholars have concentrated on the institutional analysis of specific policy areas, which would enrich integration studies with testable hypotheses on the role of institutions in the integration process. This section addresses this necessity and uses institutional analysis to shed light on the role of institutions within the multi-level system of governance in European regional policy.

The 'domestic preference formation function' and the learning process

The notion of 'learning' that has emerged recently as a crucial concept within the theoretical framework of integration in Europe (Richardson, 1996: 17–34; Kohler-Koch, 1996: 370–1; Checkel, 1998; Paraskevopoulos, 1998c) is concerned with the domestic preference formation process, the complexities of which have been overlooked by liberal intergovernmentalism to a significant extent (Moravcsik, 1993; 1995). It is considered as linked to international actors' uncertainty and thus points to the role of knowledge and information flows in facilitating cooperative relations among those actors. Indeed, institutional learning is interpreted as a function of adaptable systems of 'governance under uncertainty' (Richardson, 1996: 20).[18] As defined in chapter one, it is the process by which actors acquire new interests and identities and form their preferences through interaction with broader institutional contexts/norms (Checkel, 1998). In addition, existing evidence from the European structural policy points to the role of a learning institutional infrastructure at local level, which is not necessarily associated with the role of national or international factors, in facilitating the adaptation process (see previous section). In particular, although the degree of decentralization of the state administrative structure plays a key role in determining the learning capacity of the regional institutional infrastructure, because of the dynamic character of intergovernmental relations (discussed in chapter one), the crucial prerequisite for institutional learning and adaptation within the EU structural policy environment is certain capacities for collective action at local level. This point has been reinforced by recent research, which shows that the strength of associational culture and regional identity, as well as conflicting national/regional interests, are the underlying factors of regional mobilization at European level, rather than a funding/resource focusing logic (Keating, 1996; Marks, *et al.*, 1996a).

Within this framework, the concepts of social capital and institutional networks, by facilitating collective action and by shaping intra-regional interactions through the processes of political exchange and socialization (discussed in chapter one) constitute the prerequisites for learning and adaptation to the changing European environment. Hence, in the planning and implementation processes of European structural policy social capital and institutional networks are considered the crucial parameters upon which the Europeanization of regional and local economies and systems of governance is dependent. On the part of the EU Commission, this is illustrated by its initiative to encourage partnership at all stages of the policy-making process, which constitutes the start-up for social capital formation at regional level. More specifically, the expansion in number and scope of Community Initiatives as a tool for enabling regional actors to be involved in cooperative relations has reinforced the importance of networks on both the interregional and transnational bases.[19] This trend corresponds to the emergence of the policy network approach on almost all policy domains within the EU system of governance (Keohane and Hoffmann, 1991; Rhodes *et al.*, 1996; Peterson, 1995; Kassim, 1994; Kohler-Koch, 1996; Richardson, 1996; Kenis and Schneider, 1991; Windhoff-Heritier, 1993). Thus, institutional networks and social capital are introduced, within the 'new governance' agenda of EU studies (Hix, 1998), as conceptual tools for facilitating learning and adaptation processes through their capacity for resolving collective action problems: by structuring institutional interactions in the case of the former, and by providing stable rules and procedures (social norms) that facilitate the exchange and flow of information and reduce uncertainty in the latter. Subsequently, since they affect preference-formation and institution-building processes, they constitute intrinsic elements of the attempt to 'socialize' the rational-choice new institutionalist approach to integration in Europe.

The rational-choice new institutionalist approach

Within the EU policy-making process rational-choice new institutionalists accept the fundamental assumptions of liberal intergovernmentalism about the primary role of member-state governments in the EU decision-making process and therefore emphasize actors' (member-states') preferences as the explanatory variable for both policy outcomes and institutional change. However, they go on to determine the conditions under which EU institutions, once created, have an impact on the policy choices of the member-states that could not be predicted from the preferences alone (Pollack, 1997). In this respect, EU institutions serve as an intervening variable between the preferences of member-state governments and choices about policy-making and institutional change (Pollack, 1996: 430). Thus, they constitute a crucial factor for the development of collective activities across a wide spectrum of public policy and hence for building collective governance in the EU (Bulmer, 1994), by structuring interactions and exchange relations among member-states. Subsequently, rational-choice institutionalists are mainly focused either on two-level game modelling, that is the way in which domestic institutions are used for strengthening the member-state governments' position in bargaining within the European Council (Schneider and Cederman, 1994), or on the extent to which the decision-making procedures (cooperation, co-decision) have an impact on the redistribution of power among key EU institutional actors (EP, ECJ) (Garrett and Tsebelis, 1996). Additionally, as for EU structural policy, rational-choice institutionalism focuses on the impact of particular institutional choices on the distribution of power among supranational, national and subnational levels of governance (Pollack, 1995). In sum, rational-choice institutionalism adopts a rather 'thin' approach to the institutional function, in the sense that it views EU institutions as merely the appropriate tools for structuring exchange relations among member-states, thus facilitating collective governance. This interpretation of institutions, however, by assuming actors' preferences as fixed and exogenous from the broad institutional environment, underestimates the role of institutional interactions and subsequently it is incapable of harnessing the influence of the socialization function on the formation of actors' preferences and identities at the supranational, national or subnational levels.

Institutional thickness and the socialization function

Social capital and institutional networks constitute crucial components of the socialization function within the EU policy-making process in two ways. First, although the emergence of the network metaphor on the study of policy-making in the EU has been initially conceived of as a reflection of the necessity for mapping exchange relations among the actors, the real added value of network analysis is linked to its capacity for capturing the system of institutional interactions. In that sense, however, the network paradigm overrides the rational-choice new institutionalist approach in a constructive way, on the one hand by taking into account and mapping the rationality-based exchange process, and on the other, by capturing the main features of the broad institutional environment in terms of institutional interactions and interdependencies among the actors. In doing so, the network metaphor becomes an important component of the socialization function. On the other hand, social capital, being initially itself a by-product of the exchange process, is transformed into a public good, thus influencing actors' preferences and identities and, subsequently, constituting a semi-independent variable that, by affecting actors' preference formation, facilitates the stability of intra-network relations and hence the learning and adaptation processes within institutional networks, which, in turn, function as an intervening variable between actors' preferences and policy outcomes.

Thus, in the field of the EU policy-making process, social capital and institutional networks, as crucial components of the socialization function within the learning process and hence as intrinsic elements of the domestic preference formation function, play an important role in building forms of collective governance at the supranational, national and subnational levels: as a by-product of the interactions among the actors in the case of the former, and as a tool for structuring actors' preferences in the latter. In that sense, they are viewed as the appropriate concepts for softening rational-choice institutionalist assumptions about 'institutional thinness'. Yet, the arising crucial issue is related to the role of history and path dependence logic in the creation of social capital and hence in the enhancing of the learning process. The concept of learning, evolutionist in principle, does not contradict path dependence analysis. Its fundamental function of 'learning to cooperate' (Sabel, 1993b: 120–40) is based on a 'limited rationality dynamic model' of game theory for promoting norms (namely social capital), similar in many respects to Axelrod's (1997: 40–68) evolutionary approach to norms, which provides mechanisms (sanctions, socialization) for stability and continuity of norms over time and emphasizes their role, as informal institutions, in affecting actors' preferences. It is in that sense that learning is familiar with historical institutionalism (Rose, 1990; Pierson, 1996; Bulmer, 1994; 1998). However, it should be distinguished from the deterministic interpretations of history, since it is based on the process of making collective action a rational choice. Additionally, the notions of civic engagement and strong civil society, based on the presence of social capital, constitute intrinsic elements of Western culture, which cannot be confined within the dualism of the rationality-based models of markets and hierarchies (Finnemore, 1996).

Under the above considerations and by adapting the general theoretical understanding of network dynamics, as established in chapter one, to the European policy-making environment, the proposed theoretical model of a learning institutional infrastructure in the multi-level system of governance of European structural policy is based on a local functional network, since functional networks, by shaping public–private relations, incorporating multiple types of resource and thus facilitating collective action, provide the nucleus support structure for learning and adaptation (see chapter one). Hence, where there is a lack of this type of network, as in the Objective 1 regions of the smaller and more centralized member-states, the adopted development strategies are usually driven by central state administrative structures and therefore, irrespective of their effectiveness and efficiency (for example, Ireland), inhibit rather than facilitate bottom-up learning and adaptation processes (Leonardi, 1995a).

On the other hand, European regional policy is considered a fundamental change in the system parameters that represents simultaneously a threat to pre-existing institutional arrangements in both the economic and political spheres, and an opportunity for institution-building and network-creation, especially in the less favoured Objective 1 regions. In particular, by challenging embedded structures and well-established interests at regional and local levels, the Structural Funds programmes cause instability in intra-network relations, which, in turn, on the one hand leads to resistance to change on the part of some organizations for which change means loss of security and power, while, on the other opens up the process of institutional restructuring, especially in regions with poor institutional infrastructure, by weakening the position of firmly established interests. This process facilitates the building of new institutions because under specific conditions, which seem to be relevant to the Objective 1 regions, the process of institution-building presupposes the redundancy of the old institutional infrastructure (Storper, 1995).

In these conditions the presence of multiple and collective leadership roles within the network can prevent the de-stabilization of intra-network relations, while, simultaneously, the collective response to the crisis can effectively moderate local repercussions of the changes. In this role as moderator of the tensions between learning and monitoring the power relations that the changes may engender (discussed in chapter one), an effective leadership should: first, satisfy all groups who have a stake in what is occurring; second, create a strategic vision and convince all those involved; and third, allow space for independent actions that adhere to the general strategic vision (Bennett *et al.*, 1994b: 292–3). Defined in this way, leadership requires the decentralization of power and responsibility and a high level of involvement of the participants. Hence, learning institutional networks in such a policy environment should combine a core of actors (intra-regional functional network) linked with strong ties, and a range of other local actors connected through looser ties to the core network.

The diagram in Figure 2.1 illustrates the way in which a learning institutional network at the local level, based on the processes of exchange and socialization, can facilitate the adaptation process of the region within the multi-level governance structure we are witnessing in European regional policy. In particular, the diagram reveals the way in which intra-regional interactions should be shaped. There is a group of actors (intra-regional functional network) that is linked with strong ties, while some of them[3,4,5] are loosely connected with other peripheral actors. This structure of local interactions reflects both the need for local leadership involving public and private actors and the importance of linkages with other peripheral local or non-local actors for access to new resources (information, knowledge, new ideas). Furthermore, the diagram demonstrates the distribution of power

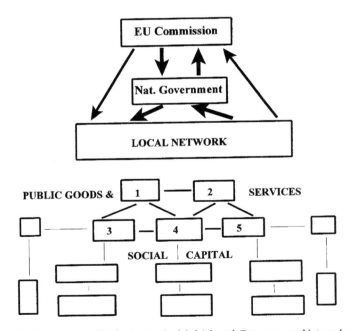

Figure 2.1 Learning and Adaptation in Multi-Level Governance Networks
Source: based on expansion of Garmise's (1995a) model.

among the actors based on the process of exchange, whereby an actor's power is strengthened by his/her ability to combine external, as well as internal linkages and, therefore, access to multiple resources. Hence, the distribution of power within the network plays a key role in shaping intra-regional interactions and achieving collective action. Finally, the role of social capital is to facilitate collective action among the actors through the socialization process, through which they become actively involved in the provision of public goods and services that support the local productive system.

Within this theoretical framework, the concept of 'institutional thickness', as an important feature of the local institutional infrastructure, is considered a crucial precondition for the processes of learning, adaptation and Europeanization of the regional systems of governance within the multi-level governance structure of European regional policy. Subsequently, institutional thickness constitutes the cornerstone for achieving convergence and hence socio-economic cohesion within the EU. This 'thick' interpretation of the institutional function, which involves the presence of dense, intra-regional functional institutional networks, with a learning capacity and facilitated by the presence of social capital endowments, implies the capacity of the local institutional infrastructure for adaptation of both its structural and policy output functions in response to changes occurring in the global or European environment. In that sense, institutionally thick regional and local systems of governance are expected to be more apt to face the challenges and grasp the opportunities that the European policy-making environment presents. This implies that within such an institutional environment local networks provide an effective range of services, while the local system of governance as a whole is more capable of integrating more resources from the EU Structural Funds.

In addition, given that EU regional policy imposes a rather enduring and longstanding challenge on the cluster of interests that may underpin the old institutional establishments across Europe, the resistance to change should be seen as a temporary, rather than permanent condition. In that sense, European regional policy is viewed as a positive external shock for promoting institutional and policy-making innovation at the regional level, especially in the regions of highly centralized member-states, most of which are eligible for assistance under Objective 1. Hence, even if the pre-existing institutional capacity for learning and institution-building was poor, regions facing the challenges of Europeanization and being involved in EU programmes and initiatives would begin to build institutional infrastructure and participate in networks of all kinds to increase their development potential by gaining access to EU funds.

However, the definition of learning as a twofold process involving institutional and policy adaptation suggests a two-stage approach to the study of institutional networks and the implementation of European regional policy (CSF, 1989–93). The first stage is an investigation of national conditions which affect the local policy environment and the development of local institutional capacity. Of particular importance is the structure of the state. The second stage is to evaluate the local institutional infrastructure by mapping the institutional networks and identifying the presence of social capital, as well as by measuring local learning capacity through an investigation of how policy and institutional relations have evolved. Therefore, the following sections will assess the impact of the state structure on shaping local institutional capacity and establish the methodology for mapping institutional networks, identifying the presence of social capital and evaluating the learning capacity of the institutional infrastructure.

The structure of the state and local capacity for learning

The structure of the state in terms of both its constitutional dimension and the dynamics of intergovernmental relations constitutes an important component for the formation of so-called 'domestic policy networks' (Anderson, 1990: 417) or the 'European domestic policy' (Jeffery, 1997: 13) frameworks, which have been identified as crucial parameters for moulding the territorial division of powers within states and hence the shaping of the institutional capacity of subnational authorities across Europe. Furthermore, the effectiveness and efficiency of public administration at the regional and local levels play a key role in either enforcing or inhibiting the local institutional infrastructure, even though they are affected to a significant degree by the form of intergovernmental relations.

Within the system of intergovernmental relations, the territorial division of powers is closely linked to the distribution of resources among levels of government and in that sense it affects directly both the level of and scope for autonomous action by subnational authorities and patterns the nature of relations among the levels of government. In particular, if the system of interactions among local actors and the local decision-taking process are dependent on higher tiers of government for crucial resources (financial, administrative) or for favourable attitude, there is less space for horizontal cooperation, learning and building of a bounded system of policy-making at the subnational level (Anderson, 1995: 462). Thus different state structures can account for the differentiation of institutional capacity among European regions.[20]

Thus, within centralized states, the structure of intergovernmental relations is expected to be dominated by vertical networks. Although these networks can impose cooperative relations between centre and periphery, they discourage the creation of horizontal networks at local level and thus are seen as a major impediment to local institutional capacity in two ways. First, while horizontal networks bring together actors of equivalent status and power, the vertical link unequal agents in asymmetric relations of hierarchy and dependence. Within these structures the build-up of social trust is discouraged, because the flow and reliability of information among levels of government and the sanctions that support the norms against opportunism are inhibited.[21] The example of patron–client relations that involve vertical interpersonal exchange and reciprocal but asymmetric obligations is relevant to this point. Second, vertical networks demonstrate a bureaucratic hierarchical structure, within which all aspects of public policy are accomplished. Subsequently, there is little space for horizontal cooperation at local level. Conversely, institutional thickness, upon which the learning process is based, presupposes the presence of horizontally interconnected institutions that represent the broad range of local economic and social actors and responsive subnational authorities that can provide interchangeable leadership roles. Van de Ven (1975) notes:

> Vertical patterns are usually highly structured by clearly defined contracts, charters, laws, administrative policies and procedures. They are usually bureaucratically organized with rational planning, specified goals, prescribed means, and clear authority and sanctioning patterns. As a result, horizontal integration, particularly at the local level, is difficult to achieve (cited in Aldrich and Whetten, 1981: 389).[22]

Therefore, in centralized states the dynamic system of intergovernmental relations tends to have a vertical, hierarchical and bureaucratically organized structure, within which local authorities depend on higher levels of government for resources. Thus the institutional infrastructure at local level is usually dominated by intergovernmental rather than functional networks, which means less space for a bounded local system of governance. Thus, interregional comparisons within centralized states should take into account the character of the state and hence the possible differentiation should be interpreted in relative terms.

In evaluating, however, the qualities of regional and local institutional infrastructure, a secondary parameter, namely the degree of efficiency of local public authorities, should be taken into account. This is crucially dependent on the character of the local political system (for example extent of clientelism) and the way in which public officials and civil servants are selected – whether the recruitment system is dominated by professional or political considerations – which play a key role in determining the effectiveness and efficiency of local public administration. Furthermore, given the requirements of the learning process in terms of openness, quick interpretation of knowledge and information and taking initiatives, the extent to which local public authorities can be successfully involved in the process is dependent on the qualities of human capital. Hence, the quality of the local system of public administration constitutes an integral part of the evaluation of local institutional capacity.

Social capital, institutional learning and European regional policy: the methodology

As discussed in this chapter, the capacity of regional systems of governance across Europe to adapt successfully to the changing European environment (European structural policy) is dependent upon:

a) the presence of thick institutional networks at the local level which shape the system of interactions, by achieving collective action among public, private and voluntary-community actors and by coordinating and managing all resources in the area;
b) the capacity of these institutional networks to learn, that is to adapt both their structures and policy outcomes to meet the changing requirements and rules of the game that European regional policy presents;
c) the presence of social capital endowments – trust, norms and networks of civic engagement – at regional and local levels that constitute the prerequisites for both the processes of achieving synergy and collective action among the actors, and of facilitating learning and adaptation of the network as a whole; and
d) the structure of the state, especially the territorial and functional division of power and resources.

However, since, European regional policy represents an enduring chal- lenge for regional systems of governance, even poor (in institutional capacity) regions, once they are involved in EU programmes and in- itiatives, start to build an institutional infrastructure and participate in interregional and/or transregional networks.

To investigate these theoretical hypotheses the comparative case study approach has been adopted as the most appropriate methodol- ogy for identifying possible differentiation in the adaptation process. Its main advantage is that it allows the researcher an in-depth analysis of complex social and political phenomena by using varied data, such as interviews, statistics, documents and surveys (Yin, 1994). In the European regional policy area, however, which involves qualitative research, it enables for a comparison between complicated systems of interactions, focusing on both interactions among actors and interac- tions between structural and cultural features.

Why national interregional case study? The choice of cases

The research study is based on the binary comparison of two regions (NUTS II) within the same country, Greece. Two reasons make the example of Greece particularly relevant for an assessment of the impact of institutional networks and social capital on facilitating the learning and adaptation of subnational systems of governance and determining the outcomes of regional development strategies in the Europe of 2000. First, though Greece has been a member of the EC since 1981 and a recipient of major funding programmes, its economy has not responded adequately to the flow of EC investment funds and it lags behind the other peripheral states (Lyberaki, 1993). Second, Greece is characterized by a centralized and weak national administrative structure and the lack of a viable system of subnational government. Thus, even though a series of important institutional changes were introduced in 1986–87 as a consequence of the implementation of IMPs and CSFs (the country was divided into thirteen programme-regions with appointed regional councils headed by a government-appointed regional secretary), the planning role of the regional council and the region as a locus of politico-economic governance has yet to be established.

However, the degree of adaptation and mobilization of subnational governments for influencing EU policy-making is not analogous to the constitutional position nor even the structure of intergovernmental relations within specific member-states (Jeffery, 1997), and hence there can be perfectly clear patterns of interregional differentiation within a particular – even centralized – member-state (Klausen and Goldsmith,

1997). This underlines the increasing importance of other variables, such as the qualities of the system of intra-regional interactions (institutional networks), in determining the degree of adaptability of regions across Europe. Therefore, it makes sense to undertake interregional comparison within the same state structure.

Additionally, since the researcher is investigating the validity of the hypotheses in different contexts, binary comparison is related to the comparison of nations/states with similar structures, and hence allows for greater theoretical sophistication and a subsequent redefinition of the initial research hypotheses (Dogan and Pelassy, 1990). Yet, with binary comparisons two important parameters should be taken into account: first, the appropriateness of the subject to one case more than the other, and second, the difficulty of extracting general truths and theoretical propositions based on specificities of particular contexts (Dogan and Pelassy, 1990). With the former, because of their importance for the dynamic process of adaptation to the European environment, social capital and institutional learning constitute common 'comparative independent variables' (Windhoff-Heritier, 1993) for both regions, hence comparison is valid. With the latter, even though it can be difficult to generalize, when the research is based on specific contexts, case studies are usually used for extracting and testing theoretical assumptions and propositions (Yin, 1994). Furthermore, in this

research study there is a wide range of shared contextual independent variables, such as the almost complete Europeanization of structural policy, the upgraded role of the EU Commission in policy-making and the same national political and administrative environment, that can validate general theoretical conclusions.

The choice of the specific cases has been based on several criteria. First, both cases have been under the same institutional framework of assistance within EU structural policy (IMP Aegean Islands, CSF Objective 1), and over the same period of time. Second, they have had more or less similar development potential, being based on similar kinds of physical resource. Third, local authorities in both cases have been involved in the functions (planning, monitoring) of EU policy-making over the same period of time. Finally, each case was in a different stage of institutional and economic development when the first integrated EU programmes began to be implemented. These comparable cases are the Southern Aegean Islands (SAI) and the Northern Aegean Islands (NAI) regions.

Furthermore, beyond the repercussions of the multi-fragmentation of space (especially in the Southern Aegean), such as the fragmentation of cultural, political, and economic patterns among the islands, there are important common features that differentiate the profile of each region, in terms of history and prosperity. The Southern Aegean Islands (SAI) region consists of two island-complexes and simultaneously prefectures, the Cyclades and the Dodecanese. Although there are significant intra-regional (among the islands) differences in the rate of development, it is one of the most converging regions of the country and also with a good ranking among European regions (NUTS II). Conversely, the Northern Aegean Islands (NAI) region, which consists of three big islands (Lesbos, Chios and Samos), each of which, along with some smaller islands, constitutes its own prefecture, lags behind as much within Greece as at the European level. The main qualitative difference in economic development between the SAI and NAI regions lies in the speedy adjustment of the economic structure of the former in the development of the service (tertiary) sector of the economy, in particular tourism, as against the latter which has continued to rely on traditional (for each island) productive sectors (such as agriculture with an emphasis on olive oil for Lesbos, or shipping-maritime industry for Chios), demonstrating, in general, an inability to adapt to the changing environment. On the other hand, the Dodecanese, the most prosperous of the two island complexes of the SAI, was incorporated into Greece only in 1947, being until then under Italian rule, and some of the islands in the Cyclades complex (Syros) have strong traditions of trade and cultural relations with western Europe. On the contrary, the NAI followed the path of other Greek territories, being under Ottoman rule until the beginning of the twentieth century.

Measurement

To identify the interactions between structure and culture at both intra-regional and interregional levels, possible synergistic relations among public and private actors, as well as interactions between the external shock caused by the implementation of the Structural Funds' programmes and the existing institutional infrastructure, a two-stage approach has been adopted: first, carrying out network analysis, and second, identifying the presence of social capital.

Network analysis was based on semi-structured in-depth interviews with representatives of all the prominent organizations at regional level, such as subnational governments, local development agencies, chambers of commerce, university and research institutions, and other regional institutions having a say on regional policy issues in general and on planning and implementing the EU Structural Funds' programmes in particular. Elite interviewing constitutes an important methodological approach to testing hypotheses and carrying out qualitative research[23] (Oppenheim, 1996).

Based on the responses, adjacency matrices were created: a statistical tool that identifies the presence or absence of linkages among the organizations. The emerging pattern of linkages reveals the role and position of each organization and the nature of inter-organizational relationships (Knoke and Kuklinski, 1982: 17). By using adjacency matrices and by employing the UCINET software program (Borgatti, *et al.*, 1992) the research performed Social Network Analysis (SNA), which can measure the degree of institutional thickness (density calculations), distribution of power among the actors (centralization measures), structural equivalence among the actors (structural equivalence measurements), and finally the graph of the network structure, for both the processes of general exchange and implementation of the Structural Funds' programmes in the two regions.[24]

The presence of social capital, on the other hand, is usually identified either by mass survey data or by data on membership in voluntary-community organizations. The interview schedules employed social capital identification questions. However, because the interviewees did not constitute a sample, with the exception of some extreme characteristics, these data cannot constitute the basis for social capital identification. Thus, because of lack of financial resources required for mass surveys, the research relied on data on membership in voluntary organizations – which has been facilitated by a research project that is being carried out in Greece[25] – and on qualitative analysis of the fieldwork research.

Finally, for the identification of the networks' policy learning capacity, the following criteria have been specified that reflect the discussion in chapter one. First, given the importance of dialogue and communication for the learning process, the presence of fora for dialogue, such as conferences and committees focusing on specific policy areas, are considered as crucial indicators for the identification of learning (Jenkins-Smith and Sabatier, 1993). Second, the building of new institutions and the expansion of the already existing institutional networks, by bringing in new actors in response to changing external conditions that necessitate new policy areas and subsequently new sources of information and knowledge, are seen jointly as an important criterion for learning capacity. Third, problem-identification procedures and the gradual achievement of general consensus among the actors about the problem, which can be seen as the previous stage of the Sabel's 'learning to cooperate', constitutes the third indicator of learning (Jenkins-Smith and Sabatier, 1993). Finally, the presence of a good amount of formal and informal communication channels among the policy actors of the public sphere in a broad sense and private interest actors (firms), whereby the public–private divide is overcome, is seen as the last but not least prerequisite for institutional thickness and learning.

Conclusions

This chapter discussed the theoretical aspects of European regional policy and defined the concepts of learning, adaptation and Europeanization of regional systems of governance, which constitute the core concepts of this book. Subsequently, it established the main hypothesis of the book: that social capital and dense functional intra-regional networks are identified as independent and intervening variables respectively of the local capacity for learning and adaptation within the European regional policy environment. Furthermore, the Europeanization of public policy and the structure of the state have been considered as providing opportunities for and constraints on the local institutional capacity for learning. Hence, some secondary hypotheses related to the role of the Europeanization process and the structure of the state in facilitating or inhibiting the learning and adaptation capacity of the local institutions were established.

Finally, this chapter outlined the methodology of the research study. A comparative case study approach has been used, because of its ability to integrate a variety of data sources and to allow an in-depth analysis of complex social and political phenomena. To identify the interactions between structure and culture the book adopts a two-stage approach: first carrying out social network analysis, a statistical technique which can measure the density of the network and the distribution of power among the actors, and second, identifying the presence of social capital. The network analysis is based on semi-structured in-depth interviews with local elites, while for the identification of social capital the study has relied on data on membership in voluntary organizations and qualitative analysis by fieldwork research. Additionally, a set of criteria for measuring the local learning capacity was identified.

3
Greece: Restructuring under Pressure or the Response to an External Shock

Introduction

This chapter deals with two important features affecting, directly or indirectly, the system of local institutional interactions (local institutional networks) and its learning capacity (adaptability): first, the structural – structure of the state and intergovernmental relations – and cultural – civic culture and social capital – specificities of the Greek socio-political system; and second, the main aspects of national regional policy, as it has gradually evolved after the Second World War and the civil war, as well as the impact of the Europeanization process, especially after the introduction of the IMPs (1985). The chapter is divided into three sections. Section one presents the main features of the state structure and the system of intergovernmental relations and assesses their impact on the learning capacity and Europeanization of local systems of governance. Section two focuses on the gradual transformation of national regional policy as a consequence of the pressures from EU membership. Finally, section three discusses the impact of cultural characteristics on facilitating or inhibiting structural and political adaptation.

State structure and intergovernmental relations: from local clientelism to clientelist corporatism

As chapter two has established, the distribution of power and financial resources between different levels of government and the political and administrative capacity of regional and local authorities may facilitate or inhibit the learning and adaptation processes of subnational systems of governance.

The highly centralized and weak administrative structure and the lack of a viable system of subnational government are generally considered as impediments to Greece's adjustment to the new European environment and the successful exploitation of the opportunities it presents for modernization and economic development. However, Greece's entry into the EU and, in particular, the gradual Europeanization of regional policy, have constituted external shocks to the structure of the state and its public administration. In that sense the slow process towards administrative restructuring and adjustment, which started in the 1980s, is interpreted as a response to the challenges of the European environment. This section is itself divided into three subsections: the first focuses on the origins of the modern Greek state structure and the distribution of functions and competences between different levels of government; the second examines the way in which financial resources are allocated and resource-dependence relations between the tiers of government are shaped; finally, the third evaluates the capacity of bureaucracy and public administration, and the quality of the subnational political elites, for institutional learning and adaptation.

From local clientelism to state clientelist patronage

In Greece there are mainly three levels of subnational government: the region (NUTS II level-13), the prefecture (NUTS III level-55) and the municipality commune (437 demoi and 5388 koinotites).[1] Given that the regions (*perifereies*) were established for the purposes and under the pressure of the implementation of European regional policy programmes (IMPs and CSFs) only in 1986, with their core functions concerning regional development and planning, the prefecture and the first tier of local government (municipalities and communes) constitute the traditional forms of subnational government, originating either in the period of Ottoman occupation or in the period of the creation of the modern Greek state in the first quarter of the nineteenth century, which was marked by the tension between centralization and decentralization.

Thus, the coexistence of municipalities (*demoi*) and a plethora of non-viable communes (*koinotites*) constitutes the main characteristic of the Greek system of local government. This can be traced back to the distinctive features of the economic, political and social structures of the Ottoman empire, where the combination of a highly centralized economic and political structure with autonomous small villages, from the middle of the sixteenth century, through the increasing, commercialization of agriculture, produced a more or less total autonomy for local potentates (*pashas*) at the expense of both the state and the peasants.[2] Moreover, this process is viewed as a crucial factor for the creation and further reinforcement of local clientelistic networks (Mouzelis, 1978; Hadjimichalis, 1987). In particular, the communes in Ottoman Greece constituted nuclei systems of local government that performed a wide range of functions, involving the provision of public goods and services (education, public works, water provision) financed by the raising of their own taxes. The common feature of their administrative structure, however, was the predominant role of local landowning elites (local potentates-*prouchontes*) in choosing local leadership, given the indirect and guided election procedures. Thus, owing their existence to the financial and administrative requirements of the Ottoman system of administration (that is the collection of taxes), and their survival to the tolerance of the empire's central authority (Christofilopoulou, 1990), the Greek communes should be seen simultaneously as quasi-democratic forms of local governance and nuclei bases for the formulation of local clientelism. Paradoxically enough, however, the ideological expediencies that accompanied the creation of the modern Greek state and emphasized the role of the communes in the Ottoman era as cells for the preservation of Greek language, religion and culture[3] were used simultaneously by the opponents of ideas of decentralization (Kontogiorgis, 1985: 75).

Thus, the structure of the newly founded Greek state started, even from the first steps, to reflect the inherent inconsistencies and discrepancies of the long Ottoman period between the political (institutional), economic and social spheres. Hence, not surprisingly, the westernizers' – modernizers[4] approach to the tension between centralization and decentralization of the state structure was identified with centralization which, beyond the trends of the age in favour of highly centralized nation-states, in the Greek case was seen as a necessity, given the lack of class-based linkages between state and civil society and the well-established personalistic, clientelistic, hierarchical networks at local level (Petropoulos, 1968; Mouzelis, 1978). Moreover, the major asymmetry between, on the one hand, the political/institutional infrastructure, transplanted from the already matured capitalist countries of western Europe, and, on the other hand, the pre-capitalist structure of Greek economy and society led to an imposed 'from above' model of modernization that gradually became a consistent pattern for promoting political and economic innovation in Greece.

Within this framework, the institutional foundations laid down by Capodistrias,[5] the first Governor of Greece (1828–31), and King Otto

(1833–62), were based on the perception of a centralized and unitary state structure with emphasis on core institutional aspects, such as the army and public bureaucracy. In intergovernmental relations this trend was substantiated with the establishment of the prefectural system, based on the departmental conception of *nomoi* involving the prefecture and the province as intrinsic features of the territorial and administrative state structure, headed by central state-appointed prefects (nomarchs) and heads of the provinces (eparchs) respectively. Furthermore, the creation of a new unit of local government, the municipality (*demos*), consisting of more than one commune, was seen as an attempt to assault the powerful local *prouchontes*.

However, the communes survived over time and their role was further reinforced by the so-called 'liberation of the communes' reform introduced by Prime Minister Venizelos in 1912, in an attempt to liberate the communes from the organizational oppression of demoi, that had in the meantime become strongholds of his monarchic political opponents. What the Venizelos reform implicitly brought about was the transfer of clientelistic relations from local to national level, following the gradual establishment of the parliamentary system and the creation of national political parties. Thus, local clientelistic networks became gradually the bottom tier of the hierarchical, clientelistic networks, upon which the national political system and the organization of the political parties were based (Mouzelis, 1978). Hence, Venizelos's reform is considered a source for the structural problems facing the contemporary Greek administrative system (a large number of fragmented and non-viable communes[6]).

Within this hierarchical state structure, the role of the prefecture has always been central in the system of centre–periphery relations, performing the functions of all ministries, and headed by the prefect, who was – until 1994 – the appointed delegate of central government. Thus, since the provision of services and the distribution of central government funds were decided by the prefect and his officials and the prefectures are the electoral constituencies for general elections, the normal channel for the satisfaction of local needs was through political pressures exercised by local politicians and local authority executives, focusing mainly on the incorporation of municipal works into the Public Investment Programme of the prefecture and thus breeding hierarchical clientelistic networks at local level.

In the political upheaval of the post-civil war period in the 1950s and 1960s, the emphasis placed by the dominant ideology on state neutrality was used as a tool to cover up the correlation between expansion of political clientelism and the strengthening of state repression. Two consequences were: the reform of the prefects' status, through specific criteria and methods of recruitment; strengthening it as that of the civil servant and the predominance of the ideology of 'apolitical' local government, which emphasized the administrative role of local institutions and the tightening of the prefectural supervision of local authorities, involving both *ex ante* and *ex post* control of municipal decisions.

The above features of post-war centre–periphery relations, which were, to a significant extent, dominant even in the first period after the restoration of democracy (1974–81), created a policy environment favourable for local governments' control by political clientelism, financial dependence on the central state and administrative supervision by the Ministry of the Interior. In this respect, the Greek system of local government is considered similar to the French one, given the existence in both systems of a schism between administrative and political functions of local authorities and their approach to decentralization as a functional reproduction of the central state at the local level (Christofilopoulou, 1990).

Yet, the process of democratic stabilization and the opening up of European prospects have constituted the crucial determinants for restructuring the state and the reformulation of intergovernmental relations after the restoration of democracy in 1974. The first post-dictatorship period (1974–80) was characterized by a series of reluctant reforms undertaken by the New Democracy right-wing government, involving mainly the reinstatement of key pre-dictatorship legislation and the modernization of existing institutions. Thus, the first step was the restoration of the 'quasi-civil servant' status of the prefects, according to which prefects were chosen by the government from a 'List of Prefects' drawn up by a group of judges called the 'Council of Prefects', who used specific criteria for their appointment and evaluation.

Furthermore, with regard to the first tier of local government, a new Municipal Code was introduced in 1980 with a provision for a reluctant transfer of functions. Urban transport, nurseries, old-age centres, housing and municipal marketplaces were among a series of new competences transferred to local government. Additionally, the new Code provided for the division of local authority functions into 'exclusive' and 'shared' competences, that is functions performed either by local government or by other public sector organizations. Under this distinction, the only exclusive functions introduced by the new Code were: urban transport, municipal sports facilities and youth centres, the construction of municipal buildings and parking meters. Conversely, a series of crucial local development functions, such as tourist development of municipal land, public housing, culture, nurseries, hygiene and health care centres, pollution and building controls were characterized as shared competences. This distinction contributed to a considerable overlapping of functions among different levels of government, which emerged as a crucial issue for centre–periphery relations after the reforms of the 1980s.

Finally, the ability, given to local governments, to create municipal enterprises – an important step towards enhancing the entrepreneurial character of local authorities with far-reaching repercussions for getting access to and managing of EU resources – and the establishment of the Municipal Enterprises of Water Supply and Sewerage for managing the water supply and sewage systems in towns of more than 10,000 inhabitants were the last important innovations of this first post-dictatorship period.

To sum up, the general characteristic of this first post-dictatorship period was the partial resurgence of pre-dictatorship clientelist networks and national party-driven patronage coupled with some reluctant modernizing reforms.

Intergovernmental relations and the emergence of state clientelist corporatism

Entry into the EC in 1981 coincided with a major change in Greek politics: the coming to power of the first PASOK government. Thus, the period of Greece's response to the challenge of adjustment to the new European environment in the 1980s was marked by the presence of a new, socialist government, that came into power with a strong commitment to and a widely publicized programme of decentralization. The changes occurring in the system of intergovernmental relations in the post-1981 period are characterized by the tendency towards a more corporatist system of regional interest representation (Andrikopoulou, *et al.*, 1988), which, however, being still based on the previous clientelist relations have led to what may be called clientelist corporatism.[7]

This trend became initially evident through the changes in the nature and role of prefectural councils introduced in 1982. Instead of being composed mainly of civil servants, they were transformed into advisory councils representing the various organized interests of the prefecture. The new councils include local government representatives, that make up half the council, the mayor of the leading municipality of the prefecture, two representatives of the Local Association of Municipalities and Communes-LAMC, whilst the remaining members are elected representatives of professional organizations, chambers of commerce, agricultural cooperatives and labour movement organizations at the prefecture level.

This reform in the composition of the councils, however, coincided with a second change, involving the deinstitutionalization and 'politicization' (Christofilopoulou, 1990: 88) of the prefects' status. The appointment and evaluation of the prefects were no longer the responsibility of any specific governmental institution (Council of Prefects). Instead, the prefects were directly appointed and dismissed by the government, without any criteria for recruitment and time limits on their term in office.

The reformulation of the nature and role of the prefect and the prefectural councils was accompanied by a third reform involving the relations between the prefecture and the first tier of local government. In particular, the *ex ante* and *ex post* controls of the prefects on the expediency of municipal decisions were significantly restricted[8] and the prefectural tutelage limited to checks on the legality of municipal decisions. Even though these reforms signalled a functional transformation of the role of the prefecture, they did not fulfil the virtues attributed by the wording of the law to the prefectural councils as 'organs of popular representation', given that they were not directly elected institutions. Instead, what the reform really brought about was a shift from the well-known clientelistic relations between local state (prefecture) and society (civil society, interest groups) towards an interest group-corporatist representation at the prefecture-level policy-making process (Verney and Papageorgiou, 1993: 113).

At local government level the main goal of the PASOK reforms was the opening up of the system for citizens' participation in decision-making on local issues. Thus, provincial councils and the creation of directly elected district and neighbourhood councils were innovated at sub-prefectural and sub-municipal levels. Furthermore, a wide range of incentives for voluntary mergers of small demoi and neighbouring communes, as well as for inter-municipal cooperation and the establishment of municipal enterprises involving public–private partnerships at local level, were introduced, nevertheless with poor results.

Moreover, the major reform, introduced in 1986 for the creation of an elected second tier of local government at the prefectural level – the so-called Prefectural Local Authorities – was not implemented until 1994, when the elections were held under a different legal framework.

Finally, the last important reform of this period, the establishment of the administrative regions as central administrative units for regional planning and development, along with the provision for directly elected prefectural councils, constituted Greece's response to the increasing pace of Europeanization of regional policy in the 1980s and the subsequent reorientation of the planning, implementation and monitoring processes. Thus, the country was divided into thirteen regions,[9] headed by General Secretaries of the Regions, directly appointed and dismissed by the government, whilst the regional councils that were set up, in addition to the General Secretaries, consist of the prefects of each nomos of the region and one representative of the Local Association of Municipalities and Communes of each nomos. In the regional Monitoring Committees of the Structural Funds' operational programmes, however, interest group-representatives of each nomos of the region (chambers of commerce, agricultural cooperatives, trade unions) are actively involved in the process.

The structure of the system of intergovernmental relations in Greece, as formed in the 1980s, is presented in Figure 3.1. What this graph reveals, is that, despite several reforms, involving the opening up of the system to civic participation and providing encouragement for the formulation of local interactions, because of the persistent reluctance of the state to decentralize, centre–periphery relations are hierarchically structured, and highly centralized, since the various bottom-up features are abrogated by the final control of the central state. Thus, the administrative hierarchy which traditionally exists between the levels of government is found mainly in central government, the prefecture and the local authorities, whilst the newly created region constitutes the institutional aspect of the top-down approach to strategic regional planning. The only directly elected form of subnational government within the system is the first tier of local government, whose interests at the central government level are represented through an umbrella organization, the Central Association of Municipalities and Communes, in a traditionally neo-corporatist manner. As it might have been expected – and as will be shown in the following section of this chapter – the processes of regional planning and democratic programming in Greece in the 1980s have been profoundly influenced by this structure of intergovernmental relations.

The distribution of functions between different levels of subnational government, after the reforms of the 1980s and early 1990s, constitutes a crucial issue for the shaping of local interactions, the level and scope of inter-organizational learning and adaptation, and hence, for the

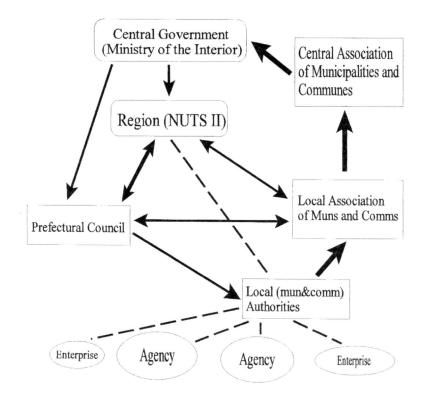

Administrative Hierarchy
Neo-corporatist Interest Representation
Formal Non-hierarchical Linkages
Informal (Advisory, Administrative) Linkages

Figure 3.1   Intergovernmental Relations in Greece Prior to the Last (1994) Reform
Source: Paraskevopoulos, C. J. (1998b).

Europeanization function of local governments. Additionally, the European dimension and its interaction with the process of administrative restructuring has dramatically expanded the functional limits of subnational governments in Greece.

Table 3.1 below shows the distribution of functions among various levels of government after the reforms of the 1980s. There are three main features of this distribution. First, with the exception of tradi-

Table 3.1   Distribution of Functions by Level of Government in Greece

Policy Areas	National Government	Regional Council	Prefectural Council	Local Government
TRADITIONAL				
Law and Order, Public Admin.	XXXXX			
Foreign Affairs, Defence	XXXXX			
Monetary Policy	XXXXX			
Foreign Trade, Fiscal Policy	XXXXX			
Statistics, Media, Communication	XXXXX			
ECONOMY-SECTORS				
Agriculture, Fisheries	XX	X	XX	
SMEs	XXX			XX
Commerce, Trade, Markets	XXX		XX	
Tourism	XX		XX	X
Banking, Insurance	XXXXX			
Employment, Industrial Relations	XXX		XX	
Economic Planning	XXXXX			
SOCIETY				
Education	XX		X	XX
Health–Welfare	XX		XX	X
Social Services	X		XXX	X
Social Insurance	XXXXX			
Culture, Leisure	X		XX	XX
TERRITORY				
Regional Planning	X	XXX	X	X
Urban Planning–Housing	X		XX	XX
Public Works	X		XXX	X
Public Transport	XX		XX	X
Roads	XX		XX	X
Water and Sewage				XXXXX
Energy	XXXXX			
Environment	X		XX	XX

Source: adapted by the author from Municipal Code, Law 1622/86.

tional state functions most functions are shared by central government, prefecture and first tier of local government. A wide range of economic, social and even territorial functions are shared predominantly between central state and prefecture. In particular, the powers of the prefectural councils include: planning and regional development, agriculture, tourism, health, social welfare, labour and commerce, transport, culture and education. Some of these functions are shared with the municipality, whose powers, however, remain minimal. Second, subsequently, in almost all policy areas there is functional interference by the central state. Third, the functional role of the region is limited to that of strategic regional planner, which places it at the margins of the local system

of governance, consisting mainly of the prefecture and the local authorities. Thus, the high degree of functional overlap has become a crucial
characteristic of the Greek system of subnational government after the
reforms of the 1980s (Psychopedis and Getimis, 1989). This overlapping
has several consequences for the system of intergovernmental relations,
which may inhibit or facilitate the degree of effectiveness within the
system and the formation of intra-regional or interregional interactions
that are seen as the necessary prerequisites for the building up of learning institutional policy networks at local level.

These consequences are threefold. First, the strong overlaping of
functions, the imperceptible bounds of responsibilities and the subsequent coordination problems create dysfunctions in the system that
often inhibit rather than facilitate its effectiveness. Psychopedis and
Getimis (1989: 99) note:

> The transfer and diffusion of powers among new decentralized insti-
> tutions at the local level does not necessarily lead to the improve-
> ment of their performance. The conflict between the new
> institutions regarding the decentralized powers, the problem of
> strong functional overlap and the dispersion of responsibilities to
> various separate and isolated institutions continue to be considered
> the crucial issues of local institutions.

Second, the unclear distribution of functions opens up possibilities for
dynamic flexibility in the system of intergovernmental relations,
within which local authorities are given space for bounded and relatively autonomous policy-making through the establishment of rules
of the game among participants, thus providing the necessary environment for building cooperative policy networks in areas of common
concern. Within this policy environment, characterized by a disorga-
nized stability, the differentiation in innovation capacity among subnational governments is crucially dependent on the availability of
economic resources and civic culture endowments, that can facilitate
the formation of inter-institutional interactions by exploiting the
benefits of institutional learning. The opportunities provided by the
European policy framework and, in particular, by the Europeanization
of regional policy play a catalytic role in this process. Finally, resource
interdependence and the subsequent bargaining requirements among
levels of government or institutions within the same level provide the
foundation for dialogue and communication, and consequently
the basis, at least, of a learning environment. Hence, the functional
overlapping of the Greek subnational system of government – a

consequence of the fragmentary and often incoherent decentralization policy since the early 1980s – represents simultaneously the danger of inefficiency and a chance for the flexible adaptation of subnational governments. The most crucial factor in this process is the presence of civicness (social capital endowments) at the local level.

The reform of 1994[10] and the elections for the second tier of local government, which were held in the same year, have changed significantly the landscape of intergovernmental relations in Greece. Figure 3.2 sets out the structure of intergovernmental relations after

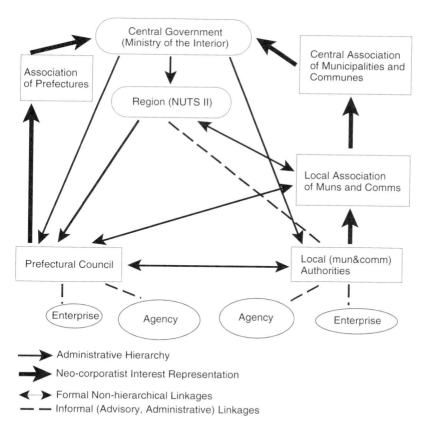

Figure 3.2 Intergovernmental Relations in Greece after the 1994 Reform
Source: Paraskevopoulos, C. J. (1998b).

the 1994 reform. The main features of the reform concern the role of the old prefectural councils, which have been renamed *Nomarchal Local Authorities*. The nomarchal local authorities constitute the elected second tier of local government with their own financial resources and the right to establish their own agencies, as well as to participate together with other local actors in enterprises. However, there is no administrative tutelage or hierarchical control between the second and the first tier. The abolition of the hierarchical relationship between the old prefecture and the local authorities implies anticipation of conflicts between the two tiers that could arise from the existing strong overlap of their functions. However, a sort of administrative tutelage of the region (Regional General Secretary) has been established, with regard to the legality of the decisions of the prefectural councils which points to the start-up of a gradual process leading to the substitution by the region of the old prefecture as a central state representative at local level.

Thus, the newly reformed system of intergovernmental relations consists of two directly elected tiers of local government with unclearly allocated and strongly overlapping responsibilities and a third tier (region), directly controlled by the central state. Within this institutional structure, the distribution of competences among the three levels, especially among prefecture and local governments, should be performed within the framework of territorial and functional subsidiarity. Finally, the transfer of almost all functions of the traditional 'local state' (prefecture) to the new nomarchal authorities[11] has refocused the debate on two traditionally crucial issues for the subnational government in Greece: the problem of financial resources and the political and public administration capacity.

The system of local government finance and centre–periphery relations

The local government finance system in Greece has always been the crucial administrative field that reflects the centralized state structure, as well as its interconnectedness with the resource-dependence relations between centre and periphery and the shaping of hierarchical clientelistic networks at national and local levels.

In the post-war period the centralization trend is indicated by both the limited role of local governments in managing their own finances and the level of local government revenue as a percentage of the central state budget. Thus, local government revenue as a percentage of the state budget in the post-war period dropped from

9.3 in 1948 to 6.6 in 1974, to be increased again to 11.1 in 1984 (Tatsos, 1988: 22).

The revenue of local government is categorized in 'regular' and 'extraordinary' (Ministry of the Interior, 1987). The first consists of income from property, local taxes, charges and regular central government grants, while the second – most of which was abolished in the 1989 reform – is mainly grants from the Public Investment Programme of the Ministry of National Economy distributed by the prefectures, or specific grants given to local authorities by other public actors (such as Ministry of Culture) for specific municipal works purposes.

Given the centralization of the fiscal system, Greek local authorities had minimal power to tax. On the other hand, the various charges imposed on all inhabitants for several services constitute a rather stable, but relatively limited, source of revenue. Thus, central government grants have constituted the main source of local government revenue.[12] Since both regular and extraordinary transfers were to a significant extent at the discretion of central government and subsequently a permanent source of uncertainty for local economic planning, they facilitated the development of clientelist relationships between local authorities officials and central state political elites. Hence, the 1989 reform of local government finance was focused on strengthening local governments' financial autonomy by rationalizing the revenue system. Thus, the return of the existing tax on immovable property to municipalities was accompanied by the abolition of the regular and most of the specific and extraordinary grants and their substitution by a new revenue-sharing system: the so-called 'Central Autonomous Resources of Local Government' scheme.[13] Moreover, the grants from the Peripheral Investment programme of the Ministry of National Economy have been replaced by one-third of the local government share of income tax, which is separated from the Central Autonomous Resources. Finally, and more importantly, local authorities are allowed, but not obliged, to introduce additional taxation for the completion of specific municipal programmes.

This major reform of local government finance, however, did not result in a substantial increase of revenue, given the political reluctance and administrative incapacity for raising the tax on immovable property – the only tax given wholly to local government. For this reason the responsibility for its collection was later returned to the central state services.[14] Subsequently, some local authorities in an attempt to strengthen their financial autonomy have tried to pursue policies involving the provision of social services (day care, transport, cafeterias and so on) as an indirect source of revenue. Nonetheless, the rationalization of the system of grant revenue accompanied by the enactment of 'objective' criteria for its distribution has contributed to the institutionalization of a redistributive function of those transfers seeking to equalize the differences between rich and poor.

Within the EU policy-making environment, however, reform of the system of local government finance constitutes a major challenge for both local political leadership and other public, private and voluntary (civil society) actors involved in reshaping the system of local interactions on a reciprocal basis, because it means the imposition of specific local taxes on the one hand and commitment to the provision of public goods and services on the other. This process will be facilitated by the financial status of the new prefectural councils.

The financial function of the prefectural councils up to the 1994 reform was twofold: first, distribution of the funds provided by the Peripheral Public Investment Programme, and second, administrative-legal control of the budget of local authorities (municipalities and communes). These functions were in line with the dual role of the prefecture, on the one hand, as the institutional formulation of what has been called 'local state' (Psychopedis and Getimis, 1989) and, on the other, as the appropriate administration field for incorporating local needs into central decision-making and thus absorbing the local pressures. Both functions are performed through the Public Investment Programme, which provides the ground for the regulation of local problems by bridging the gap between local needs and availability of resources (Psychopedis and Getimis, 1989: 84–5). The means to achieve these objectives lie with the functional and territorial differentiation of the Public Investment Programme, which is facilitated by its division into the programme of the central state and the regional public investment programme. What this differentiation implies is that, within the framework of the decentralization policies pursued in the post-1981 period, the central state undertakes the regulation of problems arising in policy areas where the economies of scale are high (such as large-scale investments), whilst simultaneously leaving the regulation of local scale problems (e.g. small-scale infrastructure) to the local state (prefecture). Furthermore, in formulating the Peripheral Public Investment Programme, local needs are taken into account, even within the limitations of the clientelist system.

After the 1994 reform, however, and the subsequent abolition of the budgetary control of local authorities by the prefecture, there has been a distinction of the nomarchal local authorities revenue similar to that of the municipalities: in regular and extraordinary revenue. The regular revenue consists of taxes, charges, income form property, the central autonomous resources and the specific annual financial transfer for the costs of exercising central state functions, while the extraordinary revenue consists of loans, specific transfers of other public actors and the resources from the EU.

To sum up, maintenance of the financial dependence of subnational governments on the central state transfers accompanied by strong functional overlap has constituted an intrinsic element of the system of intergovernmental relations in Greece. Nonetheless the opening up of the system to bottom-up initiatives based on flexible schemes for mobilization of endogenous resources (additional taxation, use of modern cooperative financial tools) presents a challenge to the local system of governance. Hence, the learning, adaptation and Europeanization processes rely on formal or informal networks at the local level that can achieve synergistic effects among the actors by combining public and private resources. The success of this process, however, is crucially dependent on the presence of a strong civil society, the capacity of local political elites and the administration system.

Subnational political elites and the quality of public administration bureaucracy

Greek municipal and communal councils are elected every four years according to a double-ballot majoritarian electoral system.[15] In municipalities of more than 5000 inhabitants the winning list is that which gains the absolute majority of the votes. The head of the winning list becomes mayor or president of the commune. In municipalities where no list receives absolute majority in the first ballot there is a second ballot among the leading candidates a week later. After each municipal election, the local authorities elect the governing boards of Local Associations of Municipalities and Communes (LAMC), their corporate organization at the nomos level, which in turn elect their representatives in the Central Association of Municipalities and Communes (CAMC), the umbrella organization of local authorities on a nationwide basis. Both the CAMC and the fifty-one LAMC, however, lack the appropriate organization and scientific expertise to provide the needed technical support and consultation to their members, or to present local authorities' interests efficiently at central government level.

Although there is no formal appearance of the names of political parties on the lists – a practice consistent with the post-war dominant ideology of 'apolitical' local government – local elections are dominated by intense 'party politicization', especially in the urban areas. Thus, municipal councils are usually run by party coalitions, which are formed either before the first ballot, or in the second ballot, when no separate list corresponding to major political parties wins the majority of the votes in the first ballot (Christofilopoulou, 1990).

The role of political parties as vehicles of political clientelism has always been decisive for the huge expansion of the inefficient state bureaucracy,[16] as well as for the incorporation of civil society and allocation of resources. Thus, the interrelated and mutually reinforcing processes of political clientelism and the expansion of a legalistic and inefficient bureaucracy are considered the main features of the system of public administration, with serious repercussions for the functioning of the public sector. First, the normal recruitment criteria, rendered unusable by political intervention and subsequent bureaucratic growth, have resulted in a bureaucracy that is relatively autonomous from the political patrons, resisting the implementation of reformist political decisions insofar as these decisions affect their interests (Flogaitis, 1987). This, in turn, creates the so-called 'bureaucratic vicious circle'[17] (Flogaitis, 1987: 52–4) according to which bureaucrats' resistance to reformist measures leads to their non-implementation, thus increasing their ineffectiveness, which results in yet more reform efforts. Second, the legalistic character of the system, the so-called 'notorious legalism of public administration' (Athanasopoulos, 1983: 137[18] (cited in Christofilopoulou, 1990: 286)), constitutes a major impediment to the system, given the dependence of public policy-making on the bureaucracy's expertise in legal formalities. Third, the hierarchical structure of the system accompanied by very small wage differentials and absolute job security discourages civil servants' initiative, most of whom try to find secondary work in the parallel economy. Finally, as a consequence of these factors, in contrast with most European countries, there is no functional relationship between public administration and civil society. Thus, the political parties play the role of interlocutors between public-sector bureaucracy and civil society by attempting to bypass the rigidities of the public administration and thus bridging the gap in state–society relations.

Within this framework, the functions of local authorities have had to be accomplished between the Scylla of party-dominated political clientelism and the Charybdis of a highly centralized, hierarchically structured system of public administration, with far-reaching repercussions for local policy-making. Thus, being public law entities primarily under the administrative control and tutelage of the Ministry of the Interior,[19] and therefore obliged to follow the rigid procedures of the public sector for personnel recruitment and salaries, local governments cannot attract competent, well-educated, appropriate staff.[20] Consequently, they lack the planning and project development capacity necessary for the preparation of project proposals for participation in EU or national development programmes, thus facing enormous difficulties in tapping resources vital for local development. Furthermore, these deficiencies block and ultimately undermine important development projects, whilst, on the other hand, the undertaking of planning functions by the central state bureaucracy results in huge delays in the transfer of EU or national funds. Finally, because of the bureaucratic inefficiencies of the state structure, the decision-making process is much more time-consuming than in the case of other local actors (that is private or voluntary).

Under these circumstances, the role of political parties and local MPs is similar to that observed at the national level, that is the role of interlocutors between the central state bureaucracy and local authorities which facilitates the transfer of resources by circumventing bureaucratic channels. In this process, local government executives (i.e mayors) are increasingly involved in political brokerage similar to that observed by Sidney Tarrow (1974: 46–7) in Italy, using contacts with their own or other political party deputies to achieve objectives corresponding to local needs. The crucial importance of political parties, however, is not simply confined to their role in transferring necessary resources, but also applies to their ideological and organizational impact on the management of local issues and the quality of local elites.

Thus, in the post-war period local government constituted the traditional forum for the centre and left-wing parties that were almost permanently in opposition during the 1950s and 1960s. The majority of urban demoi in this period were under the control of coalitions between centre and left-wing parties. This 'castle of democracy' approach to local government, however, although it was seen as an appropriate political tool against the authoritarianism of the post-war state and the predominance of the 'apolitical' approach to local government, in fact contributed to the marginalization of issues crucial for local governance by merely using local governments as fora for opposition on issues from the national political arena.

With the restoration of democracy in 1974 a new, profoundly altered political landscape emerged, which was marked by the reformulation of the old and the emergence of new political parties.[21] During the first post-dictatorship period (1975–81), that was a substantially preparatory period for accession into the EC, decentralization and local government issues remained at the margins of public debate. The vast majority of municipalities were under the control of coalitions between the Pantellenic Socialist Movement (PASOK) and the parties of the communist left, whose 'politicization' approach to local government contradicted the attitude of the New Democracy right-wing government that local government was merely a branch of public administration (Christofilopoulou, 1990). However, the opportunistic strategy of PASOK of exploiting these alliances at the local level by presenting the image of a bloc of so-called 'progressive democratic forces' against the 'authoritarian' government led to the significant underplaying of local government issues as subordinates in the framework of general confrontation with the government. A similar approach, in many respects, had been adopted by the major party of the communist left, the Communist Party of Greece (KKE), whose commitment to centralized state and central planning had led to a passive attitude on the part of local governments, since local issues were seen as dependent upon change of government at central state level. Additionally, the policies of these main opposition parties (PASOK and KKE) were crucially influenced by their common position against Greece's entry into the EC. Within this political climate there is no easily identifiable differentiation in administrative capacity at local government level among right- and left-wing political parties. Rather, whatever the differentiation in institutional performance, it should be attributed either to personal initiatives or to the impact of differentiation in cultural or institutional capacity on shaping interactions among local actors. Moreover, the tendency to use local government as a springboard for personal political elevation, which has been a common characteristic of all political parties in the post-dictatorship period, should be attributed as a deficiency in the policy approach of all parties to local government.

In the second post-dictatorship period, after 1981, which is characterized, with the exception of the 1990–93 period, by the predominant role of PASOK in Greek politics, local government has been continuously the preferential policy area of PASOK in collaboration with the left-wing parties, even though, since 1986, New Democracy has proved particularly competent in increasing its influence in major urban municipalities (Athens and Salonika).

Therefore, beyond the necessities imposed by EC membership, the reluctant reforms introduced by the PASOK governments during the

1980s should be partly attributed to PASOK's powerful position in local governments, based on its well-established mechanisms for political mobilization at the local level, since 1974. These local strongholds constituted the first tier of the centralized clientelist structure of PASOK in the 1980s upon which populist mobilization was based. Mouzelis (1995: 19) notes:

> Papandreou managed to build the first non-Communist mass party organization in Greece, with PASOK's branches extending into the remotest Greek villages. This ... contributed to the further centralization of political parties. Clientelistic bosses gradually saw their control over local votes being undermined by a populistically controlled, centralized party structure, which replaced traditional patrons with better-educated party cadres who derived their authority from above (from Papandreou's charisma) rather than from the grass-roots level.

Within this framework, very frequently during the 1980s, local governments were used as the appropriate base for mobilization and support of PASOK's policies at national level and especially in foreign affairs,[22] thus underplaying their functions at the local level. However, the gradual shift of PASOK's European policy towards complete acceptance of EU orientation of the country since the late 1980s, and especially during its last – matured – term in office after 1993, has contributed to the change in local governments' attitude and the refocusing of their interest on local rather than national policy issues. Within these changing attitudes, EU membership is no longer considered as a threat to local development, but rather as a challenge for the reformulation of local interactions.

In conclusion, because of Greece's highly centralized administrative structure, the role of the political parties as mediators between centre and periphery is crucial. However, there is no identifiable, identical pattern of administrative capacity at the local level among political parties. What matters is the strength or weakness of systems of interactions at the local level, which determine local institutional capacity and the way in which local demands are mediated at national or European level. In a country, where centralized planning remains predominant, the way in which central–local relations are shaped is particularly evident in the framework of regional policy, the gradual Europeanization of which is the subject of the following section.

Regional policy in Greece: national and European contexts

The centralized, hierarchical structure of the Greek administrative system corresponds to the pattern of regional disparities between centre and periphery, the main feature of which is the concentration of population and economic, social and cultural activities, primarily in the greater Athens area and secondarily in Salonika. The origins of the regional problem are traced to the transformations occurring at the beginning of the twentieth century that led to the early take-off of industrial capitalist development. This process was boosted by the coincidence of several factors, such as the collapse of Asia Minor in 1922 and the subsequent waves of 1.6 million refugees, the acceleration of land reform and an enormous influx of foreign funds (Mouzelis, 1978; Hadjimichalis, 1987). Since industrial activities were concentrated in the major cities – Athens, Piraeus, Patras, Volos and Salonika – the industrial boom of this period constituted the first crucial factor for the formulation of what were called 'development axes of the country' (Patras–Athens–Salonika). During the post-civil war period, the emigration waves and the subsequent concentration of population in the Athens and Salonika areas combined with administrative centralization contributed to the intensification of the regional problem, until it gradually became the most serious national issue. Hence, the need for a national regional policy.

The evolutionary process for the formulation of a national regional policy, based on fiscal and monetary incentive packages (investment grants, interest-related subsidies, depreciation allowances) for attracting private investments in the periphery and creating basic economic and social infrastructure through the Public Investment Programme, can be divided into three pre-EC membership sub-periods: the first from 1948 to 1960, the second from 1961 to 1974 and the third from 1975 to 1979.

During the first post-war period, regional development policy was focused mainly on the abolition of indirect taxes imposed on the circulation of goods and services (the equivalent of VAT), on increasing depreciation allowances for regional industry and on fiscal concessions for reinvesting profits, while interest rate subsidies for industrial loans were introduced.

The second period (1961–74) was characterized by an upgraded role of regional planning at the national level. This trend was substantiated by the operationalization of Regional Development Agencies (RDA) at prefecture level under the control of the then Ministry of

Coordination, and by the creation of the Industrial Areas Network undertaken by the Bank for Industrial Development. Furthermore, with the institutional framework of that period the entire country was divided into four incentive zones and for the first time investment grants, conditional on each region's level of development, were introduced (Paraskevopoulos, 1988).

After the restoration of democracy in 1974 emphasis was placed on the improvement of incentive schemes for development of the border regions, and especially Thrace, for national reasons. Furthermore, in an attempt to rationalize the system of investment grants, the manufacturing branches were distinguished as of high, medium and low assistance (Paraskevopoulos, 1988). In the same period, however, the introduction of the first post-dictatorship regional development plan (1978–82) signalled a shift in spatial and regional planning towards the nodal or 'growth-poles' approach to regional development[23] (Konsolas, 1985: 383–5). In particular, the main goal of the plan was the reduction of regional disparities through the development of a rival network to the cities of Athens and Salonika. Thus, specific quantitative population goals were set up for primarily selected dynamic urban centres, the so-called 'Centres of Intensive Development Programmes' e.g. Patras, Larissa), which were to be transformed into poles of self-sustaining development. Additionally, another network of less dynamic centres, consisting mainly of the capitals of the *nomoi*, the so-called 'Municipal Urban Centres', were formed in which special programmes for the improvement of infrastructure were provided. The remaining urban areas of the country were organized into 'Systems of Agricultural or Agro-Industrial Urban Centres'.

Although the idea of central economic planning had been introduced in 1964 following the establishment of the National Centre for Planning and Economic Research (KEPE), the five-year plans gradually became synonymous with highly centralized exercises on paper because they did not take into account real conditions and thus were not finally implemented. This rule applied to the first post-dictatorship plan (1978–82) which was not actually implemented. However, it foresaw and indirectly influenced the developments, given that most of the urban centres selected by the plan for intensive development programmes, during the 1980s, gradually became growth poles through concentrating population and economic resources from their broader provinces.

In the first period after accession to the EC, which coincided with the coming into power of the PASOK government, the maintenance of the national character of regional policy, based on centralized 'top-down' control, became evident in the modification of the system of regional development incentives that was introduced by law 1262/82.[24] The innovations brought about by the reform were threefold; first, the broadening of the range of activities qualified for incentives by including, in particular, the non-state public sector of the economy, that is the entrepreneurial initiatives of local authorities and various cooperatives and associations; second, the increasing involvement of regional and prefecture councils in the decisions concerning the approval of applications, which, however, reinforced the role of central administration bureaucracy (Ministry of National Economy), since both the regional and prefecture councils were not directly elected bodies and there was no provision for the involvement of local governments (Andrikopoulou, 1992); third, a re-designation of the four broad incentive zones, according to their level of development.[25]

The top-down character of decision-making, based on the dominant role of the Ministry of National Economy and its Regional Development Agencies at prefecture level and the exclusion of elected local authorities, coupled with the lack of coordination between the main ministries of National Economy and Interior responsible for regional development have constituted intrinsic elements of regional incentive policy (Psychopedis and Getimis, 1989: 53–4). The coincidence of the above characteristics and the lack of information flows, communication and dialogue between actors at the local level led to the reduction of regional development policy in a series of fragmented and uncoordinated actions (*ibid.*). Since the incentives system and the Public Investment Programme constitute the main instruments of regional policy, the combination of centralized decision-making and the lack of local networks leaves little space for endogenous decision-taking, which is viewed as the main prerequisite for integrated development strategies (see chapter one).

Moreover, interestingly enough, the gradual Europeanization of regional policy in the 1980s, in contrast with most of the northern member-states, did not result in the reduction of regional incentive expenditure, but rather to its significant increase.[26] This trend, which seems to be consistent with the expansionary fiscal policy followed by the PASOK governments in the 1980s and not affected by the short austerity programme of 1986–88, should be attributed to the well-established political clientelist relations (see previous section) and subsequent protective role of the state. Additionally, the persistence of the national incentives scheme as a quasi-national branch of regional policy has to a significant extent led, on the one hand, to a low contribution of the private sector to the sub-programmes or measures of IMPs and CSFs (see chapter two), and on the other, to the waste of national and European financial resources, since both the national contribution to EU programmes and the regional incentives scheme are financed through the Public Investment Programme.

The system of regional planning and the key role of the Public Investment Programme were at the centre of the institutional reforms imposed by the Europeanization of regional policy with the introduction of the six IMPs in 1985 and the CSFs in 1989. The very substance of the Greek centralized planning procedures was challenged by the principles of European structural policy, and especially by the operationalization of partnership and subsidiarity to facilitate the mobilization of subnational governments in planning and implementation processes (see chapter two). The integrated approach initialized by the IMPs implied the start-up of the institutional learning process for Greek subnational authorities by requiring their active participation in planning and monitoring procedures. The maintenance of the same approach in formulating the Regional Development Plans (RDP) of CSFs created conditions of permanent pressure upon the central state for decentralization and restructuring of the planning system. The major reform of intergovernmental relations in the 1980s (see previous section) coincided with the restructuring of the planning system that was initialized by the 1983–87 five-year plan. Thus, even though the IMPs and RDPs were primarily conceived of as programmes for promoting economic development, their most important function in the Greek case has been that of 'a financial "stimulus" to promote the reform of sub-national governmental structures' (Papageorgiou and Verney, 1993: 141).

The main features of the new planning system were twofold: first, the opening up of procedures of democratic planning at each spatial level, which would be facilitated by the institutional changes in intergovernmental relations (elected prefectural councils); second, the maintenance of the hierarchical, 'top-down' structure, within which the coherence and complementarity of the plans in terms of time schedule and territorial level would be achieved. Thus, the functional limits of the new system were set by its attempt 'to combine "top-down" control with "bottom-up" definition of priorities' (Andrikopoulou, 1992: 198).

As is shown in Figure 3.3, while annual and medium-term plans are to be drawn up at each territorial level, each tier of government decides the allocation of Public Investment Funds to the next lower level. These decisions are constrained by expenditure ceilings defined for each level of government by the Ministry of National Economy. Under

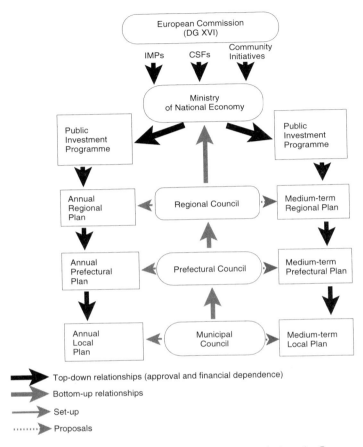

Figure 3.3   Regional Planning and Centre–Periphery relations in Greece
Source: Paraskevopoulos, C. J. (1998b).

these conditions, what the decentralization and democratic planning reforms implicitly brought about was the identification of specific projects at each level of government, subject to the expenditure constraints of the higher tier. Moreover, given the lack of directly elected planning bodies at prefectural level until the 1994 reform and the division of the Public Investment Programme into national and prefectural components, the real impact of democratic planning on the regionalization of the budget was the co-management (controlled by the centre) of the Public Investment Programme by the Ministry of National Economy and the prefectures.

This structure of regional planning and budget management, dominated by the central role of the Ministry of National Economy,[27] has been a major impediment to the implementation and monitoring of both the IMPs and the Regional Operational Programmes (ROPs) of the CSFs. In particular, the absence of direct links between the EU Commission and subnational governments has created major coordination problems and seriously inhibited the development of learning and adaptation capacities by the subnational elites, which are essential to endogenously driven integrated development strategies. Thus, during the formulation of the IMPs the centralization of decision-making was accompanied by a lack of both formal and informal channels of information exchange and communication on an intra- or inter-regional basis, that is a lack of intra- and inter-regional horizontal institutional networks (Papageorgiou and Verney, 1993). This local institutional infrastructure inadequacy caused piecemeal drafting of the IMPs by the Ministry of National Economy, when it should have been an outcome of integrated planning within which local needs would have been taken into account.[28] Consequently, the implementation of two-thirds of the IMPs budget was allocated to central agencies, while the remaining one-third was managed by the prefectures (*ibid.*: 148). Furthermore, in the monitoring procedures the lack of direct communication between the regional monitoring committees[29] and EU bureaucracy became evident, since the channels of information between supranational and subnational level passed through the central Inter-ministerial Committee. All these dysfunctions led, in substance, to distortion of the scope of the IMPs, which were designed for enhancing the learning and adaptation functions at subnational level by the operationalization of the integrated approach. Thus, rather than being integrated strategic plans for development, IMPs were essentially lists of proposals by the prefectures based on demands from local authorities and other local agencies (Konsolas, 1992). Hence the eventual outcome – the lowest implementation rate in comparison with the other beneficiaries (France and Italy) (Leonardi, 1995a) – should be attributed to the limited Europeanization of the Greek administrative system and lack of local institutional capacity. These weaknesses are indicated by the low rate of private-sector involvement in IMP structural interventions.[30]

The lessons learned from the implementation of the IMPs, the upgraded role of the Regional Secretariat in drawing up the Regional Operational Programmes and the administrative support provided by programme managers and evaluation consultants have brought about the main improvements embodied in the implementation of the first

CSF (1989–93). However, the unfavourable political and economic circumstances, especially during the initial phase, the well-known administrative weaknesses and continuing hierarchical structure of the
planning procedures functioned as counter-forces causing internal and
external inconsistencies, significant delays and inefficiencies (CEC,
1995; Ioakimidis, 1996). With the Regional Operational Programmes,
on the one hand, control of the Ministry of National Economy over
the financial resources of the CSF and more importantly over
Community Initiative funds and, on the other, the low quality of the
local institutional infrastructure in learning and adaptation (absence of
learning intra-regional networks) played an important role in inhibiting endogenous decision-making, the formulation of integrated
development strategies, and eventually the Europeanization of subnational governments. Nevertheless, there are signs of some differentiation in effectiveness among regions and prefectures (CEC, 1995),
which point to the crucial role of civic culture and the strength of
civil society that can facilitate or inhibit the formulation of the
system of interactions among the actors at local level. The cultural
peculiarities and the strength of civil society in Greece are the
subjects of the next section.

Civil society and the cultural schism

The question of civil society constitutes a crucial as well as neglected
side of Greek history. Even though in R. Inglehart's (1988)
classification of European countries according to levels of mutual trust
Greece appears to be rated higher than above all parts of Italy, research
on social trust and civic engagement is completely overlooked.
However, the clientelistic political system, the lack of administrative
transparency and the inadequate institutional infrastructure, which are
the usual explanations for the relative divergence of Greek economy
(Lyberaki, 1993) and society, seem to be closely linked to an 'extremely
weak civil society' (Mouzelis, 1995: 19).

Indeed, since the construction of the modern Greek state in the first
half of the nineteenth century, its history has been dominated by a
cross-cutting cultural schism – Diamandouros's 'cultural dualism'[31] –
between two powerful and conflicting cultural trends: the Western on
the one hand and the Byzantine–Ottoman on the other (1994: 8). The
first is linked to the Western Enlightenment traditions of civicness,
rule of law and constitutionalism, as they have been reformulated over
time since their original Hellenic roots, and the second to the pre-

capitalist, despotic tradition of strong state, clientelism and the Orthodox Church that is a combination of the later Byzantine and Ottoman heritages (Mouzelis, 1986, 1995).

During the independence struggle, the cultural schism was evident in the conflict between the revolutionary block of 'westernizers', within which the enlightened Greek diaspora of the West played the key role, and the reluctant block dominated by the Orthodox Church (Mouzelis, 1978; Diamandouros, 1994; Clogg, 1979). The first block consisted of the enlightened Greek diaspora bourgeoisie, the Western-oriented, Western-trained intelligentsia, who provided both the leadership and the necessary material resources for the struggle, and the masses of peasantry and ruined artisans who were primarily interested in safeguarding their traditional rights against the increasing power of local gentry. The second (reluctant) block comprised: the Orthodox Church, whose hostility to any attempt to overthrow Ottoman rule should be attributed to its fear of loss of privileges and subsequently political power; the Phanariotes, whose reluctance is easily explainable by their privileged position in the administrative hierarchy and their close relations with the Church; and the local gentry, who because of their landowning power status were extremely reluctant to join the nationalist mood (Mouzelis, 1978; Filias, 1974; Diamandouros, 1994).

Two other important developments deserve reference, if the main features of the multifaceted processes that crucially influenced the structure of state–society relations are to be understood. The first is the protagonist role of Greeks in European commerce, which had been boosted, primarily, by highly favourable international circumstances that started as early as the end of the sixteenth and the beginning of the seventeenth centuries. This development had a direct impact on what has been called the 'early take-off' period of Greek capitalist accumulation, (Moscof, 1972,[32] cited in Mouzelis, 1978: 10–11), involving a significant shift from the distribution sphere to productive economic sectors. This second important development, which started in the mid-eighteenth century, was marked by increasing investment in the ship-building industry and handicrafts (mainly textiles), among which the Ambelakia cooperative is the most famous case.[33] However, the Ambelakia and other cooperative handicraft industrial associations are directly comparable with and represent the Greek version of the sixteenth-century proto-capitalist industrial movement in Europe and in particular the English industrial districts that did not flourish because of the predominance of the paradigm of mass production that marked the dawn of the English Industrial Revolution (Mouzelis, 1978).

Thus, the failed attempts at industrial development based on ship-building and handicraft cooperative activities signalled the pre-dominance of the distinctively comprador character of the Greek indigenous bourgeoisie and subsequently of Greek capitalism, which is not irrelevant to the structural and cultural characteristics of the modern Greek state.

Within this framework the cultural differentiation, a substantially Greek *v* Hellenist antithesis, has had far-reaching repercussions on Greece's transition to modernity and its capacity to adapt to changes in the global or European environments. The predominance of Diamandouros's famous 'underdog culture'[34] during the period of tran-sition, and even during the later period after the Second World War and the civil war, determined to a significant extent the 'qualities' of contemporary Greek economy and society. Furthermore, the emer-gence of the subcultures of clientelism and populism (Mouzelis, 1995; Lyrintzis, 1993), coupled with the quasi-capitalist character of the Greek economy characterized by the dominant role of the state, have led to the 'atrophic civil society' – 'hypertrophic state' interplay (Campbell, 1964). Additionally, the peculiar combination of populism, clientelism and elements of state corporatism (Mavrogordatos, 1988; 1993; Schmitter, 1995) after the emergence of PASOK in the 1980s led to what may be called state-clientelist corporatism which has added to the deterioration of state–society relations at the expense of the latter (Paraskevopoulos, 1998a). Deriving from this analysis and emphasizing the weakness of civil society, similarities have been identified between Greece – as an exception from the other southern European countries – and Latin America, over, in particular, the transition from authoritar-ianism (Schmitter, 1986).

Under these considerations, mutual trust, norms of reciprocity and networks of civic engagement, which constitute intrinsic elements of civicness, are difficult to identify. Conversely, the Greek version of individualism and free-riding, within the framework of a still pre-modern society, is counterbalanced by the well-publicized substitute concepts of *filotimo* and *besa*,[35] which, however, being primarily irra-tional and non-contractual in both the formal and informal senses, cannot be seen as convincing substitutes for mutual trust (Tsoukalas, 1995). Hence, the irresponsible, authoritarian and anomic behaviour identified by Banfield with familism in southern Italy may be relevant to the Greek case as well.

Yet, notwithstanding these unfavourable circumstances the process of Europeanization is interpreted as an external shock for society and the economy because it imposes pressures for change (Kazakos, 1991). Furthermore, reactionary attitudes towards trade unionism and subject-oriented new social movements provide evidence of 'from below' post-modern reactions that challenge well-established patterns of behaviour (Mouzelis, 1995). These trends are expected to create conditions of instability and change in the political system, which, even in the post-Papandreou era and despite the current 'from above' movement towards a more prompt adaptation, is still dominated by cross-sectional rivalry between modernizers and populists.

Conclusions

This chapter has demonstrated that the combination of a centralized state structure and a weak civil society in Greece creates conditions that breed hierarchical clientelist networks, which in turn constitute a major impediment to the learning, adaptation and Europeanization functions of the socio-political and economic structures. In particular, the well-established clientelist networks, upon which the political system is traditionally based, have been the crucial determinant for shaping state–society and centre–periphery relations, since they function as mediators between the inefficient state bureaucracy and society (interest groups, civil society). Within this framework subnational governments' functions have had to be accomplished between the Scylla of party-dominated political clientelism and the Charybdis of a highly centralized, hierarchically structured system of public administration.

However, the gradual process of Europeanization of regional policy in the 1980s has constituted an external constraint on administrative restructuring and adjustment of the hierarchically structured Greek political and economic systems. Hence, the 1989 reform of local government finance, the establishment of the directly elected second tier of subnational government at the prefectural level, and the initiation of democratic planning at the regional level have led to the opening up of the local governance system to bottom-up initiatives. Nevertheless, they are crucially dependent on the strength of civil society and the formation of the system of interactions among the actors at regional and local levels on a horizontal basis.

Although my analysis suggests that the peculiar individualism of the Greek people has led to a country of free riders, in which civil society and social capital are major problems for society's learning and adaptation capacity, the following chapters identify a regional differentiation in institutional learning and adaptation evolving from different traditions in institution-building, in the strength of civil society and in adaptation between the regions.

4
Institutional Capacity and Policy Environment in the Southern Aegean Islands

Introduction

Although the centralized state structure, as outlined in chapter three, acts as an important constraint for local institutional capacity in Greece, given the dynamic character of the system of intergovernmental relations, the characteristics of the system of intra-regional interactions play a decisive role in the dynamism of local systems of governance and their capacity for adaptation. This chapter maps the institutional infrastructure in the Southern Aegean Islands region, highlighting its political, economic, institutional and cultural (social capital) features.

Local characteristics and political climate

The Southern Aegean Islands region (NUT II) comprises 78 islands, of which only 43 are inhabited, with a population of 257 481, or 2.51 per cent of the entire country's population (1991). It consists simultaneously of two island-complexes and prefectures: the Cyclades with a population of 94 005 inhabitants, and the Dodecanese with a population of 163 476 (1991). The demographic picture of the region[1] is one of the best in the country since the early 1970s. After a substantial decrease during the decade 1961–71 (7.01 per cent or 0.7 per annum) because of both internal and external emigration flows, the population of the region increased significantly (12.6 per cent or 1.26 per annum) in the decade 1971–81. Finally, during the decade 1981–91 its population increased by 10.25 per cent, or 1.0 per cent per annum, while all the other regions had lower rates of increase in the same period. At the prefectural level, the Dodecanese, after a small decrease in population in the decade 1961–71 (1.63 per cent) – by far the smallest among the five prefectures of the Aegean islands in the same period – since the early 1970s has demonstrated the best demographic picture in comparison with all the other Aegean island prefectures, with an increase of 19.88 per cent during the decade 1971–81 and 13 per cent in the decade 1981–91. The Cyclades prefecture, on the other hand, shows a better performance when compared with the Northern Aegean islands, but lags behind the Dodecanese. In particular, after a substantial decrease during the decade 1961–71 (–13.63 per cent), its population increased significantly during the decades 1971–81 (2.46 per cent) and 1981–91 (6.27 per cent).

In education, the region lags behind country averages. In particular, according to the 1991 population census, it demonstrates a lower percentage (7.1 per cent) in university graduates when compared with the national mean (11.5 per cent) in 1991. The picture is the same in secondary education (27.95 per cent : 31.5 per cent respectively), while the region has a higher level of illiteracy than the national mean (7.75 per cent : 6.8 per cent).

The administrative and economic centre of the region is shared among the most prosperous islands. The capital city of Syros island (Ermoupolis) is the capital of both the region (seat of the regional secretariat) and the Cyclades prefecture, while Rhodes is the capital of the Dodecanese. In terms of economic development, because of the significant intra-regional disparities (among the islands), the economic centre of the region is shared among a leading group of developed islands consisting of Rhodes and Kos in the Dodecanese, and Mykonos and Santorini in the Cyclades. Additionally, the island character and subsequent fragmentation of space has important consequences for the administrative structure of the region at the sub-prefectural level. It comprises ten provinces (provincial councils): seven in the Cyclades complex (Andros, Santorini, Milos, Naxos, Kea, Tinos and Paros) and three in the Dodecanese (Kos, Karpathos and Kalymnos). However, the subordinate character of the province *vis-à-vis* the prefecture and the first tier of local government (municipalities), and the short life of the directly elected sub-prefects (the first election took place in 1994) have resulted in a limited role within the regional system of governance.

A significant aspect of spatial fragmentation within the region is illustrated by difficulties in communication between the two island-complexes and the subsequent lack of communication and transport linkages between the capitals of the prefectures (Syros and Rhodes). Under these circumstances, although the old dispute between the

Cyclades and the Dodecanese about the seat of the regional secretariat is interpreted as a symptom of the traditional parochialism of the Greek periphery, it may be viewed as a consequence of the centripetal structure of the Greek administrative and transport systems as well. Thus the island character of the region should be seen as an aggravating factor in the deterioration of structural problems deriving from the Greek socio-political system (see chapter three). Within such a policy-making environment, to reveal the local specificities and particularities the research should place emphasis on the prefectural level, given that the regional secretariat's initiatives, especially since the early 1990s, focused on cohesive and integrative actions to meet the development challenges facing the entire region, are limited by its rather marginal role within the local system of governance (regional secretary and council directly appointed by central government).

Therefore, at the prefectural level, Dodecanese, arguably the most prosperous of the two Southern Aegean island-complexes, was incorporated into Greece in 1947 having been until then under Italian rule. This is considered a crucial factor in the shaping of its political, economic and civic environment since the 1950s and 1960s. In particular, two prerequisites for economic development, the special tariff regime for products imported into the prefecture since 1947 and the advanced infrastructure left by the Italians (land registry, transport network, ports, airports, theatres, public buildings), have been crucial parameters for the formulation of local political, economic and social climate factors (Getimis, 1989). As one of the interviewees underlined:[2]

> the physical infrastructure and cultural environment inherited from the Italians have constituted a unique asset for the tourist development of the Dodecanese, which, under a different – not that of the Greek state structure – policy making environment, would had secured the future of the Dodecanese islands as the leading tourist destination in Europe.

Furthermore, local governance institutions, and especially the city councils of Rhodes and Kos, as well as private-interest organizations (Chambers of commerce) have proved particularly competent in comparison with their counterparts in other regions.

In addition, within the Cyclades complex, some islands (Mykonos in the 1960s) started to demonstrate a policy-making environment similar to the Dodecanese, while some others (e.g. Syros) have had strong cultural and trade relations with western Europe originating in their role as niches of early capitalist development in the mid-nineteenth century (1830–60) (Kardasis, 1987).

The politics of the Dodecanese were dominated by the centre and centre-left political parties, in contrast to most of the other Greek regions which were characterized by the predominant role of either the extreme right or extreme left, and this contributed to the creation of a moderate political climate, an important characteristic of the Dodecanese in the post-civil war period. Thus, during the pre-dictatorship years, it was considered a stronghold of the big coalition of small centre-wing political parties, the Centre Union, whilst the political influence of both right and extreme left-wing political parties was rather marginal. In the post-dictatorship period, however, the process of building a two-party system in Greek politics resulted in the marginalization and later elimination of the Centre Union and gradual replacement by PASOK as the predominant party in Dodecanese politics.[3] Therefore, the Dodecanese has had a policy-making environment identical to that of Greece as a whole, facilitated by a political climate that was not seriously affected by the political upheaval of post-civil war Greece.

The Cyclades prefecture, on the other hand, having been a strong-hold for right and centre-right political parties during the post-civil war period until 1981, in the post-1981 period followed changes in the political climate that were characterized by a shift towards the centre-left of the political spectrum and the gradual emergence and endurance of PASOK in Greek politics.

At the prefectural level, since the 1994 elections, both prefectural councils have been dominated by either PASOK or by the centre-left coalition consisting of PASOK and the Coalition of the Left.[4]

Finally, at the local level (municipalities and communes), the Dodecanese is characterized by a strong tradition of PASOK domi-nance. Even after the last (1994) election, the vast majority of the 17 municipal and 57 communal councils of the prefecture is domin-ated by either PASOK or by coalitions between PASOK and the Coalition of the Left. Furthermore, in Cyclades, although the majority of the 10 municipal and 107 communal councils are governed by PASOK or by coalitions with the Coalition of the Left, there is an important presence of New Democracy mayorships in Mykonos and Andros.

To sum up, the Southern Aegean Islands region demonstrates a rela-tively good (for the Greek case) policy-making and institution-building environment, especially at the prefectural level. The Dodecanese has a strong tradition of collaborative relations among the local actors, which should be partly attributed to historical and cultural reasons, while the Cyclades islands have demonstrated similar trends, especially since the early 1960s.

Economic structure, boundedness and adaptation

The Southern Aegean Islands region is one of the most converging regions in the country in economic and welfare indicators and demonstrates a relatively good ranking among the European regions (NUTS II). This is illustrated by the macro-economic indicators in Table 4.1. Thus, in the interregional comparison based on the GDP index (EU 12 = 100) the three-year (1989–91) GDP average in PPS

Table 4.1   Principal Indicators per Region (NUTS II)

Regions	GDP three-year average 1989–91 (EUR12 = 100)			Share of sectors in total employment (1991)			Unemployment rate	
	per inhab. (PPS)	*per pers. empl. (PPS)*	*per pers. empl. (ECU)*	*Agr.*	*Ind.*	*Serv.*	*Rate 1993*	*Change 1988–93*
1. East. Macedonia & Thrace	43.3	42.2	31.4	43.0	20.3	36.7	5.5	–3.5
2. Central Macedonia	46.8	53.1	39.5	25.1	28.4	46.5	6.2	–0.6
3. Western Macedonia	50.2	62.3	46.4	29.5	32.2	38.4	8.1	2.1
4. Ipeiros	36.2	41.1	30.6	34.8	22.5	42.7	9.9	4.9
5. Thessalia	43.7	49.2	36.6	36.1	24.5	39.4	7.0	0.1
6. Ionian Islands	43.7	41.3	30.7	35.7	17.7	46.6	4.0	0.6
7. Western Greece	40.8	42.1	31.3	39.0	19.4	41.7	8.8	1.6
8. Sterea Ellada	58.0	73.0	54.4	38.3	27.2	34.5	7.1	0.2
9. Peloponese	47.3	51.2	38.1	45.5	19.5	35.0	5.7	–0.1
10. Attiki	52.3	56.2	41.8	1.3	29.6	69.2	10.0	0.0
11. Northern Aegean Isls.	35.2	42.3	31.5	20.7	17.3	61.9	9.0	3.6
12. Southern Aegean Isls.	52.2	67.2	50.0	8.4	23.7	68.0	3.6	–1.5
13. Crete	45.5	48.8	36.3	45	15.9	39.1	4	0.5
GREECE	48.1	52.8	39.3	22.2	25.7	52.1	7.8	0.1

Source: CEC, 1994a.

per inhabitant of the region is 52.2, well above the country's average. Additionally, in terms of unemployment, the region demonstrates a low rate (3.6) when compared with the country's average (7.8), while it has the second best rate, among the Greek regions, in the change of unemployment for the period 1988–93 (–1.5). Furthermore, the Southern Aegean Islands also are among the most converging regions in Europe in the interregional ranking of the EU regions according to their level of unemployment (CEC, 1994a: 195–7).

The good economic performance in macro-economic indicators, however, should not be simply reduced to a symptom of EU regional policy interventions. Conversely, it should be linked to pre-existing trends in the development process of the region since the late 1960s and early 1970s, which have been accelerated by the flow of EU funds, especially in the late 1980s and early 1990s. Thus, as Figure 4.1 shows, the average annual change of GDP during the decade 1970–80 (5.30 per cent) was well above the country's average (4.57), while in the decade 1980–91 the region experienced the highest rate of average annual change among the Greek regions (23.16 per cent) and, consequently, well above the country's average (20.07).[5] Finally, in

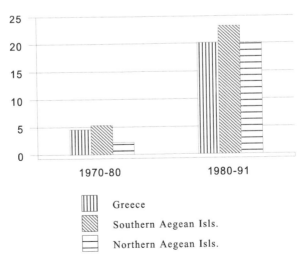

Figure 4.1   Average Annual Change of GDP in Greece, Southern Aegean and Northern Aegean, 1970–91
Source: NSSG, national accounts.[5]

the post-1991 period, the share of the region in the national GDP increased substantially from 2.73 per cent in 1991 to 2.78 per cent in 1994.

However, the processes of convergence and catching up in the Southern Aegean region are better illustrated by its ranking within the per capita GDP index (country = 100) over time and by its performance with regard to specific welfare indicators. Thus, as Figure 4.2 shows, although the region had a relatively good ranking – sixth among the thirteen regions and definitely above the Northern Aegean – in 1970, it was lagging behind the country's average. During the period 1970–81 it rose to third position within the index, just behind the Attika and Sterea Ellada regions, and reached the country's mean, while in the period 1981–91 it exceeded the country's average.

In welfare indicators, the Southern Aegean Islands was the first region in telephones per 100 inhabitants in 1991 and the second region in per capita savings, just after Attika in 1990 (Figure 4.3). However, following the traditional weakness of the Greek periphery in

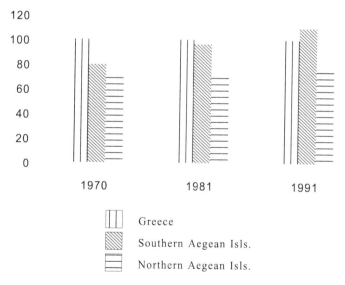

Figure 4.2 Per capita GDP Index for Greece, Southern Aegean and Northern Aegean, 1970, 1981 and 1991
Source: adapted from Athanaslou *et al.* (1995).

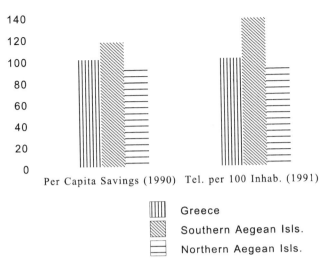

Figure 4.3   Welfare Indicators for Greece, Southern Aegean and Northern Aegean
Source: adapted from Athanaslou *et al.* (1995).

social services, according to 1991 data, it lags behind in medical personnel, which is concentrated primarily in the Athens area and secondarily in Salonika (Central Macedonia).[6]

The crucial factor, however, that may account for the Southern Aegean's good economic performance and closing of the divergence gap is the prompt adaptation of the region's economic structure, characterized by the shift towards development of the tertiary (services) sector of the economy, with particular emphasis on tourism since the 1960s. This trend is particularly evident in the sectoral distribution of employment, which is illustrated by the spectacular increase of employment in the tertiary sector from 38 per cent in 1971 to 50 per cent in 1981 and 68 per cent in 1991 (see Table 4.1). Conversely, employment in the primary sector (mainly agriculture) of the economy decreased dramatically from 36 per cent in 1971 to 21.1 per cent in 1981 and 8.4 in 1991. Furthermore, as the Location Quotients[7] based on employment data show, the region of Southern Aegean Islands along with Attika – with values of the quotient varying from 1.24 to 1.46 respectively – were the only regions of the country with a clear orientation towards the tertiary sector of production in the 1980s (1981 and 1987) (Konsolas *et al.*, 1993: 46–7).

Nonetheless, the specific weight of tourism in the productive structure of the regional economy is illustrated by the region's share of hotel units and foreign tourists' B&B (Figure 4.4). The Southern Aegean is the region with the highest number of hotel units in the country, accounting for 24 per cent of the total capacity,[8] whilst, simultaneously, it is the main destination for foreign tourists with a 32.8 per cent in 1991.[9]

Finally, in macro-economic indicators the sector of 'Miscellaneous Services', which is linked mainly to the tourist industry, accounts for 36.53 per cent of regional GDP[10] (Figure 4.5). Hence, it constitutes the leading sector of the economy with 'Commerce' being the complementary services-oriented sector and 'Agriculture' accounting for a rather marginal percentage, for the Greek case, of regional GDP.[11] Furthermore, on an interregional basis, whilst the Southern Aegean share in the national GDP was 2.78 per cent in 1994, its contribution to the specific sector of 'Miscellaneous Services' on a national basis amounted to 10.57 per cent for the same year.

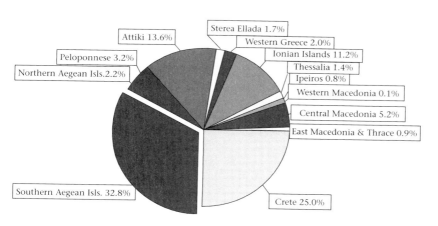

Figure 4.4   Regional Distribution of Foreign Tourist B&B in Hotel Units (1991)
Source: NSSG (1991). Tourism statistics.

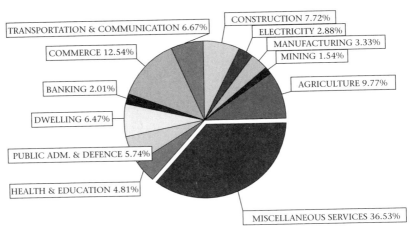

TRANSPORTATION & COMMUNICATION 6.67%
CONSTRUCTION 7.72%
ELECTRICITY 2.88%
COMMERCE 12.54%
MANUFACTURING 3.33%
MINING 1.54%
BANKING 2.01%
AGRICULTURE 9.77%
DWELLING 6.47%
PUBLIC ADM. & DEFENCE 5.74%
HEALTH & EDUCATION 4.81%
MISCELLANEOUS SERVICES 36.53%

Figure 4.5   SAI Regional GDP by Sector of Production (1994)
Source: NSSG (1994): National accounts: Section of regional accounts.

At the prefectural level, the specific features of the economic struc-ture and local system of governance of the Dodecanese can, to a significant extent, account for the developmental path of the entire Southern Aegean Islands region, given the specific weight of the prefec-ture within the regional economic and political structure. The first important feature of the Dodecanese economic structure is its prompt adaptation towards the tertiary sector of the economy and particularly the tourist industry. This process, which started in the 1960s, was facil-itated, to some an extent, by the advanced infrastructure left by the Italians and by the special tariff regime[12] as discussed above since its incorporation into the Greek state in 1947 (Getimis, 1989). Thus, as Figure 4.6 reveals, employment in the tertiary sector, which in 1971 was already the leading sector of the Dodecanese economy, increased from 43.3 per cent in 1971 to 68.2 per cent in 1991, while the share of the primary sector dropped dramatically from 29.7 per cent to 7.8 per cent respectively. Hence, the economic structure of the Dodecanese is similar to that of Attika, rather than to the country's average.

Furthermore, the emphasis on the development of the tourist industry becomes evident from the data on the sectoral composition of GDP. Thus, in 1994, the share of the 'Miscellaneous Services' sector 'mainly tourist industry', accounted for 46.15 per cent of the prefec-tural GDP, whilst in the same year the share of the primary sector

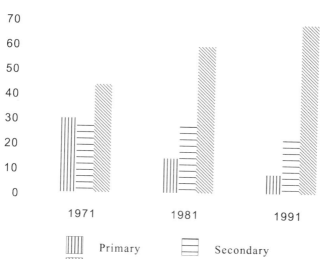

Figure 4.6 Employment by Sector of Production in Dodecanese
Source: Theodori-Markoyiannaki, E. (1986), and NSSG, 1991 Census.

dropped to just 5.15 per cent. Additionally, the Dodecanese prefecture accounted for the 18 per cent of the national annual inflows of foreign exchange in the period 1988–92.[13]

The emphasis on tourist development, however, has had important consequences for the other sectors of the economy. Thus, as the data on industrial specialization at the prefectural level reveal, the viability of the industrial sectors in Dodecanese depends on their complementarity to the tourist industry (Paraskevopoulos, 1988; Getimis, 1989). In that sense, the industrial specialization in traditional Greek industry branches, such as those of food, beverages, non-metallic mineral products and furniture, should be thus attributed. The criterion of complementarity applies also to the primary sector, mainly agriculture, even though this trend has been substantiated recently (since the late 1980s). Conversely, during the initial take-off period, the increasing need for agricultural products owing to the expansion of the tourist industry had led to an increased imports trade, becoming the dominant sector of trade at the expense of exports, which were limited to just 3 per cent of imports (Finas, 1981).

The concentration of tourist development on the islands of Rhodes and Kos, however, constitutes the second important feature of the Dodecanese economic structure. In particular, even until the early 1980s, tourist development in the prefecture was dominated by that of Rhodes and Kos, with the greatest part (86 per cent) of the prefectural tourist product concentrated in Rhodes (Logothetis, 1983). Nonetheless, this trend started to change in the late 1980s and early 1990s, given that the negative impact of overconcentration on quality and the gradual shift of consumer preferences towards small-scale tourism (Stokowski, 1994) have contributed to the diffusion of tourist development to the other islands of the prefecture.

Finally, the last and most crucial feature of the local economic structure, which is related to the functional performance of the Dodecanese local governments, and hence to the degree of boundedness of the local system of governance, is council tax. The council tax (4 and 2 per cent on the value of prefecture imports and exports respectively) which has been imposed by all – both city and communal–local councils is an important financial resource for all local governments of the prefecture and points to a comparatively bounded and endogenously driven system of local governance. It should be noted that in 1985 and only for councils of Rhodes island council tax revenue reached a total of 800 million DRS (Rhodes council a total 55 per cent) (Getimis, 1989: 137). Thus, the revenue from both council tax and income tax has led the local governments of Dodecanese (*demoi* and communes) to have the highest rate in the country in revenue per inhabitants (ibid.).

In this swing of the pendulum towards tourism-oriented development some islands of the Cyclades complex followed gradually. This process was led by Mykonos in the 1960s, favoured by a number of concurrent factors, while Santorini and other islands joined later. Nonetheless, the tourist development in Cyclades is less intense than in Dodecanese. This is because of diversification of the types of development among the Cyclades islands, with some islands being based on the tourist industry (Mykonos, Santorini) and some others remaining mainly agriculture-oriented (Naxos). Hence, the Cyclades complex is characterized by the considerable role of agriculture in the productive structure of the prefectural economy.

As Figure 4.7 reveals, despite the increasing importance of tourism in the prefectural economy since the 1970s, the agricultural sector retains a significant share of the Cyclades GDP varying from 25.46 per cent in 1970 to 21.40 per cent in 1994. Additionally, the Cyclades tourist sector accounted for only 12.75 per cent of the sectoral regional GDP

(Miscellaneous Services) compared with the 87.25 per cent of Dodecanese. Conversely, the Cyclades GDP in agriculture constitutes the great share (67.76 per cent) of the sectoral GDP at the regional level. However, in terms of the share of the main sectors in employment, the tertiary sector has jumped from 32.5 per cent in 1971 to 66.6 per cent in 1991, while, according to the latest data available for 1998, the tourism and commerce sectors account for 52.48 per cent of the total employment figures.[14]

Finally, there is a considerable degree of endogenous decision-making which, however, is mainly confined to the Mykonos–Syros island complex. This may be interpreted as a consequence of the specific weight of Mykonos and Syros within the prefecture's socio-economic structure: Syros as the administrative centre (seat of the prefect) and Mykonos as the leading island in the tourist industry, which has resulted in the increasing weight of Mykonos local institutions, and especially the mayor and municipal council, in the decision-making process of the prefecture.

In conclusion, the relatively good economic performance of the Southern Aegean Islands region is mainly because of the prompt adaptation of its economic structure towards the tertiary sector of the economy, with particular emphasis on the tourist industry.

Figure 4.7 Cyclades Prefecture: Agriculture and Tourism in the GDP
Source: NSSG: Regional Accounts 1970, 1980, 1990 and 1994

108   *Interpreting Convergence in the European Union*

This process was facilitated by capacities for endogenously driven mechanisms of economic governance, primarily in the Dodecanese and secondarily in the Cyclades.

Local institutional networks and their learning capacity

This section draws the institutional map of the region and evaluates the structural features of local institutional networks of general exchange. By measuring structural features such as density, centralization and structural equivalence we show how the formulation of local institutional interactions through the processes of exchange, resource interdependence and power distribution affects the level of collective action and hence the learning and adaptation capacities at both regional and prefectural levels.

Institutional networks in the Southern Aegean Islands

The assessment of the structure of local institutional networks at the regional and prefectural levels is based on social network analysis (SNA) and, in particular, on density, centralization and structural equivalence measures, which reveal crucial features of the network structure, intrinsically linked to its collective action, learning and adaptation capacities (see chapter two). These features are indicators of the way in which interactions between the institutional actors are formulated and public–private relations are shaped at the local level. Additionally, by using the multi-dimensional scaling technique all these features are illustrated within the graph of the network.

The most prominent public and private actors at the regional and local levels in reputation, position and role within the local system of governance were entered into the matrix.[15] Thus, at the regional level, twenty-one actors were identified as central to the system of governance. The sub-group of public actors comprises: the regional general secretariat (SRGS); the Dodecanese and Cyclades prefectural councils (DPREFC and CYPREFC); the local Dodecanese and Cyclades associations of municipalities and communes (DAMC and CYAMC); the city councils of Rhodes and Kos (RCITY and KCITY) in the Dodecanese and Ermoupolis and Mykonos (ERCITY and MYCITY) in Cyclades; and the University of the Aegean. Additionally, the group of the most important private-interest organizations consists of the Dodecanese and Cyclades chambers of commerce (DCHAMBER and CYCHAMBER); the Rhodes and Mykonos hotel owners' associations (RHOTELA, MYHOTELA); the Dodecanese and Mykonos tourist agents' associations

(DTOURA, MYTOURA). Finally, the Dodecanese and Cyclades development agencies (DDA and CYDA), which are mainly focused on the management of EU Structural Fund programmes or initiatives have become important actors, especially since the 1988 reform of the Structural Funds and the increasing need for management and monitoring of the Regional Operational Programmers and Community Initiatives.

As Table 4.2 reveals, the network at the regional level is characterized by low density (0.367 per cent) and high centralization (70 per cent) indicators. What these indicators underline is that there are no actual intra-regional networks but only ones within each prefecture. In particular, because, on the one hand, of the administrative structure of the state (see chapter three) and, on the other, the fragmentation of space due to the island character of the region, at the regional level the network is highly centralized around the Regional Secretariat. Two lessons should be drawn from this observation: first, that the

Table 4.2   Centrality Measures of General Exchange Network in the SAI

Organizations	*Network Centrality* %
1. Reg. Gen. Secretariat	100
2. Dodecanese Pref. Council	55
3. Cyclades Pref. Council	50
4. Dodecanese Chamber	45
5. Cyclades Chamber	45
6. Dodecanese Ass. Munic. & Comm.	45
7. Cyclades Ass. Munic. & Comm.	45
8. Rhodes City Council	40
9. Dodecanese Tourist Ag. Ass.	40
10. Kos City Council	35
11. Rhodes Hotel Owners Ass.	35
12. Kos Hotel Owners Ass.	35
13. Mykonos City Council	35
14. Ermoupolis City Council	30
15. Mykonos Hotel Owners As.	30
16. Mykonos Tourist Agents As.	30
17. Cyclades Training Centre	20
18. Dodecanese Development Ag.	15
19. Cyclades Development Ag.	15
20. University of the Aegean	15
21. Ermoupolis Development Ag.	10
Total Network Centralization	70

Source: Paraskevopoulos, C. J. (1998b)

prefecture, mainly because of historical reasons, remains the main locus of economic and political governance; and second, that the region has not yet been legitimized as a key actor within the subnational level of governance. Thus, it constitutes the meso-level between the two main levels of governance: the central state and local government, consisting of the prefecture and municipalities.

It should be noted that the extremely low specific weight of the University of the Aegean can be explained by its location. Its main departments are located on the Northern Aegean Islands and thus it constitutes a relatively more important actor for the Northern than for the Southern Aegean Islands region. Furthermore, the marginal role of the Dodecanese, Cyclades and Ermoupolis development agencies should be interpreted as a result of their almost exclusive role in the management of programmes financed by the EU Structural Funds.

Thus, as Figure 4.8 based on the multi-dimensional scaling reveals, the regional secretariat is the central actor – mainly because of its role within the administrative hierarchy – and the real networks are those at the prefectural level.

Institutions and institutional networks in the Dodecanese prefecture

The institutional infrastructure of the Dodecanese prefecture is part of the heritage left by the Italians.[16] The term 'Italian heritage' should

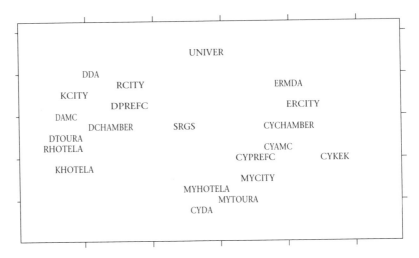

Figure 4.8   Institutional Networks in SAí Region

include not merely the physical infrastructure (road networks, airports, water and sewage systems), but also a series of pivotal institutions, such as the system of land registry.[17] Thus the Dodecanese is the only prefecture in Greece with a land registry system, which has been a crucial factor in protecting the physical environment, regulating public and private use of land and providing public spaces in the cities. Additionally, beyond the city councils, which have proved particularly competent in comparison with their counterparts in other regions, private-interest organizations have a strong presence in the Dodecanese region. These include the chamber of commerce, the hotel owners' associations and the tourist agents' associations, which are active participants in the local system of governance.

The chamber of commerce was established in 1949 and has 20,287 members from all the islands of the Dodecanese complex. Although it is seated in Rhodes, it has three provincial offices in the Kos, Kalymnos and Karpathos islands and provides its members with a wide range of services, such as administrative assistance, expert advice and information on important issues. Despite the fact that in Greece, as in most of the continental European countries, the chambers of commerce are public law institutions, the Dodecanese Chamber is the most historic and prominent private-interest organization and simultaneously one of the key actors in the institutional structure of the prefecture. In particular, having overcome its role as a unionist and corporatist body representing the merchants' interests, it is an important actor in the development process and the initiator of almost all fora for information, dialogue and communication in the prefecture. Hence it has been the key actor in decision-making processes in almost all policy areas and beyond its role within the regional council, it also participates in all decision-making bodies, such as the economic and social committee of the prefecture, health-related committees, as well as in prefectural and provincial tourism committees. Finally, it is the only Greek chamber with membership status in the Union of the Mediterranean Chambers (ASCAME), as well as in EUROCHAMBRES, whilst it simultaneously participates, along with the other chambers of the Aegean islands, in the only existing interregional network (among the Southern and Northern Aegean regions): the Chambers' Association for the development of the Aegean Islands.

The Rhodes and Kos Hotel Owners' Associations constitute the second 'pillar' of the private-interest institutional infrastructure of the Dodecanese. They were established in 1949 and 1956 respectively and, along with the Chamber, have been crucial institutional components of productive restructuring, that is the move from development based on agriculture and trade towards tourism, since the 1950s. The associations, with roughly 650 members (450 of which are Rhodes members), have been key actors within the local system of governance. The Rhodes Association in particular plays a key role in initiatives and projects related to the tourist industry. Thus, it was an initiator, along with others (such as the Local Association of Municipalities and Communes of the prefecture), of an advisory committee – in substance an informal prefectural council – dealing with development issues alongside the formal prefectural council. This committee has been an important forum for dialogue and communication in the prefecture since 1984.

Finally, the Tourist Agents' Association, which is virtually the tourist department of the Chamber, is considered an important actor in tourism-related local initiatives, along with the Chamber and the Hotel Owners Association.

Within this framework, the existing evidence, in comparison with other regions, on distinguished institution building and network creation on a bottom-up basis should be linked to intrinsic qualitative features of the institutional infrastructure in Dodecanese. This evidence should include the following. First, the city councils, and especially the Rhodes and Kos councils, have undertaken pioneering initiatives in creating infrastructure and providing social services. The Rhodes council, in particular, has created the first municipal transport company in Greece (RODA) based on an initial Italian plan. Second, in a paradigm of horizontal networks at the local level, a mini-network has been created by the Hotel Owners' Association (RHOTELA), the Tourist Agents (DTOURA), the Chamber and the Association of Municipalities and Communes, focused on policy-making initiatives for the tourist industry. The institutional form of this network is the Organization for Tourist Promotion,[18] which is financed by a special council tax. Finally, the Dodecanese Cooperative Bank, which has been created on a Chamber initiative in cooperation with the Rhodes City Council, may be seen as a Greek version of rotating credit associations at the local level.

The quality of the local institutional infrastructure, however, is illustrated by specific indicators of institutional performance at the prefectural level, such as the distribution of financial resources among the main sectors of the local economy (investment *vis-à-vis* consumption) and the priorities of the prefectural public investment programme. In particular, without taking into account the grants and subsidies of national regional policy (law 1262/82), public investment expenditure for the years 1983, 1984 and 1985 accounted for 46 per cent, 51.5 per cent and 61.8 per cent of the total state expenditure in the prefecture respectively. Conversely, public consumption and functional administrative expenses accounted for 28.5 per cent, 28.8 per cent and 29.5 per cent respectively, and income support subsidies for 21 per cent, 16.9 per cent and 21 per cent respectively (Getimis, 1989: 157). This investment-oriented structure of public expenditure in Dodecanese diverges significantly from the country's average and especially from that of Attika region, where public investment expenditure does not exceed 25 per cent and 11 per cent of the total expenditure respectively (ibid.).

Additionally, with regard to sectoral prioritization of public investment expenditure, the prefectural public investment programme demonstrates a more coherent and consistent orientation towards 'first priority' local problems, when compared with the orientation of central state public investment. In particular, the sectors of transport/communication and water/sewage, which have been the most crucial local issues given their impact on the tourist sector, were the first priorities of the prefectural public investment programme in the mid-1980s, whereas central state investments had no coherent orientation corresponding to local needs (Getimis, 1989: 153–4).

The structure of the institutional networks in Dodecanese reflects the qualities of the local institutional infrastructure. Thus, the density measure of the general exchange network (0.727), which shows the degree of network cohesion, indicates that almost all the actors are connected to each other.

Furthermore, the centralization measures (Table 4.3) reveal the way in which resources and hence power are distributed among the actors and, subsequently, the central actors within the network, that is those with the greatest number of linkages (Scott, 1994). The low degree of centralization (33.33 per cent) demonstrates a horizontal, rather than vertical-hierarchical structure of the network. What the density and centralization measures indicate is that resources and power are rather equally dispersed among a wide range of actors, and subsequently this structure provides the ground for shifting alliances and creating synergies among public and private actors, which is a prerequisite for achieving collective action, and hence facilitating the learning and adaptation processes within the network.

Nonetheless, as the individual centralization measures of each actor demonstrate, certain actors hold more central positions than others. Thus, beyond the Regional Secretariat, whose central position derives from its role within the administrative hierarchy of the central state, there is a number of both public and private local actors which

Table 4.3   Centrality Measures of General Exchange Network in the
Dodecanese Prefecture

Organization	Network Centrality %
1. Reg. Gen. Secretariat	100
2. Pref. Council	100
3. Association Mun. & Comm.	90
4. Chamber	80
5. Rhodes City Council	80
6. Tourist Agents' Ass.	80
7. Kos City Council	70
8. Rhodes Hotel Owners Ass.	70
9. Kos Hotel Owners Ass.	70
10. University	30
11. Development Agency	30
Total Network Centralization:	33.33

Source: Paraskevopoulos, C. J. (1998b)

provides certain capacities for alternative leadership roles. First, the central role of the Prefectural Council, which is connected to all other actors, is complemented by the quite central position of the Association of the Municipalities which acts as interlocutor between the first and second tiers of local government and provides municipalities and communes of the prefecture with crucial services, such as technical and administrative assistance. Additionally, the Rhodes City Council, the Chamber and the Tourist Agents hold quite central positions within the network, which reflect their key role in the decision-making processes. Second, the low centrality of the University is due to its dislocation among the Aegean islands. In particular, the main University departments are located in the Northern Aegean islands (see chapter five) with the exception of the Education department, which is located in the Southern Aegean (Rhodes). Moreover, the University is a completely new institution (established in 1985), which has not yet acquired its role within the institutional structure of the region.

Finally, the marginal position of the Development Agency should be attributed to its exclusive orientation towards the management of EU regional policy programmes and initiatives.

The above structural characteristics are further strengthened by the analysis of the structural equivalence, which identifies common structural positions among the actors with regard to their linkages (Scott, 1994).

What the structural equivalence of the actors in the Dodecanese general exchange network (Figure 4.9) reveals is that, beyond the public actors of block one – region general secretariat and prefecture council – which are completely connected to all other actors and can constitute the leadership of the network, there is a second block consisting of both public – Rhodes and Kos City Councils, Association of Municipalities – and private-interest organizations – Chamber, Rhodes and Kos Hotel Owners' Association and the Tourist Agents' Association. Although these actors are not completely connected, with the exception of the two marginal actors of block three, namely the university and the Dodecanese Development Agency (DDA), they have a good rate of linkages within the network. The marginal character of the University and the DDA is because of the dislocation of the departments of the former among the Aegean islands and the specific role of the latter as an organization created primarily for the management of Structural Funds programmes (Community Initiatives).

	SRGS	DPREFC	DCHAMBER	RHOTELA	KCITY	DTOURA	DAMC	KHOTELA	RCITY	DDA	UNIVER
SRGS	1	1	1	1	1	1	1	1	1	1	1
DPREFC	1	1	1	1	1	1	1	1	1	1	1
DCHAMBER	1	1	1	1	1	1	1	1	1		
RHOTELA	1	1	1	1		1	1	1	1		
KCITY	1	1	1		1	1	1	1	1		
DTOURA	1	1	1	1	1	1	1	1	1		
DAMC	1	1	1	1	1	1	1	1	1	1	
KHOTELA	1	1	1	1	1	1	1	1			
RCITY	1	1	1	1	1	1	1		1		1
DDA	1	1					1			1	
UNIVER	1	1							1		1

Figure 4.9   Structural Equivalence of Network Actors in Dodecanese

Finally, in Figure 4.10 the graphical depiction of the network by multidimensional scaling technique reflects the above structural characteristics. The principal actors of the network (Regional Secretariat, Prefectural Council, Association of Municipalities, Rhodes City Council, Chamber and Tourist Agents) are depicted in the centre of the graph, while the other less central actors (Hotel Owners, Kos City Council) are depicted around the core centre. Conversely, the University and Development Agency are at the margins of the network.

To sum up, the Dodecanese has a good institutional infrastructure (for the Greek case), characterized by dense and horizontal local institutional networks. Despite the leading role which the Regional Secretariat and Prefecture have as a consequence of the state structure, there is a considerable presence of synergistic networks crossing the public–private divide and playing a decisive role in the local system of governance. Thus, the horizontal structure of the local network should be attributed to the upgraded structure of local institutions rather than to a differentiation of the state structure.

Institutions and institutional networks in the Cyclades prefecture

The institutional infrastructure in the Cyclades prefecture is, to a significant extent, similar to that of the Dodecanese. Despite the lack

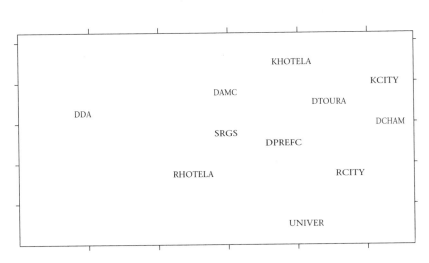

Figure 4.10   Institutional Networks in Dodecanese

of Dodecanese tradition in institution-building and the differentiation in institutional capacity and economic structure between the islands of the Cyclades complex, the central institutional actors of the prefecture are particularly active in undertaking initiatives for institutional and economic adjustment of the prefecture. Thus, beyond the Regional Secretariat and the Prefectural Council, which provide formal leadership mainly because of their role within the administrative structure of the state, a series of public (Association of Municipalities and Communes, Mykonos and Ermoupolis City Councils) and private-interest (Chamber, Hotel Owners, Tourist Agents) actors play an important role within the local system of governance. In particular, the underpinning factors that have sustained the Cyclades institutional structure should be identified, on the one hand, with the strong trade and cultural relations of Syros with western Europe in the middle of the nineteenth century (1832–57) and, on the other, with prompt adjustment of the economic structure of other islands (Mykonos, Santorini) towards the tourist sector in the early 1960s.

Thus, among private-interest organizations, the Chamber constitutes one of the most historic and prominent actors within the local system of governance. It was established in the dawn of the Syros take-off period (1836) and historically has been the first chamber of the country, totalling approximately 10,000 members. Whereas in the past it was the leading institutional actor because of its role in the export-oriented trade during the 'golden' period, it currently focuses on leading the adaptation process in Syros and the other Cyclades islands, by combining tourist development with trade and small-scale agriculture.[19] Therefore, beyond providing its members with the usual services in terms of administrative and technical assistance, the Chamber participates in initiatives focusing on self-sustainable development[20] at the local, intra-regional and interregional levels. Hence, at the local level, it participates, along with the Ermoupolis City Council and the Association of Municipalities, in a local network, the Ermoupolis Municipal Development Agency. This agency focuses on the regeneration of Ermoupolis city, famous for its architecture, and the management of related EU programmes. Second, at the prefectural level, the Chamber is actively involved, along with the Prefectural Council and the Association of Municipalities, in the creation of the prefectural training centre, the establishment of a credit association focusing on financing local development projects, as well as in the development of an energy policy centre for renewable energy sources. Finally, the Chamber participates, along with the other chambers of both the Northern and Southern Aegean islands, in the only interregional network of the archipelagos, the Chambers' Association for the development of the Aegean Islands, while it is an active participant of the Tourism Committee of the Union of Greek Chambers.

The Hotel Owners' and Tourist Agents' Associations are active participants in tourism-related initiatives undertaken especially by the city councils. In particular, they participate in the tourism committees of both Syros and Mykonos city councils, with whom they usually attend international tourism-related exhibitions. Additionally, they participate in the cooperative programmes for tourist promotion organized by the prefectural council.

With regard to the public actors of the prefecture, Ermoupolis and Mykonos City Councils have proved to be particularly competent in taking initiatives with emphasis on tourism-related infrastructure, upgrading the physical and cultural environment and improving the training capacity of the prefecture. In particular, Ermoupolis City Council developed a controversial project, financed jointly by the private sector (60 per cent) and the Municipal Enterprise for Tourist Development (40 per cent), the Aegean casino on Syros. Additionally, the mayor of Mykonos and the city council have played a key role within the Cyclades Development Agency, which has been created by an initiative of the Prefectural Council, along with the Association of Municipalities and Communes. Finally, the Prefectural Training Centre is the outcome of the joint action undertaken by the Association of Municipalities, the Prefectural Council and the Chamber.

Looking at the structural characteristics of the institutional network in Cyclades, they reflect, to a significant extent, the above mentioned qualitative features of the local institutional infrastructure. Thus, the density measure in the general exchange network (0.545), which reveals the degree of network cohesion, indicates that most of the central actors are connected to each other. Additionally, as the centrality measures of Table 4.4 show, the relatively high rate of network centralization (54.55 per cent) is mainly due to the extremely low presence of the University. As was noted in the previous section that there is no main University department located on any of the Cyclades islands, which can partly account for its marginal role within the network. Therefore, the centrality measures do not correspond to a vertical structure of the network, but rather stress the division of the other network actors mainly into two groups. The first group consists of the leading actors with the greatest number of linkages, while the second comprises the less connected actors.

Table 4.4 Centrality Measures of General Exchange Network in the Cyclades Prefecture

Organization	Network Centrality %
1. Reg. Gen. Secretariat	100.00
2. Prefecture Council	81.82
3. Association of Munic. & Comm.	81.82
4. Chamber	72.73
5. Mykonos City Council	63.64
6. Ermoupolis City Council	54.55
7. Hotel Owners Ass.	54.55
8. Tourist Ag. Ass.	54.55
9. Training Centre	36.36
10. Development Agency	27.27
11. Ermoupolis Development Ag.	18.18
12. University	9.09
Total Network Centralization:	54.55

Source: Paraskevopoulos, C. J. (1998b)

Thus, beyond the Regional Secretariat, which is the most central actor because of its position within the administrative hierarchy, the Prefecture Council and the Association of Municipalities and at a second stage the Chamber constitute the leading actors of the network, providing alternatives for leadership roles within the local system of governance. Furthermore, the Mykonos and Ermoupolis City Councils, as well as the Hotel Owners' Association and the Tourist Agents, although less central, provide the ground for public–private synergies that facilitate the learning and adaptation processes. Additionally, the relatively marginal position of the Training Centre does not reflect the expectations for its dynamic role, especially in the implementation of EU Social Fund programmes, given that it is a quite new institution. Finally, the rather marginal position of the prefectural and the Ermoupolis Development Agencies should be attributed to the orientation primarily towards the management of Structural Funds programmes, while the University[21] is at the extreme margins of the institutional infrastructure.

The main features of the institutional infrastructure that derive from the centrality measures are further strengthened by the block model of structural equivalence, which identifies common structural positions among the actors. In particular, the structural equivalence of the actors in the general exchange network (Figure 4.11) demonstrates, to a significant extent, a similar structure to that of the Dodecanese.

	SRGS	CYPREFC	CYAMC	MYHOTELA	CYCHAMBER	MYCITY	MYTOURA	ERMDA	UNIVER	CYDA	ERCITY	CYKEK
SRGS	1	1	1	1	1	1	1	1	1	1	1	1
CYPREFC	1	1	1	1	1	1	1			1	1	1
CYAMC	1	1	1	1	1	1	1			1	1	1
MYHOTELA	1	1	1	1	1	1	1					
CYCHAMBER	1	1	1	1	1	1	1				1	1
MYCITY	1	1	1	1	1	1	1			1		
MYTOURA	1	1	1	1	1	1	1					
ERMDA	1							1		1		
UNIVER	1								1			
CYDA	1	1	1							1		
ERCITY	1	1	1	1	1			1			1	
CYKEK	1	1	1	1								1

Figure 4.11   Structural Equivalence of Network Actors in Cyclades

More specifically, under the leading (public) actors of block one (Regional Secretariat, Prefecture Council, Association of Municipalities and Communes) there is a group of public and private-interest organizations (Mykonos and Ermoupolis City Councils, Chamber, Hotel Owners' Association and Tourist Agents), which, although less connected within the network, contribute to its cohesive and relatively horizontal character. This is not revealed in the density and centralization measures mainly because of the marginal presence of the University.

The graph of the network (Figure 4.12), based on the multidimensional scaling, represents the above mentioned structural features of the network. Thus, the Regional Secretariat (SRGS) is depicted at the centre of the graph surrounded by two groups of central actors which constitute the local network. The first group consists of the Prefecture Council, the Chamber and the Association of Municipalities (CYAMC). The second group comprises Mykonos and Ermoupolis City Councils, Hotel Owners and Tourist Agents. Finally, the Cyclades Development Agency (CYDA), the Cyclades Training Centre (CYKEK), the Ermoupolis Development Agency (ERMDA) and the University, are depicted at the margins of the network.

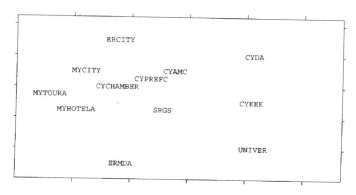

Figure 4.12   Institutional Networks in Cyclades

In conclusion, the Cyclades demonstrates a general exchange network relatively similar to that of the Dodecanese, which, with the exception of the University and the EU Funds-oriented actors, is horizontally structured, thus providing alternative leadership roles and public–private synergies.

Social capital and civic culture in the Southern Aegean Islands

Beyond the fact that research on social trust and civic engagement is completely overlooked in Greece, its identification may be misleading, given the unclearly defined boundaries between trust and its famous Greek substitute of *filotimo* (see chapter three). Therefore, research on social trust, norms and networks of civic engagement, that is social capital, should take into account specific Greek factors and peculiarities. Within this framework, it has been difficult to identify clear-cut differences in the levels of social capital among the regions concerned.

However, as is shown in Figure 4.13, which is based on registration data of membership of voluntary organizations,[22] there is a virtual superiority of the Southern Aegean Islands in all categories of voluntaristic participation.[23] In particular, the differentiation is predominantly evident in the cultural and health care-related

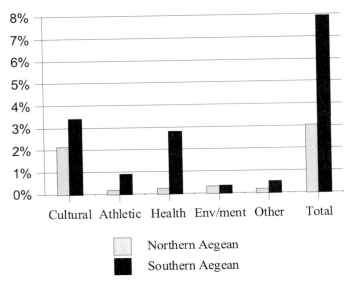

Figure 4.13   Membership of Voluntary Organizations by Category: Southern and Northern Aegean
Source: VOLMED research project (1996) and author's research.

categories, as well as, at a second level, in the category 'other', which includes crucial sub-categories, such as human rights and women's organizations. Nonetheless, what the qualitative analysis of the data underlines is that voluntarism and civic engagement in the Southern Aegean focus mainly on initiatives for providing public goods (e.g. health care).

Looking at the qualitative features of the fieldwork, however, an unclear picture emerges from the answers of our respondents – though they do not constitute a sample – to the questions about law and order (obedience to the law) and trust issues. In particular, while there seems to be a vast majority arguing for trust in the region, another vast majority is negative about obedience to the law.[24] Additionally, there is some evidence on law breaking, especially in relation to construction regulations, which mainly concern the land registry system in Dodecanese (Getimis, 1989). Moreover, the presence of social trust needs to be further researched in the light of the previously mentioned confusion with *filotimo*.

Nonetheless, the relative strength of civil society in the Southern Aegean should be attributed to the strong tradition of civicness in most of the Dodecanese islands and in some islands of the Cyclades complex (Syros, Mykonos). In the Dodecanese, it seems to be closely linked to the long period of Italian rule and the subsequent Western orientation of the local economy and society. In the Cyclades, the tradition of civicness is related to the presence of a civic class in some islands (eg Syros in the nineteenth century[25]), which influenced, to a significant extent, the prompt adaptation of other islands (Mykonos) to the development of tourism in the 1960s.

However, an in-depth assessment of the strength of civil society and the presence of social capital would require the local factors at prefectural level to be raised. Thus, as the data of Table 4.5 reveal, health-care and cultural organizations can account for the strength of civil society in both the Cyclades and Dodecanese prefectures. For the former, it is particularly evident by the important presence of health-care and social protection-related organizations in both prefectures. First, in Syros, a 200-member strong complete network providing home-care services for disabled people has been established. Additionally, huge network of civic engagement involving 2000 voluntary blood-donors in Syros (a high proportion of the population) has contributed to the substantial blood-independence of the Cyclades prefectural hospital.[26]

Furthermore, in the Dodecanese, the Association of Persons with Special Needs which has 2000 members, by operating under city council schemes, provides social protection services and has been involved in several local initiatives. Within this framework, it undertook the implementation of the HORIZON I Initiative during the period of the first CSF (1989–1993) throughout the entire prefecture.[27]

With regard to the cultural voluntarist organizations, most of them (Lyceum of Greek Women, theatre groups) were established during the last quarter of the nineteenth century and were closely linked to the presence of a civil class that was trade-oriented and strongly

Table 4.5   SAI Membership of Voluntary Organizations, 1996 (percentage of population by category)

	Cultural	*Athletic*	*Health Care*	*Env/ment*	*Other*	*Total*
Cyclades Prefecture	4.5	1.15	3.15	0.45	0.65	9.9
Dodecanese Pref.	2.8	0.75	2.5	0.3	0.45	6.8
Southern Aegean Isl.	3.4	0.9	2.8	0.35	0.5	7.95

Source: VOLMED Research Project on Voluntary organizations in the Mediterranean (1996), based on author's research.

influenced by Western cultural forms. Thus, although the civic traditions have been significantly undermined by the collapse of the old civil class in these islands, there are signs of cultural differentiation and relative civic society. Hence, in the particular case of Syros, a special city council tax, the so-called 'cultural tax', has been imposed focusing on the financial support of local cultural organizations, especially the Lyceum of Greek Women – established in 1915– and several theatre groups.[28] Additionally, most of the other social protection-related organizations in Cyclades are financially supported by the city councils.

Finally, the considerable presence of voluntarist organizations concerned with human rights and women-related issues have been included in the category 'other'. Thus, in the Cyclades prefecture women's organizations have been identified primarily in Naxos and Paros islands, which are strongly involved in cultural activities. Additionally, in the Dodecanese, the involvement of the Kos and Rhodes women's organizations in crucial local issues has been identified. The Kos women's society, in particular, is an important actor within the local system of governance since it participates in several local networks in close cooperation with the Kos City Council.[29]

This section, despite the lack of mass survey data, has demonstrated that there is a relatively civic policy-making environment in the Southern Aegean Islands region. In particular, beyond the data analysis, this trend seems to be vindicated by qualitative features arising from the fieldwork research and is attributable to the strong tradition of cultural and trade relations with western European countries in most of these islands.

Conclusions

This chapter has shown that the Southern Aegean Islands region has demonstrated a better, economic performance in macroeconomics indicators in comparison with the Northern Aegean Islands and most of the other regions in Greece. This differentiation should be attributed to the prompt adaptation of the economic structure of the region towards the tertiary sector of the economy with particular emphasis on tourism. In institutional capacity, however, it has been shown that there are no actual intra-regional networks, but only networks at prefectural level. This observation points to the fact that the Regional Secretariat remains at the margins of the local system of governance because of historical and state-structure reasons.

Thus, the Dodecanese prefecture demonstrates, for the case of Greece, a very good quality of institutional infrastructure, characterized by dense and horizontally structured general exchange institutional networks and a relatively bounded system of local economic governance, which should be, to a significant extent, attributed to its tradition in institution-building since its incorporation into the Greek state in the late 1940s. This institutional infrastructure involves cooperative relations among public and private institutional actors and provides a variety of leadership roles, which, especially after 1994 with the elected prefectural council, provides the ground for a learning environment that can facilitate the adaptation process within the framework of EU regional policy. The Cyclades prefecture, on the other hand, has a quality of institutional networks similar to the Dodecanese, but a less bounded system of local economic governance.

Finally, the good institutional infrastructure is facilitated by the presence of a relatively strong civil society and social capital endowments in both prefectures.

5
Institutional Capacity and Policy Environment in the Northern Aegean Islands

Introduction

As has been shown in chapter four, in the case of the Southern Aegean islands, despite the centralized structure of the state, local factors in institutional networks and the strength of civil society can play an important role in enhancing the learning and adaptation processes of the local system of governance. This chapter maps the institutional infrastructure in the Northern Aegean Islands region, drawing its political, economic, institutional and cultural features.

Local factors and political climate

The Northern Aegean Islands region (NUT II), with a population of 199 231 inhabitants, or 1.94 per cent of the entire country in 1991, consists of three big islands (Lesbos, Chios and Samos), each of which, along with some smaller islands, constitutes a prefecture. The Lesbos prefecture with a population of 105 082 inhabitants (1991) comprises mainly Lesbos and Limnos islands. The Samos prefecture consists mainly of Samos and Ikaria islands with a population of 41 965 inhabitants (1991). Finally, the Chios prefecture with a population of 52 184 (1991) comprises Chios island and the small islands of Innouses and Psara. The demographic picture of the region is one of the worst in the country,[1] characterized by significant population losses since the 1950s and 1960s. In particular, its population decreased significantly during the decades 1961–71 (17.30 per cent) and 1971–81 (7.34 per cent), while only in the 1981–91 decade did the region demonstrate a small increase (2.17 per cent).

At the prefectural level, the Lesbos prefecture has demonstrated the worst demographic picture since the 1960s, with population decreases of 18.14 per cent and 8.87 per cent for the decades 1961–71 and 1971–81 respectively, while only during the last decade 1981–91 did it experience a small increase in population (0.4 per cent). The Samos prefecture demonstrates a similar picture with population losses of 19.82 per cent and 2.85 per cent during the decades 1961–71 and 1971–81 respectively, and a small increase (0.6 per cent) during the 1981–91 decade. Finally, the best demographic picture in relative terms is that of Chios prefecture with population decreases of 13.30 per cent and 7.57 per cent during the decades 1961–71 and 1971–81 respectively and a substantial increase (4.7 per cent) in the last decade 1981–91.

With regard to educational features, the region lags behind the country averages with the exception of the illiteracy rate. In particular, according to the 1991 census, it demonstrates a lower percentage (7.46 per cent) in university and technical college graduates in comparison with the national average (11.5 per cent). Additionally, the situation is similar in secondary education (28.1 per cent – 31.5 per cent respectively), while the level of illiteracy is lower (5.30 per cent) than the national average (6.8 per cent).

The complete fragmentation of the administrative and economic structures between the three prefectures, illustrated by problematic transport and communication linkages, is the main characteristic of the region. Although Mytilene – the capital of the Lesbos prefecture – is the seat of the Regional Secretariat and hence the administrative centre, it does not constitute the economic centre of the region, since the development patterns among the island-prefectures are fragmented. Thus, the only similarity in levels of economic development among the islands is that they are low. Additionally, the administrative structure is affected by the degree of fragmentation of space. In that sense it involves only two provinces (provincial councils): one in the Lesbos (Limnos) and one in the Samos prefectures (Ikaria), though for reasons similar to those in the Southern Aegean the role of provincial councils remains marginal within the regional system of governance. Therefore, the existing dispute between the three prefectures about the distribution of public investment funds should be viewed as a consequence of the radial structure of Greek administrative and transport/communication systems and the structure of the intra-regional interactions. Within this framework 'the only cohesive institution of the region is the Regional Secretariat, whose relatively good administrative structure is mainly due to the stability and continuity of the personnel'.[2] However, given the limitations of the role of the Regional

Secretariat (see chapters three and four), the particularities of the policy-making environment need to be identified by looking at the analysis at prefectural level. Moreover, the important common features of the Northern Aegean islands, their liberation from Ottoman rule and incorporation into the Greek state as well as their economic dependence on trade with the Asia Minor region with which they had formed an integrated economic area, do not abrogate the crucial role of local features.

Thus Lesbos was incorporated into the Greek state in 1912, being until then under Ottoman rule. However, during the last years of Ottoman rule (1880–1912) it experienced a period of early capitalist development based exclusively on olive oil and soap production (Siphnaeou, 1996). The subsequent development of trade and cultural relations with the countries of western Europe contributed, on the one hand, to the formulation of a cosmopolitan civil class and on the other to the start-up of a premature working-class movement based on the germs of early twentieth-century socialist ideas. Nonetheless, the collapse of Asia Minor (1922) and the world economic crisis of the 1930s led to the gradual decline of the Lesbos economy and society, which was still based on the monoculture of olive oil. Additionally, the subsequent influx of refugees played a key role in the formulation of a strong socialist movement, which was an important component of the newly founded (1920s–30s) Communist Party of Greece. Under these circumstances, Lesbos, having been the headquarters of the partisan army, became one of the main theatres of the Greek civil war (1946–49) and a stronghold of the Communist Party during the post-war period. Moreover, after the collapse of the old civil class in the 1920s, Lesbos has remained an olive oil-dependent economy and society, 'demonstrating a consistently persistent lack of both institutional and policy adaptation, accompanied by the lack of local leadership that would have led the adaptation process of the economy and the society'.[3] Within this framework, the challenge of adaptation and adjustment constitutes the most crucial issue for Lesbos economic and institutional structures today.

Samos has economic and political characteristics similar to those of Lesbos. After its liberation from Ottoman rule in 1913 it was incorporated into the Greek state. The waves of refugees that followed the collapse of Asia Minor led to the development of a strong communist tradition. Ikaria island, in particular, having been used as a place for political exiles during the post-civil war period, continues to be considered one of the strongholds of the Communist Party. Thus, Samos has remained a primarily agriculture-oriented economy and society, characterized by lack in capacity to adapt, even though in the post-dictatorship period there has been evidence of a shift towards small-scale tourism.

Finally, Chios, having been liberated in the same period with the other Northern Aegean islands (1912–13), has demonstrated similar adaptation problems without, however, the agricultural and partisan tradition of the other islands. It is considered the island of shipowners and shipping-maritime industry, while on the other hand it has been characterized by a rather moderate political climate. Thus, conversely, its adaptation incapacity results from its traditional dependence on the shipping-maritime industry.

Under these circumstances, the main feature of the political climate in both the Lesbos and Samos prefectures has been the left–right divide. In particular, the extreme left–right clashes dominated the political life of both islands during the post-civil war period. Thus Lesbos was considered the 'red island', because of the strong Communist Party presence during the whole post-civil war period and even after the restoration of democracy in 1974.[4] This trend was not affected by the emergence of the PASOK phenomenon in the first post-dictatorship years, but only after 1993 when, for the first time, the Communist Party experienced a substantial reduction of its power to the benefit of PASOK and other left-wing parties (eg Coalition of the Left). However, as it will be shown in the fourth section of this chapter, the strong presence of the Communist Party[5] in the political life of the island, especially during the post-dictatorship period, 'has had important consequences for the local system of governance and its adaptation and learning capacity.[6]

The Samos prefecture demonstrates a political climate that of similar to Lesbos, characterized by the strong presence of the Communist Party, even during the post-dictatorship period. Nonetheless, the specific political feature of the Samos prefecture has been a more clear-cut left–right divide, which is shown by the right-wing New Democracy Party election percentages in the post-dictatorship period.[7] Additionally, after 1993 there has been a considerable reduction in the election percentages of the Communist party in favour of PASOK and the Coalition of the Left.

Finally, the political climate in Chios is completely different. In particular, after the restoration of democracy Chios has demonstrated a rather moderate political climate which is similar to trends at the national level. Thus, whilst in the first post-dictatorship period it was dominated by the centre-right, after 1981 there followed changes in the political climate brought about by the emergence of PASOK and the subsequent shift of the political spectrum towards the centre–left.[8]

At the prefectural level, after the 1994 election, despite the considerable presence of the Communist Party in both Lesbos and Samos, there is a clear predominance of PASOK, or of centre–left coalition consisting of PASOK and the Coalition of the Left, in all three prefectures.[9]

Finally, at the local level (municipalities and communes) Lesbos and Samos have had a strong tradition of Communist Party predominance. In particular, most of the local councils of the Lesbos prefecture are still dominated by the Communist Party, whilst only after the last 1994 election have there been some PASOK or Coalition of the Left majorities or mayorships. The climate in Samos is similar, although in the Samos prefecture there is a left–right differentiation between Samos and Ikaria islands. In Chios, however, especially during the post-1981 period, the majority of the nine municipal and thirty-two communal councils are mainly PASOK-or Coalition of the Left-dominated.

In conclusion, the Northern Aegean Islands region demonstrates a lack of the policy-making environment that would facilitate the institution-building and adaptation processes at both regional and prefectural levels. This is illustrated by the economic divergence of the region and points to the absence of crucial institutional and cultural features from the local institutional infrastructure.

Economic structure, boundedness and adaptation

Despite the close proximity and similar level of natural resources with the Southern Aegean, the Northern Aegean Islands region is one of the most diverging regions at both national and European levels (see Table 4.1). Thus, in the interregional comparison based on the GDP index (EU 12 = 100) its three-year (1989–91) average in PPS per inhabitant of the region is just 35.2 per cent, lagging behind the country's average (48.1 per cent). Furthermore, the region demonstrated one of the higher rates of unemployment (9 per cent) well above the country's average (7.8 per cent) in 1993, whilst it had the second worst rate in unemployment increase for the period 1988–93 (3.6 per cent). Additionally, at the interregional ranking within the EU (NUTS II), according to the GDP per head criterion it is the sixth most diverging region (CEC, 1994: 192–4).

This divergence in macro-economic indicators, however, is not a new phenomenon. It is linked to pre-existing trends in the economic performance of the region. Thus, as Figure 4.1 shows, the average annual change of GDP during the 1970–80 decade (2.18 per cent) was inferior to the country's average (4.57 per cent), as well as to that of the Southern Aegean (5.30 per cent). Additionally, in the decade 1980–91 the region had the same rate of average annual change as the national mean, but it was lagging behind the Southern Aegean. Finally, in the post-1991 period the share of the region in the national GDP dropped substantially from 1.33 per cent in 1991 to 1.31 per cent in 1994.[10]

The divergence gap, however, is further illustrated by its ranking within the per capita GDP index (country = 100) over time and by assessing its performance regarding specific welfare indicators. Thus, as Figure 4.2 reveals, Northern Aegean was one of the worst regions in the country in 1970, while during the 1970–81 decade it fell to the last position, lagging behind the country's average. Finally, in 1991 the Northern Aegean Islands was the second worst region in the country just above Epirus. Moreover, from welfare indicators, the region was inferior to both the country's average and the Southern Aegean in telephones per 100 inhabitants in 1991 and in per capita savings in 1990 (see Figure 4.3). Additionally, according to the 1991 data, it had one of the worst indicators of the country for medical personnel per 1000 inhabitants (Athanasiou *et al.*, 1995: 51).

Nonetheless, the crucial factor that can account for the economic divergence of the region is the lack of adaptation of its economic structure to changing conditions. Thus, despite the close proximity to the Southern Aegean and the similar climatological conditions, the region has continued to rely on each island's traditional productive sectors, which has led to the dominant role of agriculture in the structure of the regional economy. As Figure 5.1 reveals, agriculture accounts for 20 per cent of the regional GDP and hence it constitutes the leading sector of the economy. Conversely, the sector of Miscellaneous services, primarily into the tourist industry represents just 11.3 per cent of regional GDP.[11]

Additionally, although the share of agriculture in the total employment has substantially decreased during previous decades, it still remains significantly high (20.7 per cent in 1991) (see Table 4.1). Moreover, this is vindicated by the Location Quotients for the thirteen Greek regions based on employment data which show the agricultural specialization of the region in the 1980s (Konsolas *et al.*, 1993: 46–7). Conversely, the share of the region in the foreigner visitor-oriented tourist industry in 1991 was just 2.2 per cent, in comparison with the 32.8 per cent of the Southern Aegean (see Figure 4.4).

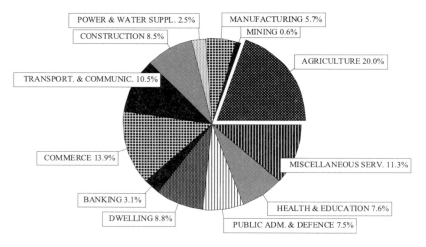

Figure 5.1   NAI Regional GDP by Sector of Production (1994)
Source: NSSG National Regional Accounts.

However, another structural factor affecting the regional economy is its dependence on defence-related activities. In particular, because of the deterioration of Greece–Turkey relations during the post-1974 period, the Northern Aegean Islands region is considered the most defence-dependent region of the EU. As Figure 5.2 based on employment data reveals, the Northern Aegean is the first defence-dependent region in Greece, with a high (29.9 per cent) share of defence-related employment (CEC, 1994a: 180). This may be interpreted as an indication of the way in which the lack of an endogenously driven, system of local economic governance and the subsequent failure in structural adjustment and adaptation of the regional economy are substituted by non-productive economic activities, such as the defence-related financial transfers of the central state.

The structural characteristics at the regional level, however, are inadequate to capture the whole range of local features, which require the qualitative characteristics at the prefectural level to be raised. Thus, the most important feature of economic structure in all three island-prefectures is the persistence of traditional productive sectors.

In particular, the strong agricultural tradition emphasizing the monoculture of the olive (olive oil) is viewed as the main feature of Lesbos's economic structure and is the explanatory variable for both its take-off period in the dawn of the twentieth century and its gradual decline after the collapse of Asia Minor (1922). As Figure 5.3 shows, the

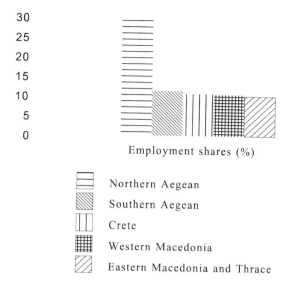

Employment shares (%)

Northern Aegean

Southern Aegean

Crete

Western Macedonia

Eastern Macedonia and Thrace

Figure 5.2 Defence Dependence of Greek Regions (NUTS II)
Source: adapted from CEC 1994a.

share of agriculture in the structural composition of the Lesbos GDP has always been high, varying from 34.2 per cent in 1970 to 27.75 per cent in 1994.[12] Additionally, the share of agriculture in the total employment still remains identically high, even though it dramatically decreased from around 60 per cent in 1971 to around 29 per cent in 1991.[13] Conversely, the share of the sector of miscellaneous services, which reflects the dynamism of the tourist industry, accounted for just 9.75 per cent of the 1994 prefectural GDP.[14]

What these data illustrate is the lack of adaptation capacity in the Lesbos economic structure, which in turn points to crucial weaknesses in the local institutional infrastructure.

Although Samos, on the other hand, has tried since the 1980s to combine agricultural with small-scale tourist development, agriculture remains its basic economic sector. Thus, even though the share of agriculture in the total employment has decreased significantly during recent decades it remains the second sector of the prefectural economy in terms of its contribution to the structural composition of the GDP. In particular, while employment in the primary sector has dropped from 57.1 per cent in 1971 to 25.1 per cent in 1991 with a parallel increase in employment in the tertiary sector (see Figure 5.4),

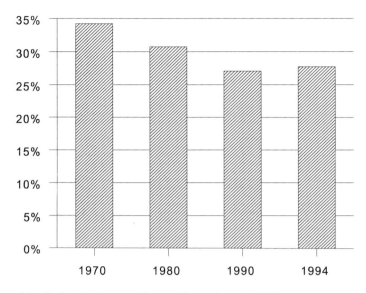

Figure 5.3   Lesbos Prefecture: Share of Agriculture in GDP
Source: adapted from NSSG: National/Regional Accounts.

agriculture accounted for 13.34 per cent of the 1994 prefectural GDP *vis-à-vis* 17.12 per cent of the Miscellaneous Services (tourism).[15]

Finally, Chios demonstrates a different economic structure when compared to the other islands, characterized by its dependence on its traditional shipping-maritime industry sector. This is illustrated by the structural composition of the prefectural GDP in 1994. As Figure 5.5 reveals, Chios's main feature is the rather transport/communication and commerce-driven economy. In particular, they are the leading sectors of the prefectural economy, accounting for 31.2 per cent of the prefectural GDP. Additionally, the share of agriculture and tourism (miscellaneous services) is limited, with the latter not exceeding 9.2 per cent of the GDP. Thus, although Chios has the lowest rate of employment in the primary and the highest rate in the tertiary sector of the economy (15.2 per cent and 59.5 per cent respectively in 1991) among the Northern Aegean islands, its tertiary sector-oriented economic structure is not related to the development of the tourist industry, but to the role of the commerce and transport/communication sectors. This point is further strengthened by the data on foreign tourist accommodation (Table 5.1). According to these indicators, Chios is the least tourist-developed island of the Northern Aegean.

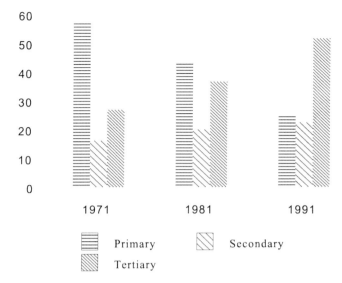

Figure 5.4 Samos Prefecture: Employment by Sector of Production
Source: adapted from NSSG employment censuses 1971, 81, 91.

These indicators are also revealing with regard to tourist development on the other islands of both the Northern and the Southern Aegean (see chapter four).

Thus Samos is the most foreign tourist-oriented island of the Northern Aegean. Conversely, the generally underdeveloped tourist industry of the other Northern Aegean islands is mainly oriented towards the domestic tourist market.

This section has shown that the economic divergence of the Northern Aegean islands should be mainly attributed to the lack of adaptation of their economic structure to changing conditions. This process is accompanied by the lack of any endogenous mechanisms for economic governance. The following sections focuse on evaluating the local institutional infrastructure, that is local institutional networks and the strength of civil society, upon which the learning and adaptation processes depend.

Local institutional networks and their learning capacity

This section assesses the quality of the institutional infrastructure of the region, by mapping the institutional networks of general exchange and measuring structural features such as density, centralization and

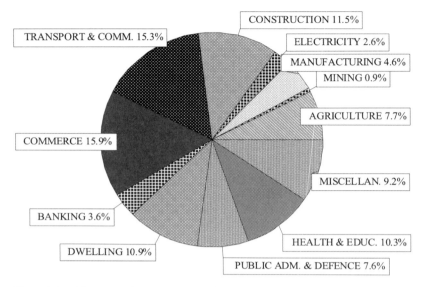

Figure 5.5   Chios GDP by Sector of Production (1994)
Source: adapted from NSSG National/Regional Accounts (1994).

structural equivalence. These features will reveal the way in which the formulation of institutional interactions through the processes of exchange, resource interdependence and power distribution affects the level of collective action and hence the capacities for learning and adaptation at regional and local levels.

Institutional networks in the Northern Aegean Islands region

The evaluation of the structure of institutional networks at both regional and prefectural levels is based on social network analysis (SNA). The above-mentioned structural measures (density, centralization and structural equivalence) indicate the degree of network cohesion, the identification of the central actors within the network and finally the network structure, and the way in which institutional interactions are formulated and public–private relations are shaped at the local level. Furthermore, all these features are illustrated within the graph of the network.

To obtain the data, the most prominent public and private actors at the regional and local levels, selected by reputation, position and role within the local system of governance, were entered into the matrix. At the

Table 5.1   NAI Permanent Inhabitants per Foreign Tourist Boarding

	1977	1981	1987	1991
Lesbos Pref.	314.2	239.2	178.5	157.1
Chios Pref.	278	183.4	251.4	269.6
Samos Pref.	119.3	46.4	29.7	41.9
GREECE	1034.8	866.5	804.2	1243.8

Source: NSSG, Population Censuses, 1981, 1991; Tourism Statistics, 1977, 1987.

regional level, twenty-three public and private actors were identified as central to the system of governance. Within this framework, the group of public actors consists of: the Regional Secretariat (NRGS), the three Prefectural Councils (Lesbos Pref. Council-LPREFC, Chios Pref. Council-CPREFC and Samos Pref. Council-SPREFC), the Local Associations of Municipalities and Communes (Lesbos AMC, Chios AMC and Samos AMC), the City Councils of Mytilene (MCITY), Chios (CCITY) and Samos (SCITY) and finally, the University of the Aegean (UNIVER). The second sub-group comprises the most important private-interest organizations: the three chambers of commerce (Lesbos-LCHAMBER , Chios-CCHAM-BER and Samos-SCHAMBER), the Lesbos Farmers' Association (LFARMA), the Chios Mastic Growers' Association (CMASTA) and the Samos Winemakers' Association (SWINE). Finally, the Lesbos and Chios Training Centres (KEKANAL and CKEK), as well as the development agencies in Lesbos (Local Development Agency-LLDA, Aeoliki Development Agency-AEOLIKI, Mytilene Municipal Development Agency-MDA) and Chios (Municipal Development Agency-CDA) constitute the outcome of public–private initiatives under the pressure of increasing need for the implementation of Structural Funds programmes.

What the low-density (0.237 per cent) and high-centralization (83.55 per cent) measures of Table 5.2 reveal, is that the structure of the network at the regional level is even worse than in the Southern Aegean. In particular, beyond the lack of intra-regional interactions, the networks are even more fragmented within each prefecture. Thus the regional network demonstrates a high degree of centralization around the Regional Secretariat. Given the common administrative structure of the state, however, and the fact that the fragmentation of space is no worse than in the Southern Aegean, this slight differentiation in network structures at regional level points to different structures of institutional interactions at prefectural level. Additionally, the relatively higher than Southern Aegean specific weight of the University (see chapter four) should be attributed to the fact that its main departments

Table 5.2 Centrality Measures of General Exchange Network in Northern Aegean Islands

Organization	Network Centrality %
1. Reg. Gen. Secretariat	100.00
2. Lesbos Pref. Council	40.91
3. Chios Pref. Council	36.36
4. Mytilene City Council	31.82
5. Samos Pref. Council	27.27
6. Lesbos Chamber	27.27
7. Chios Chamber	27.27
8. Chios City Council	27.27
9. University	22.73
10. Lesbos Farmers' Ass.	22.73
11. Samos City Council	22.73
12. Samos Chamber	22.73
13. Lesbos Ass. Munic. & Comm.	18.18
14. Chios Mastic Growers' Ass.	18.18
15. Samos Wine Makers' Ass.	18.18
16. Lesbos Training Centre	13.64
17. Chios Ass. Munic. & Comm.	13.64
18. Samos Ass. Munic. & Comm.	13.64
19. Aeoliki Dev. Agency	9.09
20. Mytilene Mun. Dev. Agency	9.09
21. Chios Mun. Dev. Agency	9.09
22. Chios Training Centre	9.09
23. Lesbos Local Dev. Agency	4.55
Total Network Centralization:	83.55

Source: Paraskevopoulos, C. J. (1998b).

are located in the Northern Aegean. Finally, the marginal role of both the Lesbos and Chios development agencies and training centres should be seen as a consequence of their almost exclusive role in the management of programmes financed by the EU Structural Funds.

Thus, in the graph of the regional network shown in Figure 5.6 the Regional Secretariat is depicted at the centre of the network as central actor, because of its position within the administrative hierarchy, and is surrounded by the three prefectural networks. However, the structure of the networks at the prefectural level differs substantially in comparison with those in the Southern Aegean (see chapter four). This is due to the different structural characteristics at prefectural level, which will be highlighted by the analysis in the following sub-sections.

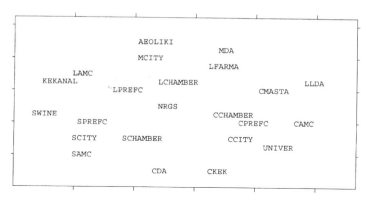

Figure 5.6   Institutional Networks in the NAI Region

Institutions and institutional networks in the Lesbos prefecture

The quantitative and qualitative features of the institutional infrastructure in the Lesbos prefecture reflect the lack of local leadership since the collapse of the old civil class in the dawn of the twentieth century and its subsequent reliance on the central state structure.[16] Thus Lesbos is characterized by a weak system of local governance, whose main feature is the lack of appropriate decision-making mechanisms and fora for dialogue and communication among local public and private actors. Subsequently the system of local interactions demonstrates symptoms of incapacity for bottom-up initiatives and abandonment to central state agencies for the necessary financial, administrative and technical resources.

The weaknesses of the system of local governance are illustrated by the low level of synergies among the actors and the subsequent lack of an endogenously driven development strategy. Additionally, the public actors of the prefecture (e.g. city councils) are incapable of providing the necessary public goods (services) that would support the local productive system; it is almost exclusively reliant on uncoordinated and fragmented initiatives undertaken mainly by specific private actors, such as the Chamber, which, however, lead to poor effectiveness and efficiency results.

Within this policy environment the Chamber constitutes the only proactive institutional actor of the prefecture, with 8400 members. Although it is seated in Mytilene, the capital of Lesbos, it has another provincial office on Limnos island. It is one of the most historic local institutions – it was established during the 'golden' age of Lesbos in

1918 – and the leader in development initiatives focused on the capacity of the local productive structure to adapt to the changing conditions in the environment. Thus, beyond providing its members with traditional services, it is the pioneer in local initiatives for shifting the productive system towards small-scale tourist development supported by the agricultural sector. Within this framework, it has undertaken initiatives for promoting the Lesbos and Limnos islands as tourist destinations, agricultural restructuring by exploitation of the islands' comparative advantages (e.g. cultivation of sweet-smelling herbs) and finally the creation of a cooperative bank to improve the financial services sector. However 'its action is restricted by the limitations and weaknesses of the local institutional infrastructure and the system of local interactions'.[17] At the interregional level, the Chamber participates, along with the chambers of the other Aegean islands, in the only existing interregional network (among the Southern and the Northern Aegean regions), the Chambers' Association for the development of the Aegean Islands.

LFARMA (Lesbos Farmers' Ass.), because of the agricultural orientation of the local economy, constitutes the second most important private-interest institutional actor of the prefecture. It was established in 1931 and consists of 61 first-degree organizations, most of which are olive oil-producing, representing around 13,500 members. Although the leadership of the association has adopted a policy for gradual agricultural restructuring, 'the lack of fora for dialogue and communication at the local level and the mentality of the local society constitute crucial impediments to achieving collective action and synergies and hence to the adaptation process'.[18] Moreover, the lack of agricultural restructuring has been identified as a crucial local issue by the degree of respondent satisfaction with specific sectors of the economic and social structure of the prefecture.[19]

It should be noted that Lesbos has been chosen as the seat of a wide range of public actors in a 'from above' attempt to enhance the development potential of the region, but with poor results. As such it is the typical case of an Aegean Ministry seat whose substantial headquarters and decision-making centre are nevertheless in Athens. Additionally, Lesbos has two basic departments of the University of the Aegean (environment and social anthropology). The case of the University deserves special reference, mainly because of the hostile environment it faced during the initial period of its presence on the island (1985–90). The identical reactions of both Greek parochialism and local mentality were rooted in well-established, short-term, individualistic economic interests closely linked to the pre-existing function of the Educational Institute on the island and its large numbers of students.[20] Nonetheless, beyond the fact that the University is a quite new institution and hence rather marginal within the local institutional infrastructure, the evidence does not seem to support the hypothesis that the location of its main departments in Lesbos would provide the ground for an educational services-based model of development.

The structure of the institutional network in Lesbos corresponds to the above-mentioned features of its institutional infrastructure. Thus the low-rate density measure of the general exchange network (0.418), which reveals the degree of network cohesion, indicates that less than half of the actors are connected to each other.

Additionally, the centralization measures (Table 5.3) reveal a high degree of network centralization (71.11 per cent), which indicates a vertical rather than horizontal structure of the network. What the low-density and high-centralization measures show is that power and resources are unequally dispersed among the actors, and subsequently, this structure inhibits the process of shifting alliances and creating synergies among public and private local actors and hence the learning and adaptation processes within the network. Thus, the local system of governance is characterized by a low degree of boundedness and endogenously driven decision-making mechanisms.

In particular, as the individual centralization measures demonstrate, the Regional Secretariat, because of its role within the administrative hierarchy of the state, holds the central position within the institutional structure of the prefecture. Additionally, the only local actors with substantial linkages within the network are the Prefectural Council and the Mytilene City Council. All the other public and private actors are loosely connected within the network, which is an indication for the lack of public–private partnerships and synergies, and hence for a low level of collective action. Thus, the Association of Municipalities, despite its formal key role within the local system of governance as interlocutor between the first and second tiers of local government, does not have the corresponding amount of linkages. The low centrality rate of the Chamber and the Farmers' Association, on the other hand, which are the only private-interest organizations within the network, indicate the generally low level of the prefecture in public–private synergies. Moreover, although the University, because of its location, constitutes a more central actor in comparison with the prefectures of the Southern Aegean (Dodecanese and Cyclades), it cannot yet be considered an integral part of the institutional structure of the prefecture.

Table 5.3   Centrality Measures of General Exchange Network in the Lesbos
Prefecture

Organization	Network Centrality %
1. Reg. Gen. Secretariat	100
2. Lesbos Pref. Council	70
3. Mytilene City Council	70
4. Lesbos Chamber	40
5. Lesbos Ass. Munic. & Comm.	40
6. University	30
7. Lesbos Farmers' Ass.	30
8. Lesbos Training Centre	30
9. Aeoliki Mun. Dev. Agency	20
10. Mytilene Mun. Dev. Agency	20
11. Lesbos Local Dev. Agency	10
Total Network Centralization	71.11

Source: Paraskevopoulos, C. J. (1998b).

Finally, the marginal position of the training centres and development
agencies is the result of their exclusive involvement in the implementation of Structural Funds programmes.

The structural features that derive from the analysis of the centrality
measures are illustrated by the structural equivalence, which identifies
common structural positions among the actors.

Thus the first important outcome of the structural equivalence of the
actors in the Lesbos general exchange network (Figure 5.7) is the
central role of the Regional Secretariat, which is completely connected
to all other actors of the prefecture. The second feature is that there are
two other groups of both public (Prefecture Council, Mytilene City
Council, Association of Municipalities, University) and private
(Farmers' Association, Chamber) actors that are loosely connected to
each other. Hence, they cannot provide the potential for an endogenously driven decision-making mechanism and the necessary
alternative leadership roles. Finally, the prefectural and municipal
development agencies (LLDA, MDA, Aeoliki) are marginalized within
the network since they are mainly oriented towards the management
and implementation of the Structural Funds programmes.

The graphic depiction of the network in Figure 5.8 vindicates the
above structural features. In particular, the Regional Secretariat is
depicted at the centre of the graph and is surrounded by the actors of

	NRGS	LPREFC	MCITY	KEKANAL	LFARMA	LCHAMBER	UNIVER	LAMC	LLDA	MDA	AEOLIKI
NRGS	1	1	1	1	1	1	1	1	1	1	1
LPREFC	1	1	1	1	1	1	1	1			
MCITY	1	1	1			1	1	1	1	1	
KEKANAL	1	1		1				1			
LFARMA	1	1			1	1					
LCHAMBER	1	1	1		1	1					
UNIVER	1	1	1				1				
LAMC	1	1	1	1				1			
LLDA	1								1		
MDA	1	1								1	
AEOLIKI	1	1									1

Figure 5.7   Structural Equivalence of Network Actors in Lesbos

the second and third groups. The development agencies, however, are depicted at the margins of the network, according to the group of actors to which they are related.

In conclusion, the Lesbos prefecture is characterized by a weak local institutional infrastructure, which has led to its dependence on the central state administrative structure for financial and technical resources. Thus the network of general exchange has a vertical structure with the central role attributed to the Regional Secretariat. Moreover, the absence of a bounded and endogenously driven policy-making environment is illustrated by the lack of local partnerships and synergies among public and private actors that would contribute over-coming the public–private divide and achieving collective action.

Institutions and institutional networks in the Chios prefecture

The Chios prefecture demonstrates a relatively better quality of institutional infrastructure than Lesbos. The undertaken initiatives – unique for the Northern Aegean islands – for the voluntary merger of most of the communes of the island in five municipalities are an indication of the qualitative differentiation in its institutional infrastructure.[21] However, this differentiation becomes evident mainly within the

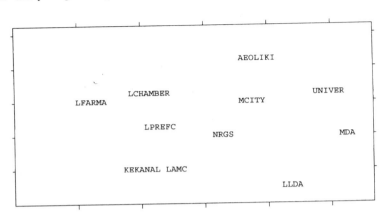

Figure 5.8   Institutional Network in Lesbos

framework of European regional policy, from the comparatively higher level of local partnership and synergy creation among the actors.

Thus, beyond the public actors, among which the City Council is the most active in local initiatives and has additionally established cooperative relations with the University, the private-interest organizations, primarily the Mastic Growers' Association and secondarily the Chamber, play a key role within the institutional structure of the prefecture. This is due to their history and traditional links with the productive system of the island. In particular, the Chamber has around 3600 members and was established in 1918 during the take-off period of the Northern Aegean islands, which was linked to trade relations with the Asia Minor region. The Chamber is an active participant in local initiatives pursued by the prefectural and city councils and focusing on crucial local issues. Within this framework, it has played a key role in procedures for extending Chios airport, in the initiative for creating trade centre in the city to facilitate development of the island's transport linkages, and in the creation of an industrial park.[22] Additionally, in cooperation with the Mastic Growers' Association, it is actively involved in promotion projects and in joint participation in international exhibitions. Furthermore, along with the other Aegean islands' chambers, it participates in the Chambers' Association for the development of the Aegean islands.

The Mastic Growers' Association, on the other hand, was established in 1938 as an umbrella organization for twenty first-rank mastic growers' cooperatives with around 3000 farmer members. It aims at the collection, standardization and promotion of the mastic, which is a traditional product of the island. The main feature of the Association is that it is an exports-oriented organization with an annual budget of 2.5 billion DRS. Hence, it constitutes the most dynamically important private-interest institutional actor at the prefectural level. Under these circumstances, the Association, in common with most of the private-interest organizations of the Northern Aegean, favours Greece–Turkey cross-border cooperation and the opening up of the Turkish market and therefore has a positive attitude towards the EU–Turkey Customs Union.[23]

Nevertheless, a strong isolation mentality accompanied by intense fear of the Turkish threat, a consequence of the deterioration in Greece–Turkey relations, are used as the explanatory variable for the poor institutional capacity of the prefecture. Thus, although the institutional infrastructure seems to be better than in Lesbos (with a density rate 0.528), the network has a vertical structure. This is illustrated by the centrality measures of Table 5.4, which reveal that beyond the Regional Secretariat and the Prefectural and City Councils there is a low degree of private actors' involvement in the local system of governance.

Thus what the individual centralization measures of each actor demonstrate is the central role of the Regional Secretariat and, at a second stage, the Prefectural and municipal councils. However, the private-interest (Chamber and Mastic Growers') organizations' relatively low rate of linkages within the network indicates the lack of public–private partnership and synergy creation. This weakness of the institutional infrastructure cannot provide the alternative leadership roles that a learning policy-making environment would require. The relatively advanced role of the University is attributed to the location of one of its main departments (business administration) on the island and, additionally, to its involvement in projects financed by the prefecture which are aimed at improving the island environment by the management of physical resources. Furthermore, the extremely weak presence of the Association of Municipalities points to its outflanking by the City Council. Finally, the Municipal Development Agency has a marginal role because it has been created by the City Council purely for the management of Community Initiatives, whilst the Training Centre is the outcome of a central state actor's (Greek Institute for Productivity) initiative and is also focused on the implementation of EU Social Fund programmes.

The main features of the institutional infrastructure that derive from the centrality measures are further illustrated by the block model of structural equivalence, which identifies common structural positions among

Table 5.4   Centrality Measures of General Exchange Network in the Chios Prefecture

Organization	Network Centrality %
1. Reg. Gen. Secretariat	100.00
2. Chios Pref. Council	87.50
3. Chios City Council	75.00
4. Chios Chamber	50.00
5. University	37.50
6. Chios Ass. Munic. & Comm.	37.50
7. Chios Mastic Growers' Ass.	37.50
8. Chios Mun. Dev. Agency	25.00
9. Chios Training Centre	25.00
Total Network Centralization:	60.71

Source: Paraskevopoulos, C. J. (1998b).

the actors. In particular, as the structural equivalence of the actors in the general exchange network (Figure 5.9) shows, the block of leading actors consists of the Regional Secretariat and the Prefectural Council, which are linked to all other actors of the prefecture (with the exception of the Municipal Development Agency). Additionally, the City Council (second block) has a rather good rate of linkages within the network, with the exception of the Mastic Growers and the Training Centre. The fragmented role of the private-interest organizations (block four) is illustrated by the loose linkages with public actors and by the strong relations among each other. Moreover, the role of the University and the Association of Municipalities is run out in the linkages with prefectural and city councils. Finally, the Municipal Development Agency and the Training Centre are marginalized within the local system of governance.

The graph of the network (Figure 5.10) vindicates the above structural characteristics. Thus, the Regional Secretariat (NRGS) and the Prefectural Council (CPREFC) are depicted at the centre of the network, whilst, with the exception of the City Council (CCITY), all the other actors are portrayed at a rather marginal position around the central actors.

To sum up, the Chios prefecture demonstrates a network structure similar to Lesbos in many respects. In particular, the vertical rather than horizontal structure of the network is related to the relatively marginal role of private-interest organizations and therefore, to the lack of public–private local partnerships. Furthermore, although one of

	NRGS	CPREFC	CCITY	UNIVER	CAMC	CDA	CCHAMB	CMASTA	CKEK
NRGS	1	1	1	1	1	1	1	1	1
CPREFC	1	1	1	1	1		1	1	1
CCITY	1	1	1	1	1	1	1		
UNIVER	1	1	1	1					
CAMC	1	1	1		1				
CDA	1		1			1			
CCHAMBER	1	1	1				1	1	
CMASTA	1	1					1	1	
CKEK	1	1							1

Figure 5.9   Structural Equivalence of Network Actors in Chios

the basic departments of the University of the Aegean is located on the island, it has not yet been incorporated into the institutional structure of the prefecture.

Institutions and institutional networks in the Samos prefecture

The institutional infrastructure in the Samos prefecture reflects its transport, communication and administrative isolation from the other prefectures of the Northern Aegean islands. Under these circumstances, traditional Greek-periphery parochialism has become more intense in the case of Samos because it is associated with the distribution of financial resources among the three prefectures of the region.[24] Thus Samos demonstrates an extremely weak institutional infrastructure, characterized by the almost complete lack of local initiatives and subsequently by major cooperation and coordination problems among the institutional actors, whose relationships are almost exclusively confined to necessary exchanges imposed by the functions of the administrative hierarchy. This policy-making environment is also adversely affected by huge divergence of the political climate among the main islands of the prefecture, that is Samos and Ikaria, into the left–right divide (see 'local factors and political climate'). However, the lack of any specific tradition in the structure of the local economy may be seen as a positive factor preventing institutional lock-in and allowing for some kind of tourist development.

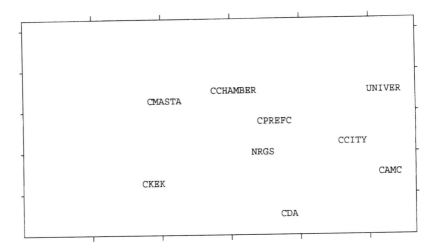

Figure 5.10   Institutional Network in Chios

Within this policy environment, the role of the Regional Secretariat is central in the institutional structure of the prefecture. Additionally, given the lack of any development agency that would combine public and private actors around specific development objectives, the Association of Municipalities has now undertaken a campaign for concentrating most of the local actors on this objective.[25] The University, on the other hand, despite the fact that one of its main departments (mathematics) is located on the island, is completely marginalized within the institutional structure of the prefecture, whilst the City Council is currently trying to pursue a form of cooperation.[26]

Moreover, the only important private-interest actor is the Association of Wine Producers. This is mainly attributed to the fact that the Chamber is a completely new institution. It was established in 1988 by the merger of the two pre-existing chambers of the prefecture and has around 4000 members. The Wine Producers Association has undertaken some initiatives to increase its exports-orientation, whilst cooperation problems with the Association of Municipalities have been identified.

Within this framework, the comparatively good rate of the density measure in the general exchange network (0.595) only partly reflects the real degree of network cohesion, since it is based on exchanges deriving from the fundamental administrative functions of each actor.

Additionally, looking at the centralization measures of Table 5.5 the central role of the Regional Secretariat is illustrated. Furthermore, the prefectural and city councils have a considerable amount of linkages within the network, while the Association of Municipalities and the private-interest actors (Chamber and Wine Producers) are linked to half of the actors. Finally, the University is marginalized within the local institutional structure and its only link is with the Regional Secretariat.

The block model of structural equivalence (Figure 5.11) demonstrates structural positions of the actors that correspond to their centrality measures. Thus, the Regional Secretariat is linked to all other institutional actors, whilst the University is clearly marginalized. The prefectural and city councils, on the other hand, are linked to all other actors with the exception of the University. Finally, the Association of Municipalities and the private-interest organizations have only formal administrative linkages with the Regional Secretariat and the prefectural and city councils. Given the lack of any development agencies, the structure of the network reveals the fragmentation of the institutions within the prefecture and the absence of local partnerships.

This policy-making environment is further illustrated by the graph of the network (Figure 5.12), based on the multi-dimensional scaling. In particular, the graph demonstrates the lack of network cohesion and the loose linkages among the actors. The Regional Secretariat (NRGS), as the leading actor of the network, is depicted at the centre of the graph. The other actors are distanced from the

Table 5.5 Centrality Measures of General Exchange Network in the Samos Prefecture

Organization	Network Centrality %
1. Reg. Gen. Secretariat	100.00
2. Samos Pref. Council	83.33
3. Samos City Council	83.33
4. Samos Chamber	50.00
5. Samos Ass. Munic. & Comm.	50.00
6. Samos Wine Producers' Ass.	50.00
7. University	16.67
Total Network Centralization:	53.33

Source: Paraskevopoulos, C. J. (1998b).

centre, whilst the University is portrayed as the most marginalized institutional actor.

In conclusion, Samos demonstrates a weak institutional infrastructure, illustrated by the vertical and hierarchical structure of the general exchange network, which has caused its dependence on the Regional Secretariat for administrative leadership. This unfavourable policy-making environment has deteriorated further in the diverging political climate among the islands of the prefecture and its isolation, in transport and communication linkages, from the other islands of the region. However, the lack of any strong tradition in terms of economic structure may be seen as a potentially positive factor that might facilitate its adaptation in the future.

Social capital and civil society in Northern Aegean islands

The identification (section 4.4) and illustration (Figure 4.13) of the differentiation in levels of participation in voluntarist organizations between the Southern and the Northern Aegean islands should be interpreted as an indication of the relative and comparative weakness of civil society in the Northern Aegean Islands region. Beyond quantitative analysis of the membership data, however, this weakness is also vindicated by qualitative analysis: particularly, the high level of voluntarist participation in organizations related to the provision of specific public goods, such as health care and social protection, in the Southern Aegean islands vis-à-vis the negligible level of such participation in the Northern Aegean.

Nonetheless, what both the quantitative and qualitative analysis of the fieldwork research underlines is a similarity in attitudes between the two regions, with regard to the crucial law and order issue (obedience to the law[27]).

Looking at the prefectural level, however, the low rate of voluntarist participation and the weakness of civil society in the Northern Aegean region seems to be related to local factors and peculiarities. In particular, primarily the Lesbos and Samos respondents and secondarily those of the Chios prefecture underlined the role of the differentiation between Southern and Northern Aegean mentalities[28] in an attempt to explain the lack of adaptation and the divergence gap of the region. The common explanations for this differentiation, however, are feelings of isolation and fear of the Turkish threat, given the deterioration of Greece–Turkey relations.

	N R G S	S P R E F C	S C I T Y	U N I V E R	S C H A M B	S A M C	S W I N E
NRGS	1	1	1	1	1	1	1
SPREFC	1	1	1		1	1	1
SCITY	1	1	1		1	1	1
UNIVER	1			1			
SCHAMBER	1	1	1		1		
SAMC	1	1	1			1	
SWINE	1	1	1				1

Figure 5.11 Structural Equivalence of Network Actors in Samos

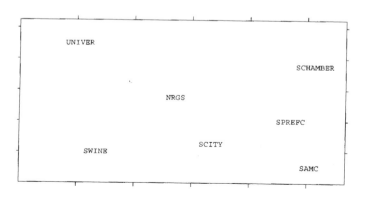

Figure 5.12 Institutional Network in Samos

The in-depth analysis of the fieldwork research at prefectural level, however, points to a different direction. Thus, as the data of Table 5.6 demonstrate, the voluntarist participation in the Lesbos prefecture is characterized by the lack of organizations focusing on the provision of social services-related public goods. Additionally, the only relatively active sector in participation is that of culture-related activities. Indeed, Lesbos is characterized by the presence of some historic, voluntary, cultural organizations, which are mainly literature and theatre-oriented.[29] The most important characteristic of Lesbos, however, is the strong evidence of lack of local leadership. This is interpreted as a consequence of the collapse of the old civil class and its non-replacement (Siphnaeou, 1996). Hence, the evidence from Lesbos seems to suggest there are neither local leadership nor networks.

On the other hand, the evidence from Chios seems to provide the best picture from among the Northern Aegean islands with a particularly strong presence of culture-related voluntarist participation.[30] Indeed there seems to be an important level of activity by literature-theatre- and music-related organizations, but negligible voluntarist participation in the provision of social services-related public goods. However, Chios demonstrates a better picture in all the other categories of voluntarist participation, such as the protection of the environment or women's issues and related social movements.

Finally, among the island-prefectures Samos seems to provide the weakest evidence on voluntary participation with some culture-related organizations. Moreover, this picture of civic engagement and civicness seems to be consistent with the evidence from the institutional infrastructure of the prefecture.

However, what adequately reflects the conditions of civicness and social capital endowments in the Northern Aegean is the evidence on the presence of social trust. In particular, by contrast with the Southern Aegean, a substantial number of respondents in the Northern Aegean gave a negative answer to the question about the level of social trust in the region. This pattern of attitudes was more evident primarily in Lesbos[31] and secondarily in Samos.

A catalytic, though overlooked, factor that seems to have influenced the formulation of crucial cultural norms, however, is the predominant role of the Communist Party of Greece (the Stalinist one) primarily in the Lesbos and secondarily in the Samos prefectures, especially during the post-civil war period. Lesbos and Samos were until recently (early 1990s) considered – and in comparative terms they continue to be – strongholds of this particular Communist Party. In Lesbos, its strong

Table 5.6 NAI Membership of Voluntary Organizations, 1996 (percentage of population by category)

Prefectures	Cultural	Athletic	Health Care	Env/ment	Other	Total
Chios Pref.	4.9	0.15	0.9	0.8	0.45	7.2
Lesbos Pr.	1.1	0.18	–	0.15	0.1	1.53
Samos Pr.	1.2	0.1	–	–	–	1.3
Northern Aegean Isl.	2.15	0.15	0.25	0.3	0.17	3.02

Source: VOLMED Research Project (1996), author's research; adapted by the author.

presence seems to be related, on the one hand, to the phase of early capitalist development of the island, which lasted until the dawning of the twentieth century and, on the other, to the flood of refugees after the collapse of Asia Minor (see 'local factors and political climate'). More specifically, the combination of this collapse and subsequent flood with the strong presence of the Communist Party seems to be a crucial factor in the formulation of the mentality and attitudes at the local level. Of particular importance in this process is the role of the ideological orientation of the Communist Party in the post-civil war period, involving a well-disposed attitude towards the ex-Soviet Union and subsequent adoption of the hierarchical and central state-dominated 'from above' model of political and economic modernization. The main specific feature of this mentality is the attitude of victim which has subsequently resulted in a passive and conspirational approach to current events.[32] Thus, the answer given by one of the interviewees to the question 'what would better describe the region (Lesbos) "honesty" or "corruption"?' was characteristic of the cultural climate on the island. He said: 'neither, only misery'.[33]

Under these circumstances Lesbos demonstrates an extremely weak civil society, closely linked to an unfavourable policy-making environment. In that sense, although it is similar and comparable to the Syros case in history and social structure, it diverges significantly from it in both the quality of institutional infrastructure (networks and social capital) and adaptation capacity (see chapter four). Samos demonstrates similarities to the case of Lesbos, which are mainly related to the impact of political culture on civic culture.

Hence, this section has demonstrated that despite the lack of mass survey data there is evidence of considerable differentiation, in civic environment, between the Southern and the Northern Aegean regions. The Northern region demonstrates a lower level of participation in voluntary organizations, in both qualitative and quantitative terms. The increased influence of the Communist Party, especially in the Lesbos and Samos prefectures, has been identified as a crucial factor that has affected the level of social capital and civicness in the region.

Conclusions

This chapter has demonstrated that the divergence of the Northern Aegean Islands region at the national as well as the European level is mainly caused by the lack of adaptation of its economic structure to changing conditions in global and European environments. Thus, the basic feature of the economic structure of the region is its dependence on economic sectors traditional to each island. This deficiency of the economic structure, however, seems to be related to the crucial institutional and political discrepancies of the region. In particular, the peculiarities of the institutional infrastructure of the region, given the common lack of intra-regional networks in Greece because of the role of the prefecture within the state structure, are attributed to specifics of the local systems of governance at prefectural level.

The Lesbos prefecture is characterized by centralized and hierarchically structured local institutional networks, which correspond to the structure of the system of local interactions in resource exchange and interdependence, as well as power distribution among the institutional actors. This structure reflects an exogenously driven local system of governance which relies on central state institutions and particularly on the Regional Secretariat for financial, administrative and technical resources. The main feature of this weak local system of governance is the lack of learning and adaptation capacities, which is closely linked to an extremely weak civil society and lack of citizens' engagement with voluntary organizations focused on the provision of social services-related public goods. Consequently, this has led to the continuous dependence of the Lesbos economy on the monoculture of the olive. A decisive role in this process should be attributed to the unfavourable political climate characterized by the predominant role of the Communist Party.

The Samos prefecture demonstrates a policy-making environment to some extent similar to Lesbos, characterized by multi-fragmented institutional networks at the prefectural level and lack of public–private synergies and local leadership. This extremely weak local institutional infrastructure is further aggravated by its almost complete isolation from the other island-prefectures of the region. However, the prefectural economy's lack of any particular tradition of productive orientation may be seen as a future asset for successful adaptation and adjustment, in avoiding institutional lock-in. An indication of that is the trend of the local economy towards small-scale tourist development supported by the agricultural sector.

Finally, Chios is partly differentiated from the other Northern Aegean islands in institutional infrastructure and civic participation, mainly in culture-oriented voluntarist organizations. In particular, it demonstrates comparatively more horizontally structured local institutional networks without, however, having yet established a learning and adaptable local system of governance. Moreover, this lack of adaptability is illustrated by the significant continuing dependence of its economy on the traditional sector of shipping and maritime industry.

Finally, the fieldwork research has clearly shown the inadequacy of the two common explanations for the divergence of the region, that is isolation and fear of the Turkish threat.

6
Catching up by Learning in European Structural Policy: Policy Networks and Adaptation in the Southern Aegean Islands

Introduction

Chapter 4 examined the institutional infrastructure in the Southern Aegean Islands region. This chapter focuses on the processes of both institutional and policy adaptation to European structural policy, with particular emphasis on the implementation and monitoring of the first CSF (1989–93). Since the CSFs have constituted a step forward in the formulation of European regional policy in respect with the initialized by the IMPs integrated approach to development, evidence from the implementation of both the IMP (1986–92) and the initial face of the second CSF (1994–99) will be used on a comparative basis with regard to the adaptation process.

From the IMP to the MOPs

The introduction of the IMPs in 1985–86 has been interpreted as an attempt to initiate the integrated approach with European regional development policy (see chapters two and three). Within this framework, the integrated approach to the development problems facing the Aegean islands determined, to a significant extent, the main priorities of the IMP for the Aegean islands, which, for planning procedures, constituted a single region. The main priority objectives of the Aegean islands IMP were: first, improvement of transport and communication linkages to combat the isolation of the islands; second, control of the over-concentration of tourism; third, promotion of those islands underdeveloped by tourism; and fourth, the development of agriculture (DGXVI, 1992; Ministry of National Economy, 1994a).

However, in accordance with the general planning and implementation problems of the IMPs in Greece, as discussed in chapter three, the degree of completion of the Aegean IMP cannot be characterized as satisfactory. Further, its implementation has demonstrated similarities with other regions (eg Crete), regarding the dominant role of central state agencies in the management of the programme (Papageorgiou and Verney, 1993). The share of central state agencies in the management of the Aegean IMP funds reached almost 93 per cent of the budget. Hence, as Figure 6.1 reveals, even at the end of 1993, the degree of completion of the actions of the IMP as a whole was just 79 per cent. In particular, looking at the measures of the specific sub-programmes, the following points must be emphasized. First, sub-programme IV for the development of agriculture, involving mainly support for small-scale irrigation systems, fisheries and advisory services, demonstrates the greatest degree of completion (87 per cent).

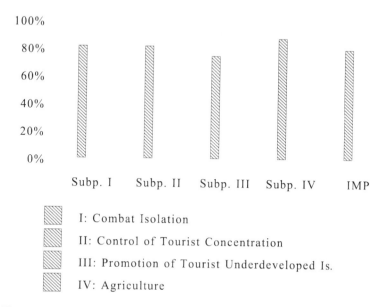

Figure 6.1   Aegean Islands IMP: Degree of Completion (31 December 1993)
Source: Ministry of National Economy (1994a).

Second, the crucial sub-programme III, which focuses on promoting tourist development in underdeveloped islands, shows the least degree of completion (74 per cent). It must be stressed that this sub-programme was mainly oriented towards supporting mostly central state agencies-driven agro-tourist projects for tourist development in the Northern Aegean islands which had poor results (for example Petra agro-tourist cooperative in Lesbos). Finally, sub-programmes I and II, focusing mainly on improving the transport and communication infrastructure, demonstrate the same degree of completion (81 per cent).

To achieve the objectives of the programme, the particular measures in the Southern Aegean islands were focused on providing advisory services to SMEs, on improving the roads, on ports and airports linkages, as well as on the tourist infrastructure (marinas, museums), by exploiting the cultural and architectural heritage, reducing energy dependence and improving living conditions (CEC, 1990a).

Although it has been difficult to identify differences in the implementation of the programme among the Southern and Northern Aegean regions because of its integrated character, some signs of an initially structural, but at a second stage effectiveness and efficiency-related differentiation have emerged. In this respect, the following points are significant. First, the Leros-project,[1] which constituted an integral, as well as crucial, part of the IMP was almost entirely (98 per cent) completed by the end of 1993, with good results for the island. Second, the emphasis on physical and social infrastructure, which will be raised in the following section as a structural feature of the MOP of the Southern Aegean, became evident even from the implementation of the IMP. In particular, the successful completion of projects for creating two new airports on Syros and Naxos islands and the substantial improvement of another one on Karpathos island, which are three of the four major interventions of the IMP in the airports-infrastructure policy area, all concern the Southern Aegean region. Furthermore, the Southern Aegean and especially the Dodecanese prefecture demonstrate a better performance in the absorption of ESF funds for training with particular emphasis on tourism (Ministry of National Economy, 1994a). Finally, the interventions in the Northern Aegean islands were mainly oriented towards improvement of the agricultural sector by small-scale irrigation schemes, the support of fisheries, and the enhancing of central state agencies-driven initiatives for the creation of agro-tourist cooperatives. This should be seen as an attempt to reform the mainly agriculture-dominated productive structure, which, however, mainly because of its top-down character, had poor results.

To sum up, even though the IMP for the Aegean islands has demonstrated weaknesses in planning and implementation similar to most of the other regions, some signs of differentiation between the Southern and Northern Aegean islands regions have been identified, which point to the pre-existing differentiation in capacity for adaptation of the institutional infrastructure. However marginal this differentiation may be, it is further illustrated by the differentiation in the involvement of institutional actors in the implementation process, as will be shown in the following section (page 171).

Planning and implementing the CSF (MOP 1989–93)

The Multi-fund regional Operational Programmes (MOPs) constitute the regional section of the Community Support Frameworks (CSFs), whose introduction marked the shift in European regional policy from the single-project to the programming approach. Furthermore, as discussed in chapter two, they opened up the process for establishing direct contacts between supranational and subnational levels of government and for active participation of the latter in the planning procedures of the programmes. In Greece there have been thirteen MOPs for the thirteen Greek regions. Each MOP consists usually of mainly three sub-programmes, corresponding to the three funds responsible for the co-financing of the Community's structural interventions, that is ERDF, ESF and EAGGF-Guidance Section, whilst financial resources are allocated according to the priority objectives specified for each region.

Within this framework, the main priority objectives put forward by the MOP for the Southern Aegean region were focused on combatting the region's isolation, the exploitation of the region's resources, the control of tourist development, the management of water resources and improving living conditions (CEC, 1990a: 42). These general objectives have been explicitly adapted through specific measures for the improvement of transport and communication, as well as the social and educational infrastructure, the improvement of water and sewage networks, the promotion of tourism, exploitation of the cultural and architectural heritage in tourist underdeveloped islands and the development of services for local SMEs. All these measures are covered by financial assistance provided by the ERDF. Furthermore, the ESF is responsible for financing vocational training-related measures, while the EAGGF focuses on measures for the protection of natural resources and the repair of damage caused by natural disasters.

As Figure 6.2 demonstrates, there is an almost clear differentiation in the distribution of financial resources among the specific measures of the sub-programmes between the Southern and Northern Aegean regions.[2] In particular, the programme of the Southern Aegean demonstrates considerable orientation towards the creation of physical infrastructure and vocational training,[3] whereas in the Northern Aegean the share of social infrastructure, business support and agriculture-related measures account for a significant part of the allocated resources. This trend should be attributed, on the one hand, to the presence of a comparatively advanced social infrastructure (hospitals, public buildings) in the Southern Aegean – which in the Dodecanese was left by the Italians – and, on the other, to the presence of an active entrepreneurship (see chapter four) that does not require business support. Instead, it stresses the need for vocational training with emphasis on tourism. Moreover, the tourist industry combined with the multi-fragmentation of space poses increased needs for technical infrastructure, which is linked to crucial issues such as the road, port and airport networks, as well as water and sewage-related problems.

Figure 6.3, which is based on 1995 ex-post data,[4] confirms the above trend. In particular, the airports, road networks, vocational training

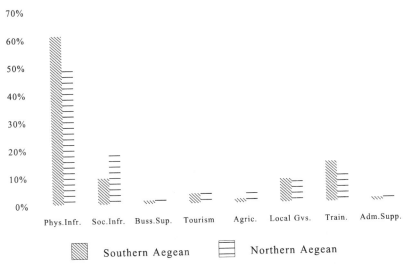

Figure 6.2   Structure of the Aegean Islands MOPs (1989–93) per sub-programme
Source: adapted from DGXVI (1992).

and environment-related infrastructure absorbed the greatest share of
the financial resources of the MOP, while agriculture and support of
tourist development are marginal. It should be noted that the category
'environment' includes water and sewage-related measures, while the
category 'airports' refers mainly to seven interventions, three in the
Dodecanese and four in the Cyclades prefectures.

Beyond, however, the crucial and revealing qualitative differences
identified in the structural orientation of the EU interventions, the two
regions of the Aegean differ crucially in another important aspect of
the implementation of Structural Funds interventions, the absorption
capacity. As Figure 6.4 reveals, the Northern Aegean region has been
lagging behind the Southern Aegean in absorption capacity during the
entire period of the programme. Subsequently, at the end of the period
(31 December 1993) the Northern Aegean absorption rate did not
exceed 57 per cent of the available funds, compared with almost 98 per
cent of the Southern Aegean.[5] This has caused serious delays, inconsistencies and the loss of substantial financial resources for the development of the Northern Aegean region.

In the funding of the MOPs and, in particular, the contribution of
the private sector to the Structural Funds programmes the Southern

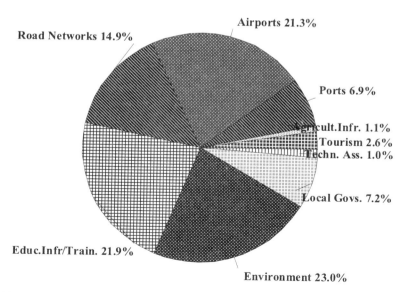

Figure 6.3 SAI MOP (1989–93): Distribution of Funds per Sector of Infrastructure
Source: Aigaio Ltd (1995).

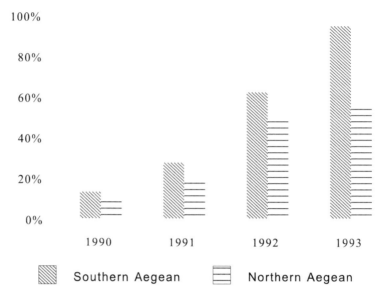

Figure 6.4   Aegean Islands Regions: Absorption Coefficients (CSF 1989–93)
Source: adapted from Ministry of National Economy (1993 a,b).

Aegean region constitutes an excellent example of the way in which the maintenance of national regional policy through the incentives system (see chapter three) leads to the distortion of EU structural interventions. As Table 6.1 reveals, the region seems to demonstrate the lowest level in the country for private sector involvement in the funding of MOP measures (0.27 per cent). Although the table derives from elaboration of the EU Commission's primary budget data that may vary significantly from the ex-post (after the implementation) final data,[6] the contribution of the private sector to the Structural Funds programmes is comparatively low in the Southern Aegean (around 3 per cent according to estimated data). This is partly attributed to the role played by the national regional policy incentives scheme, especially during the 1980s and early 1990s.

In particular, the region demonstrates one of the highest rates of the country (12.9 per cent) in private investments supported by the regional development incentives scheme for the period 1982–91 (Ministry of National Economy, 1993a: 105). These investments, however, are almost exclusively in the tourist sector of the Dodecanese

Table 6.1 Funding of the First CSF (1989–93) MOPs in Greek Regions (in %)

Regions	Private Sector Contr.	National Contr.	Total EU Contr.	ERDF Contr.	ESF Contr.	EAGGF Contr.
East Maced. & Thrace	6.03	38.51	55.46	47.53	5.22	2.71
Central Macedonia	1.23	40.58	58.19	41.65	11.64	4.90
Western Macedonia	1.83	35.95	62.22	50.50	7.77	3.95
Ipeiros	1.60	37.53	60.87	47.55	9.38	3.94
Thessalia	1.88	37.76	60.36	47.38	10.48	2.50
Ionian Isl.	3.70	37.72	58.58	50.94	5.91	1.72
Western Greece	2.75	37.40	59.85	46.17	9.66	4.00
Sterea Ellada	1.00	42.18	56.82	43.50	10.80	2.52
Peloponnese	2.77	35.54	61.70	45.30	11.77	4.61
Attika	1.72	37.15	61.13	40.76	19.88	0.50
Northern Aegean Isl.	3.41	37.51	59.08	50.21	7.32	1.54
Southern Aegean Isl.	0.27	32.86	66.88	56.35	9.67	0.85
Crete	2.21	39.54	58.26	47.90	8.24	2.12
GREECE (Total)	7.40	39.71	52.72	31.86	17.60	3.11

Source: CEC (1992a; 1992b), adapted by the author.

prefecture with particular emphasis on the island of Rhodes. Thus, since the creation of infrastructure is financed by Structural Funds money and private investments in the tourist industry are subsidized through national regional policy, beyond the abolition of any notion of entrepreneurial risk there is no motivation for the private sector to contribute to the Structural Funds programmes. Moreover, since the bureaucratic procedures of the national incentives scheme may involve a substantial amount of clientelism, access to national regional policy money through clientelist networks is considered easier. What needs to be stressed, however, is that the investments supported by the national incentives scheme may account for the expansion of the massive tourist industry mainly on the islands of Rhodes and Kos in the 1980s, but they cannot be considered as the explanatory variable for the successful adaptation of the Southern Aegean region and, in particular, the Dodecanese, since the early 1960s. Furthermore, the increased share of the EU contribution in the financing of the MOP (66.88 per cent) may be seen as an indication of the relatively better absorption capacity of the local institutional infrastructure, which should be linked to its learning and adaptation capacities (see chapter four).

The planning and implementation processes of the MOP have been crucially affected by the significant intra-regional (among the islands) disparities in the level of development. Thus, the distinction among mainly three groups of islands, according to their level of development, as it is shown in Table 6.2,[7] has been adopted by both the local and central level planning bodies.

According to this categorization, the third group (III) consists of the most prosperous islands, namely Rhodes, Kos, Santorini, Syros and Naxos, among which the economic and administrative centres of the region are shared. The second group (II) comprises islands of medium development, while the first group (I) consists of the most disadvantaged small islands. As Figure 6.5 shows, the first group of the small and less developed islands and the third group of the most developed

Table 6.2 SAI: Groups of Islands According to Level of Development

GROUP I		
AGATHONISI	KEROS	NISIROS
ANAFI	KIMOLOS	SIKINOS
ANTIPAROS	KINAROS	SCHINOUSA
ARKOI	KOUFONISIA	TELENDOS
CHALKI	LEIPSOI	THIRASSIA
DONOUSA	MARATHOS	
FOLEGANDROS	MEGISTI	TILOS
IRAKLEIA		
GROUP II		
AMORGOS	KASOS	PAROS
ANDROS	KEA	PATMOS
ASTIPALAIA	KYTHNOS	SERIFOS
IOS	LEROS	SIFNOS
KALYMNOS	MILOS	SYMI
KARPATHOS	MYKONOS	TILOS
GROUP III		
KOS	RHODES	SANTORINI
NAXOS	SYROS	

Source: adapted from Ministry of National Economy (1993a).

ones have consistently demonstrated the best performance in absorption capacity during the entire period of the Southern Aegean islands MOP (1990–93[8]).

This trend may be attributed, on the one hand, to the relatively small-scale projects undertaken on the less-developed islands and, on the other, to the clearly better quality of institutional infrastructure of the developed ones. Conversely, since the second category comprises islands of both prefectures and with relatively large-scale projects undertaken, the fragmentation of space and well-known coordination problems seem to have been the main reasons for the comparatively unsatisfactory absorption rates of this group of islands.

Beyond the outcomes deriving from analysis of the particular characteristics of the groups of islands, however, important aspects of the way in which local factors have affected the implementation of the programme emerge from the inter-prefectural comparisons, namely between Dodecanese and Cyclades. In that respect, the differentiation illustrated in Figure 6.6 between the shares of each prefecture in any

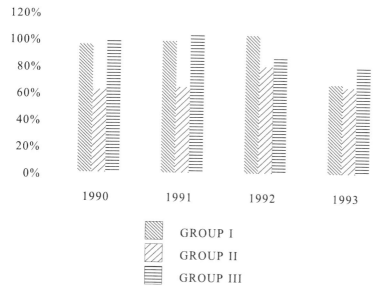

Figure 6.5   SAI: Absorption Capacity per Group of Islands
Source: adapted from Ministry of National Economy (1993a).

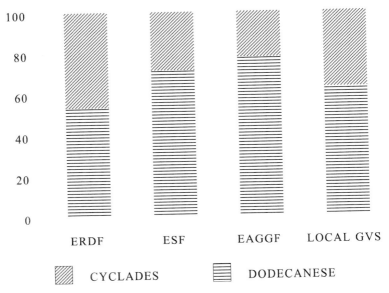

Figure 6.6   SAI MOP (1989–93): Share of Prefectures in the Sub-programmes
Source: adapted from Ministry of National Economy (1993a).

particular sub-programme of the MOP only partly may be attributed to the difference in population.

Essentially, it may be viewed as reflecting the differentiation in local needs and the capacities of the local institutional infrastructure in each prefecture. Thus, the marginally greater share of the Dodecanese in the mainly infrastructure-oriented ERDF sub-programme reflects the main priorities of the prefecture initially in the water and sewage-related infrastructure and at a second stage in the protection of the environment and educational infrastructure. Conversely, in the categories of ports, airports and road networks a rather balanced allocation of funds among the prefectures has been identified. Finally, in areas of tourist infrastructure, such as the exploitation of the cultural heritage, there are no funds allocated at all to the Dodecanese.

In the ESF sub-programme, which focuses on vocational training, the almost huge gap between the two prefectures corresponds to the existing differentiation in numbers of persons who undertook training in each prefecture. In particular, the Dodecanese has, almost traditionally, demonstrated a strong orientation towards vocational training with emphasis on tourism, which has been, to a significant extent, facilitated by the presence of the central state-run High School for Tourist Training and the appropriate institutional infrastructure. Conversely, the share of the Cyclades funds has been mainly focused on either agriculture or training about local development issues.

With the EAGGF sub-programme, on the other hand, the huge gap between the prefectures in allocated funds should be attributed to the increasing need of the Dodecanese for forestry-protection measures, whereas Cyclades funds are mainly oriented towards primary sector-related activities.

Finally, the most revealing differentiation is in the specific sub-programme for Local Government Actions. In particular, the strong tradition of the Dodecanese in institution-building at the local level and its subsequent effectiveness and efficiency in absorption of the related funds and in performing the necessary actions has had important consequences for the way in which the funds are allocated and hence it may account for the Dodecanese's greater share in the sub-programme.

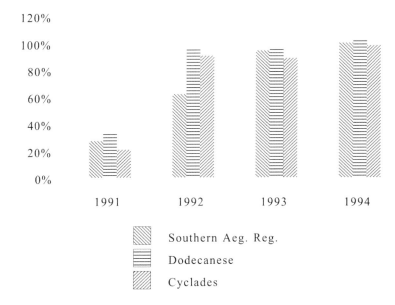

Figure 6.7   SAI MOP (1989–93): Absorption/Commitments Coefficients
Source: adapted from Aigaio Ltd (1995).

What, however, illustrates the comparatively better performance of the Dodecanese prefecture is the absorption/commitments data shown in Figure 6.7. According to these data (Aigaio Ltd, 1995), the Dodecanese has consistently demonstrated a better performance in the absorption rate of financial commitments of the MOP in comparison with both the region and the Cyclades prefecture, during the entire period of the CSF, which seems to be linked to the qualities of its institutional infrastructure.

Moreover, two of the sub-programmes of the MOP, namely the ERDF and the specific Local Governments' sub-programme, for which reliable data at the prefectural level were found, reveal a picture similar to the entire programme in absorption capacity at the regional and prefectural levels. In particular, as Figure 6.8 reveals, the Dodecanese had a higher absorption rate in comparison with both the region and the Cyclades prefecture over the entire period of implementation of the ERDF sub-programme. This differentiation reflects the strong orientation of the Dodecanese towards the infrastructure-related use of EU funds, with particular emphasis on water sewerage and educational

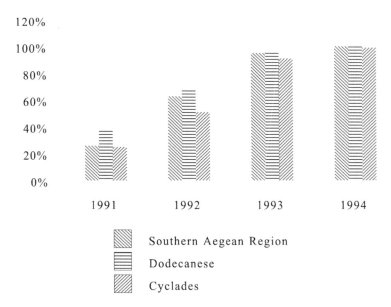

Figure 6.8   SAI MOP (1989–93): ERDF Sub-programme Absorption Rates
Source: adapted from Aigaio Ltd (1995).

infrastructure measures. Furthermore, the higher rates of differentiation during the initial phase of the programme among the Dodecanese and the Cyclades prefectures – which gradually declined by the end of the period – should be interpreted as an indication of the existing differentiation in the levels of learning and adaptation among the institutional infrastructures of the two prefectures concerned.

On the other hand, the specific Local Governments' sub-programme may be viewed as providing the most strong evidence about the differentiation in institutional capacity among the prefectures of the Southern Aegean islands. As Figure 6.9 shows, there is a huge gap in the absorption rates of the Dodecanese and Cyclades local governments over the entire period of the programme (1990–94). In particular, Dodecanese local authorities have been proved much more competent in comparison with their Cyclades counterparts in planning and hence absorbing more funds for structural interventions that reflect local needs and demands. Thus, in almost all the specific mea-

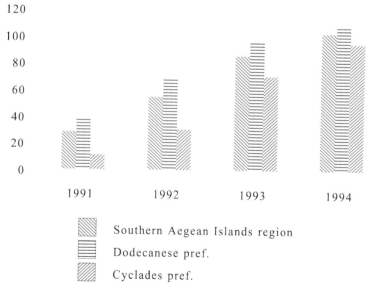

Figure 6.9   SAI MOP (1989–93): Local Government Sub-programme Absorption Rates
Source: adapted from Aigaio Ltd (1995).

sures of the sub-programme, that is 'road networks', 'social and cultural infrastructure', 'protection of the environment' and 'tourist infrastructure', there is a clear predominance of Dodecanese local governments.

Finally, as far as the Community Initiatives[9] are concerned, it has been extremely difficult to specify particular actions because of the dominant role of the central state in planning procedures and the subsequent overlapping of several ministries involved. However, as the evidence from fieldwork research at the regional and local levels will show in the following section, Community Initiatives have been important tools for the mobilization of local actors and the promotion of local partnerships within the EU regional policy environment. Further, despite the lack of specific evaluation data at the regional or prefectural levels, specific Initiatives that accompanied the first CSF stand out as having played a more important role than others in the region. Thus, LEADER, VALOREN, HORIZON, ENVIREG and REGEN/INTERREG have emerged as the most important Initiatives for the Southern Aegean region.

Since the period of fieldwork research coincided with the starting up of the implementation phase of the second CSF (1994–99), existing evidence from its ex-ante evaluations enables some preliminary observations to be made in comparative terms. The following points deserve note. First, although the second CSF (MOP) may be seen as a continuation of the first, since it focuses on the pursuit of the same main goals, there has been a shift in its approach to tourist development, involving in particular the gradual abandonment of the mass tourism model and the adoption of flexible, small-scale forms of leisure facility that are more appropriate for the smaller and less developed islands. Since this shift is accompanied by a specific integrated programme for the exploitation of physical and cultural resources, it represents an outcome of the learning process from the implementation of the first CSF, which seems to have led to adaptations to the changing patterns of demand in leisure (Stokowski, 1994). Second, this process of policy adaptation goes hand in hand with integrated actions in transport, communication and social infrastructure to promote the catching up of the less developed islands, thus reducing intra-regional disparities. Third, the interconnectedness between the sustainability of natural resources and sustainable local development has been taken into account by the new programming approach. Hence the share of actions for the protection of the environment and urban planning have been substantially upgraded within the programme. Finally, there has been a strengthening of the role of local government institutions in the planning and implementation processes through increasing support in human and technical resources provided by the specific sub-programme for local governments.

This section has demonstrated that, despite significant intra-regional disparities (among the islands) in the levels of development and absorption capacity, there is an important differentiation between the Southern and Northern Aegean island regions in both priorities for the use of the funds and absorption capacity. In particular, the Southern Aegean region shows a strong orientation towards technical and educational infrastructure in the use of funds, whereas in the Northern Aegean business support, social and agricultural infrastructure account for a considerable share of the funds. Furthermore, at the prefectural level, the Dodecanese prefecture demonstrates a better performance than the Cyclades in almost all the sub-programmes and measures of the MOP and especially in the specific sub-programme for Local Governments. Notwithstanding the comparatively low level of private sector contribution to Funds payments, because of the maintenance of the national regional policy incentives scheme, what provides the exegesis for the better performance of the Dodecanese is the differentiation in attitudes, which is illustrated by what one interviewee said: 'Structural Funds money constitutes investment for the SAI (Dodecanese). In other regions it is used as social subsidy'.[10]

We now turn to assess, in the third section, the way in which the better learning capacity of the local institutional infrastructure in the Southern Aegean region in general and of the Dodecanese prefecture in particular, as identified in chapter four, has facilitated the adaptation process of the region to a – new – policy-making environment, that of European regional policy.

Institution-building, policy networks and adaptation

By drawing the institutional map of the region and evaluating the structural features of the general exchange local institutional networks, chapter four explored the levels of collective action and hence the learning and adaptation capacities of the system of institutional interactions at regional and prefectural levels. This section assesses the degree to which the main features of the local institutional infrastructure for collective action and learning have affected the processes of institution-building and adaptation of the region to the changing environment, characterized by the gradual Europeanization of regional policy.

Institution-building, policy networks and adaptation in the Southern Aegean Islands

Although the Europeanization of regional policy and the introduction of the programming approach with the planning and implementation of the first MOP (1989–93) has been the most critical external constraint on institution-building and adaptation at the regional level, the centralized Greek administrative system and the multi-fragmentation of space have also functioned as inherent impediments to the promotion of the adaptation process in the Southern Aegean region. Thus, despite the positive impact of the European structural policy programmes on significantly improving the policy-making environment at regional level, and the substantially better network structures compared to the Northern Aegean, the combination of centralized decision-taking and fragmented policy action, which does not seem to be taken into account by the EU Commission (DG XVI), have played an important role in impeding the processes of institution-building and achieving cohesion at the regional level.[11]

The Monitoring Committee for CSF (MOP) implementation, that has been seen as the institutionalized form of the linkages between supranational (EU Commission), national and subnational elites, is the only instance of 'induced' institutional building at regional level in the Southern Aegean as well. As Table 6.3 reveals, this process has been

Table 6.3   Southern Aegean Regional Partnership for Monitoring the MOP (1989–93)

A. President: Regional General Secretary	
B. Members:	
1. Prefects:	Cyclades, Dodecanese
2. Local Ass. of Munic. & Communes:	Cyclades, Dodecanese
3. Central Government (Ministries):	National Economy, Agriculture, Employment, Interior, Envoment & Public Works, Aegean
4. Higher Education Institutions:	University of the Aegean
5. Commission of the EC (DGs):	XVI, V, VI
6. Interest Group Representatives:	Cyclades and Dodecanese Chambers, Tourist Agents, Trade Unions etc
7. Programme Manager	
8. Evaluation Consultant	

Source: Ministry of National Economy (1992; 1995).

substantiated by the broadening of the regional councils to include, beyond the prefects of the regional prefectures, representatives of the Local Associations of Municipalities and Communes and representatives of the major interest group-organizations in each prefecture (Chambers, Labour Movement Organizations).

Notwithstanding the relatively limited role of the monitoring committee, especially during the initial phase of the first CSF, in the Southern Aegean the Structural Funds programmes have facilitated the gradual process of institution-building at all levels of subnational government, which still cannot be raised at the regional level because of the lack of directly elected regional councils.[12]

Within this policy environment, even though the structure of the policy network at regional level has improved in comparison with that of the general exchange network (chapter four), it continues to demonstrate the same general characteristics. In this respect, the outcomes of the social network analysis (SNA) based on density, centralization and structural equivalence measures are revealing. Thus, although the density of the policy network, which is used as an indicator of network cohesion, has been substantially improved when compared with that of the exchange network (0.414–0.367 out of 1 respectively), essentially it remains low given that fewer than half of the actors are connected to each other within the network.

Furthermore, as Table 6.4 with the centrality measures of both the general exchange and policy networks demonstrates, despite the improvement in the degree of centralization, the policy network remains highly centralized (64.74 per cent). What these low-density and high-centralization indicators underline is that even within the European regional policy environment the network continues to demonstrate the same features, that is centralization around the Regional Secretariat and fragmentation at the prefectural level. The following lessons are drawn from this comparative analysis. First, even though the region has been a byproduct of pressures for the implementation of the Structural Funds programmes, it has not yet been institutionalized, even within the favourable (for it) policy-making environment. Second, the processes of institution-building and adaptation should be considered as slow as the learning process itself, while both the state structure and general features of the socio-political system are unfavourable. Finally, learning and institution-building are more easily achieved at the local and prefectural levels, where the development of dialogue and communication linkages may be aided by relatively favourable local factors that are more difficult to flourish at the regional level.

Table 6.4   SAI: Centrality Measures of General Exchange and Policy Networks

Organizations	General Exchange Network Centrality %	Policy Network Centrality %
1. Reg. Gen. Secretariat	100.00	100.00
2. Dodecanese Pref. Council	55.00	55.00
3. Cyclades Pref. Council	50.00	50.00
4. Dodecanese Chamber	45.00	50.00
5. Cyclades Chamber	45.00	50.00
6. Dodecanese Ass. Munic. & Comm.	45.00	45.00
7. Cyclades Ass. Munic. & Comm.	45.00	50.00
8. Rhodes City Council	40.00	45.00
9. Dodecanese Tourist Ag. Ass.	40.00	40.00
10. Kos City Council	35.00	40.00
11. Rhodes Hotel Owners Ass.	35.00	40.00
12. Kos Hotel Owners Ass.	35.00	35.00
13. Mykonos City Council	35.00	40.00
14. Ermoupolis City Council	30.00	35.00
15. Mykonos Hotel Owners As.	30.00	35.00
16. Mykonos Tourist Agents As.	30.00	35.00
17. Cyclades Training Centre	20.00	20.00
18. Dodecanese Development Ag.	15.00	35.00
19. Cyclades Development Ag.	15.00	35.00
20. University	15.00	15.00
21. Ermoupolis Development Ag.	10.00	20.00
Total Network Centralization	70.00	64.74

Source: Paraskevopoulos, C. J. (1998b).

Thus, the centrality measures of the individual actors within the network reflect mainly the degree to which the role of any particular actor has been upgraded within the EU regional policy environment. In that respect, the upgraded role of the Dodecanese, Cyclades and Ermoupolis development agencies in the policy network derives from their involvement in the management of specific Structural Funds programmes or initiatives (LEADER, URBAN), which will be raised more clearly at the prefectural level. Furthermore, the improved degree of centrality of important private-interest or associational actors (Chamber, Associations of Municipalities, Hotel Owners' Association) should be attributed to their participation in the monitoring committee of the CSF and their involvement in specific projects of the MOP at prefectural level. Finally, the marginal role of the University in the policy network reveals the degree of its legitimation within the institutional structure of the Southern Aegean region, given that it is a rela-

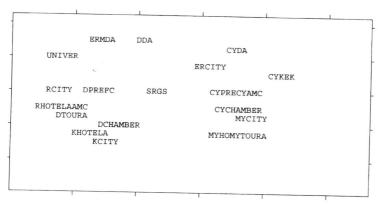

Figure 6.10 Policy Network in SAI

tively new institution, significantly dislocated or completely absent, especially in the Cyclades.[13]

The structure of the policy network in the Southern Aegean is depicted in Figure 6.10, which is based on the multi-dimensional scaling technique. The main feature of the graph is its similarity with its equivalent for the general exchange network (see chapter four). Hence, the Regional Secretariat, which remains the central actor, is depicted at the centre of the graph while the increased density of the policy network is illustrated by the structure of the actors at prefectural level.

Institution-building, policy networks and adaptation in Dodecanese

As it has been shown in chapters four and five, Dodecanese has the best institutional infrastructure in terms of qualitative features, such as capacity for learning and adaptation, which is partly attributed, on the one hand, to the presence of social capital endowments and, on the other, to the technical and institutional infrastructure left by the Italians. This strong tradition in institution building (for Greece) seems relevant to the process of adapting to the European environment because it allows the region to seize the opportunities the Europeanization of regional policy presents for modernization, economic/institutional adjustment and development. Thus, notwithstanding the limited room for manoeuvre, because of the peculiarities of the Greek socio-political structure, the Dodecanese may be viewed as one of the most successful examples of adaptation among the Greek regions.

The approach to EU regional policy as a challenge for opening up the process of institution-building, by providing the opportunity to bypass the central state structure and thus facilitating endogenous local action, became evident in Dodecanese even during the implementation of the IMP for the Aegean islands. Thus, despite the central state-dominated processes for planning and implementing the programme, in the Southern Aegean in general and in Dodecanese in particular there has been, in relative terms, a considerable presence of local non-state actors and voluntary organizations.[14]

Since the introduction of the CSF (MOP) opened up the game for supra-subnational linkages mainly in the planning and monitoring processes (monitoring committees), local governments and voluntary organizations in Dodecanese have proved competent in comparison with their counterparts in other regions in both the implementation of specific measures and institution-building, mainly around specific Community Initiatives. Thus, although the implementation of the MOP was mostly run by the prefecture, most of the local governments were involved in the implementation of MOP projects and, in particular, of the sub-programme for the protection of the environment. In the same manner they were involved in the implementation of measures for the ENVIREG Initiative. Conversely, the implementation of both INTERREG I and II Initiatives was undertaken by the prefecture.

Interestingly enough, even though rapid changes in the external conditions, such as the gradual Europeanization of regional policy for Objective 1 regions, may make old institutions redundant and create the need for new ones, in the Dodecanese, because of the pre-existing qualitative features of the local institutional infrastructure in learning and adaptation, this trend has not been vindicated.[15] On the contrary, the process of institution-building in the Dodecanese took the form of adjustment of the existing institutional structures to the requirements of the new environment. Within this framework the creation primarily of the Dodecanese Development Agency (DDA) and secondarily of the Kos Development Agency were perhaps the only important additions to the existing institutional infrastructure. Thus the DDA was created by the local Association of Municipalities (LAMC) and the Prefecture Council and focuses on developing local networks mainly around specific Community Initiatives. Hence, it has initiated joint actions with the Prefecture Council, involving the LEADER – for the islands of group I (see page 164) – and INTERREG Initiatives.[16]

Whatever the degree of adjustment of the other institutions of the prefecture may be, the role of the Chamber has been dominant within the Dodecanese institutional infrastructure. Given its almost traditional role as initiator of all the fora for dialogue and communication among the actors at the prefectural and local levels, it constitutes the leading institutional actor in adjustment and adaptation to the Europeanization of policy-making.

As Table 6.5 demonstrates, beyond its role within the local general exchange network (see chapter four), the chamber is a pioneer in its development and expansion of its institution-building capacity at the transnational level. Within this framework, it has participated in numerous EU programmes and initiatives, such as the ECOMOST and ECOLOGIC HOTELS programmes of the DG XXIII focusing on transnational cooperation in the field of ecological tourism, as well as the MERCURE-TACIS and EUROFORM programmes along with other European regions. Additionally, it has organized, along with the Hotel Owners' Association of Rhodes, a series of conferences on issues arising from the impact of tourism on development.[17]

Finally, a major step forward in the process of institution-building is under way in Dodecanese, involving a joint initiative of the basic institutional actors on a Prefectural Council plan for opening an office in Brussels.[18]

The structure of the policy network in the Dodecanese reflects the relatively successful adjustment of its institutional infrastructure to the changing conditions and the resulting level of institution-building. The density measure, which indicates the degree of network cohesion, in the policy network (0.800) is even higher than in the general exchange network (see chapter four). This density indicator demonstrates that almost all the actors are connected to each other within the network.

Furthermore, the centrality measures (Table 6.6), which reveal the way in which resources are distributed among the actors and subsequently the dominant actors within the network, demonstrate a similar structure to that of the density measure. In particular, the degree of policy network centrality is even lower than that of the general exchange network (24.44 per cent–33.33 per cent). This low degree of centralization reflects an even more horizontal structure in the policy network than that in the general exchange network (chapter four). Therefore, what the high-density and low-centrality measures of the policy network indicate is that within the European regional policy environment resources and power are even more evenly dispersed

Table 6.5 Community Initiatives and Transnational Networks in Dodecanese

Actors	Initiative
a) Dodecanese Chamber Nice (France) Irish Spanish Portuguese	a) Economic Observatory (art. 10)
b) Dodecanese Chamber Majorca Chamber	b) ECOMOST (Tourism & Environment)
c) Dodecanese Chamber Chamber Cote d' Azur	c) MERCURE
d) Dodecanese Chamber Kiev Chamber	d) MERCURE-TACIS
e) Dodecanese Chamber Chamber Cote d'Azur	e) EUROFORM

Source: adapted from unpublished documents of Dodecanese Chamber and Interview with the President.

among the local actors. Hence, the possibilities for shifting alliances, creating synergies and achieving collective action are even higher within the policy network. In that sense European regional policy may be viewed as a positive external shock that facilitates the processes of crossing the public–private divide, achieving the specific synergies and collective action among public and private actors that are essential to the necessary learning and adaptation processes within the network structure.

Looking at the centralization measures of each individual actor on a comparative basis between general exchange and policy network the following points emerge. First, beyond the Regional Secretariat and the Prefectural Council, which, because of their position within the administrative structure of the state, provided the 'traditional' leadership of the general exchange network, the role of all the other, both public and private, actors has been significantly upgraded. Second, this almost horizontal structure of the network opens up opportunities for synergies among powerful public and private actors and hence for the provision of varying leadership roles. Third, this is crucially dependent on the role of the state structure and the dynamism of the system of interactions at local level. Fourth, the upgraded role of the DDA creates possibilities for this to be crucially extended within the local system of governance, which would be favoured by the complete

Table 6.6   Dodecanese Prefecture: Centrality Measures of General Exchange and Policy Networks

Organization	General Exchange Network Centrality %	Policy Network Centrality %
1. Reg. Gen. Secretariat	100.00	100.00
2. Pref. Council	100.00	100.00
3. Association Mun. & Comm.	90.00	90.00
4. Chamber	80.00	90.00
5. Rhodes City Council	80.00	90.00
6. Tourist Agents' Ass.	80.00	80.00
7. Kos City Council	70.00	80.00
8. Rhodes Hotel Owners Ass.	70.00	80.00
9. Kos Hotel Owners Ass.	70.00	70.00
10. University	30.00	30.00
11. Development Agency	30.00	70.00
Total Network Centralization:	33.33	24.44

Source: Paraskevopoulos, C. J. (1998b).

Europeanization of regional policy. Within such a policy environment, the DDA could function as complementary to or even substitute for the Association of Municipalities, providing local governments with technical and administrative assistance. Finally, the role of the University remains rather marginal even in the policy network. The only joint involvement of the University and local actors of the Dodecanese prefecture in projects financed by the Structural Funds seems to be the sewage system of Lipsi island.

The structural features that derive from the centrality measures are further reinforced by analysis of the structural equivalence, which categorizes actors according to their structural positions within the network. Thus, the structural equivalence (Figure 6.11), when compared with the general exchange network (chapter four), reveals the following features of the policy network.[19] First, with the exception of the University (fourth block), almost all other actors are connected to each other. Second, because of the centralized administrative structure of the state (even in the implementation of the Community Initiatives and Pilot Projects the state plays the key role), the public actors (Regional Secretariat, Prefecture Council, City Councils) provide the leadership of the policy network. However, almost all the actors of the

	S R G S	D P R E F C	R C I T Y	D D A	K H O T E L A	D T O U R A	D A M C	D C H A M B E R	R H O T E L A	K C I T Y	U N I V E R
SRGS	1	1	1	1	1	1	1	1	1	1	1
DPREFC	1	1	1	1	1	1	1	1	1	1	1
RCITY	1	1	1	1		1	1	1	1	1	1
DDA	1	1	1	1			1	1	1	1	
KHOTELA	1	1			1	1	1	1	1	1	
DTOURA	1	1	1		1	1	1	1	1	1	
DAMC	1	1	1	1	1	1	1	1	1	1	
DCHAMBER	1	1	1	1	1	1	1	1	1	1	
RHOTELA	1	1	1	1	1	1	1	1	1		
KCITY	1	1	1	1	1	1	1	1		1	
UNIVER	1	1	1								1

Figure 6.11   Structural Equivalence of Policy Network Actors in Dodecanese

second and third blocks can provide varying leadership roles in the future. Third, the upgraded status of the Dodecanese Development Agency (DDA) indicates its successful involvement in the LEADER and INTERREG initiatives and its possible role as interlocutor among public and private actors to achieve synergies at the prefectural level. Finally, the structure of the network provides the ground for crossing the public–private divide among the actors, thus facilitating collective action, learning and adaptation.

The graph of the network, as depicted in Figure 6.12, vindicates the structural features arising from the structural equivalence. The first observation is that the graph of the policy network represents a more balanced network structure, in comparison with that of the general exchange network (chapter four). Furthermore, beyond the General Secretariat and the Prefecture Council, which are depicted at the centre of the graph, with the exception of the University, no other actor is marginalized within the network. Hence, the graph corresponds to the cohesive, horizontal and balanced structure of the Dodecanese policy network.

In sum, the Dodecanese prefecture demonstrates a high degree (for Greece) of institution-building and adaptation, which, however, is not characterized by the increasing redundancy of old institutions and the emergence of new ones, but rather by the successful structural adjustment of the pre-existing institutional infrastructure. On the other hand, the structure of the policy network is better than in the general

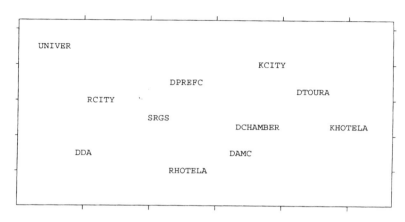

Figure 6.12   Policy Network in Dodecanese

exchange network, which means it has a structure that is more horizontal, cohesive and balanced between public and private actors.

Institution-building, policy networks and adaptation in Cyclades

As established in chapter four, the Cyclades prefecture demonstrates
significant similarities to the Dodecanese in the qualitative features of
institutional infrastructure. In particular, even though Cyclades lacks
the Dodecanese tradition in institution-building, its institutional infrastructure is characterized by a significant number of synergies between
the actors and public–private partnerships. The relatively good quality
of the Cyclades institutional infrastructure may be attributed to the
prompt adjustment of the economic and institutional structure of
some islands (Mykonos) towards the tourist sector since the 1960s and
to the historical trade and cultural relations of others (Syros) with
western Europe.

The processes of institution-building and adaptation to the European
policy-making environment, though less prompt than in the
Dodecanese, had already become evident during the implementation
of the IMP for the Aegean Islands. Thus, like the Dodecanese, Cyclades
was the second prefecture of the entire Aegean islands region with
non-state public and voluntary organizations involved in the implementation of the programme.[20]

The introduction of the CSFs and MOPs marked the start of the
learning process for local institutional infrastructure, which proved

almost as competent as the Dodecanese in mobilizing around specific programmes or initiatives of European regional policy. The planning and monitoring (Monitoring Committee) processes of the MOP constituted an opening up of direct linkages between the supranational and the subnational levels of government. In this respect, local governments of the Cyclades prefecture, despite the fragmentation of space and the differentiation of economic and institutional structures, exploited the comparative advantage of the easier access to the capital of the region (Ermoupolis, Syros) and hence the seat of the Monitoring Committee. Even though the implementation process of the MOP as in every region in Greece was primarily run by the Prefecture, local governments were actively involved in the implementation of specific measures, in projects of the MOP and, especially, in the subprogramme for the protection of the environment. Furthermore, as in the Dodecanese, most of the Cyclades local governments and particularly those of the small and less-developed islands were involved in the ENVIREG Initiative projects, focusing on tackling the water and sewage problems of the smaller and most disadvantaged islands.

With regard to the process of institution-building, the response of Cyclades to the challenges imposed by the rapidly changing environment were rather different from those of the Dodecanese. In particular, there has been only a gradual process of building new institutions, mainly because of the lack of the appropriate institutional infrastructure. Thus, the Cyclades Development Agency (CYDA) is the outcome of a cooperative network between the Prefectural Council and local Association of Municipalities and Communes.[21] On the other hand, the Ermoupolis Development Agency (ERMDA) was created by the Ermoupolis City Council and the Chamber. Moreover, a series of development agencies seem to be under way, such as the Naxos Development Agency. In sum, the gradual Europeanization of regional policy brought about new institutions focusing mainly on the development of local networking around specific Community Initiatives.

Within this policy environment, the Cyclades Development Agency has been currently involved in LEADER Initiative projects, whereas the Ermoupolis Development Agency is currently involved in implementing the URBAN Initiative in the city of Ermoupolis to regenerate the old city centre.[22] Finally, several hotel owners' associations of the Cyclades complex have been involved in PRISMA Initiative projects to promote tourist activities.

The structure of the policy network in Cyclades corresponds to the relatively successful adjustment of its institutional infrastructure to the

Europeanization of regional policy. The density measure, which is used as an indicator of the degree of network cohesion, has significantly improved in the policy network in comparison with that of the general exchange (0.636–0.545 respectively). What the density measure of the policy network indicates is that more than half of the institutional actors are connected to each other within the network.

Moreover, with regard to the centrality measures (Table 6.7), which demonstrate the way in which resources are distributed among the actors and hence the dominant actors within the network, there is a lower level of centralization in the policy network in comparison with that in the general exchange network (43.64 per cent–54.55 per cent respectively). This change indicates that within the regional policy environment, the structure of the network tends to become more horizontal, given the higher degree of actors' involvement in exchange relations with other actors of the network. Therefore, European regional policy creates favourable conditions for resource interdependence and hence for achieving those synergistic effects and collective action that are viewed as prerequisites for learning and adaptation. What should be stressed, however, is that the relatively high degree of centralization in both the general exchange and policy networks is a result of the extremely low presence of the University within the network.

Looking at the centralization measures of any individual actor at both the general exchange and policy network, the following points should be emphasized. First, under the Regional Secretariat, which is the most central actor within the networks, there is a significant presence of institutional actors apart from the Prefectural Council (especially in the policy network). In particular, primarily the local Association of Municipalities and the Chamber, and secondarily the Mykonos City Council, are well-connected, important actors within the prefecture and especially in the policy network. Second, there is, especially in the policy network, a considerable presence of important public and private actors under the leading actors (Regional Secretariat, Prefectural Council, Association of Municipalities) that form the basis for future public–private alliances at the local level. Third, the upgraded role of both development agencies (CYDA and ERMDA) within the policy network indicates that under certain circumstances (a favourable policy-making environment such as that of a completely Europeanized regional policy) they can play the crucial role of interlocutors between public and private actors, thus achieving synergies and providing local actors with crucial technical and administrative assistance. In that sense, they may be seen as substitutes for the role of

Table 6.7   Cyclades Prefecture: Centrality Measures of General Exchange and Policy Networks

Organization	General Exchange Network Centrality %	Policy Network Centrality %
1. Reg. Gen. Secretariat	100.00	100.00
2. Prefecture Council	81.82	81.82
3. Association of Munic. & Comm.	81.82	90.91
4. Chamber	72.73	81.82
5. Mykonos City Council	63.64	72.73
6. Ermoupolis City Council	54.55	63.64
7. Hotel Owners Ass.	54.55	63.64
8. Tourist Ag. Ass.	54.55	63.64
9. Training Centre	36.36	36.36
10. Development Agency	27.27	63.64
11. Ermoupolis Development Ag.	18.18	36.36
12. University	9.09	9.09
Total Network Centralization:	54.55	43.64

Source: Paraskevopoulos, C. J. (1998b).

the Association of Municipalities and Communes at prefectural level. Finally, the role of the University remains extremely marginal, even within the policy network.

The main structural characteristics that derive from analysis of the centrality measures are further strengthened by the structural equivalence, which identifies common structural positions among actors within the network, according to the structure of their relationships. Thus, the structural equivalence (Figure 6.13), when compared with the general exchange network (chapter four), reveals the following structure of the policy network. First, the University is the only marginalized actor within the structure of the policy network. Second, there are some similarities to the policy network structure in the Dodecanese, in the sense that under the leading (public) actors (Regional Secretariat, Prefecture Council and Association of Municipalities), there is a group of public and private-interest organizations (Mykonos and Ermoupolis City Councils, Chamber, Hotel Owners' Association and Tourist Agents), which, although less-connected within the network, contribute to its cohesive and horizontal character.

However, with the exception of the University, there is a group of actors, namely the Ermoupolis Development Agency, the Training

	SRGS	CYAMC	CYCHAMBER	MYHOTELA	MYCITY	CYDA	MYTOURA	CYPREFC	UNIVER	ERCITY	ERMDA	CYKEK
SRGS	1	1	1	1	1	1	1	1	1	1	1	1
CYAMC	1	1	1	1	1	1	1	1		1	1	1
CYCHAMBER	1	1	1	1	1		1	1		1	1	1
MYHOTELA	1	1	1	1	1	1	1	1				
MYCITY	1	1	1	1	1	1	1	1		1		
CYDA	1	1		1	1	1	1	1		1		
MYTOURA	1	1	1	1	1	1	1	1				
CYPREFC	1	1	1	1	1	1	1	1		1		1
UNIVER	1								1			
ERCITY	1	1	1	1	1			1		1	1	
ERMDA	1	1	1							1	1	
CYKEK	1	1	1				1					1

Figure 6.13 Structural Equivalence of Policy Network Actors in Cyclades

Centre and the Ermoupolis City Council, which for several reasons is still clearly less connected within the network. Hence its position for shifting alliances and achieving synergies and collective action is rather weak. Conversely, since the status of the Cyclades Development Agency has been substantially upgraded within the policy network, it constitutes a more important and cohesive actor in the sphere between public and private actors, and contributes to the network cohesion as well. Within this framework there is a rather limited number of actors in comparison with the Dodecanese that can provide varying leadership roles and facilitate the stabilization of relations among the key institutional actors, which is required by the learning process.

The graph of the network (Figure 6.14), based on a multi-dimensional scaling technique, depicts the main structural features arising from structural equivalence. In particular, the main characteristic of the policy network seems to be a slightly more balanced structure when compared with the general exchange network (chapter four). On the other hand, it clearly illustrates that beyond the University, which is marginalized, the Ermoupolis Development Agency (ERMDA) and the Training Centre (CYKEK) are at the margins of the network, as they were in the general exchange network.

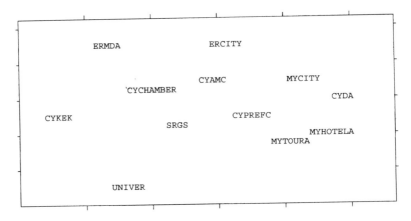

Figure 6.14   Policy Network in Cyclades

Conclusions

This chapter has demonstrated that, despite general weaknesses in the implementation of the first integrated development plans of European regional policy (IMPs and MOPs) in Greece, there have been signs of some differentiation among the regions of the Aegean islands. In the case of the IMP – which concerned the entire Aegean islands region – the differentiation between the Southern and Northern Aegean was identified in structural priorities and effectiveness in the use of resources.

In the case of the MOPs, however, where comparisons are easier, despite the intra-regional (among the islands) differences, a clearer differentiation initially among the Southern and Northern Aegean regions and at a second stage among Dodecanese and Cyclades has been identified, which seems to be related to the structure of priorities, the absorption capacity and the efficient use of resources per subprogramme.

As analysis of the institution-building and adaptation processes in the Southern Aegean islands region has shown, the capacity for adaptation within the European regional policy environment is crucially dependent on specific features of the system of institutional interactions at both regional and local levels, such as its learning capacity. The network analysis at both the regional and prefectural levels of the

Southern Aegean has demonstrated that regions best able to adapt to changing conditions are those that possess learning institutional networks, that is networks able to change in step with changing conditions.

Moreover, even if there are no such networks at the regional level, Europeanization may be seen as an externally driven process for promoting institution-building and adaptation capacity at the local level. This process, however, is dependent on the presence of crucial socio-cultural factors at the local level, such as trust, norms and networks that can facilitate collective action, and hence the learning and adaptation processes.

7
Neither Learning nor Leadership: Policy Networks and State-driven Adaptation in the Northern Aegean Islands

Introduction

By focusing on the implementation and monitoring of the first CSF (1989–93), this chapter examines the degree to which the main features of the local institutional infrastructure in the Northern Aegean Islands region (chapter five) have affected the institutions and policy-adaptation processes within the European structural policy. Given, however, the innovative character of the CSFs as a step forward in the integrated approach and the generally poor results of the implementation of the first CSF in the region, the evidence from the implementation of the Aegean IMP and the initial phase of the second CSF (1994–99) is assessed to make an overall comparative evaluation of the adaptation process over a longer period of time.

Planning and implementing the IMP in the Northern Aegean

As identified in chapter six, for the planning procedures of the IMPs the entire Aegean islands area were designated a single region. Hence the common priority objectives of the Aegean islands IMP are the improvement of transport and communication linkages to combat the isolation of the islands; the control of tourist development; the promotion of tourism in the tourist-underdeveloped islands; and finally, agricultural development.

However, beyond the generally low degree of completion of the pro-gramme as a whole (79 per cent) and its four sub-programmes in the entire Aegean islands region (chapter six), the Northern Aegean has demonstrated important qualitative aspects in both the orientation of the funds and in the effectiveness and efficiency of the implementa-tion of the programme. First, the low degree of completion of sub-programme III (74 per cent), that was identified in chapter six, is to a significant extent attributed to the poor results of the programme in the Northern Aegean islands. In particular, given the primary focus of the sub-programme on the promotion of tourist development in the underdeveloped islands, its core was a specific measure for the promo-tion of agro-tourism in the islands of the Northern Aegean. However, the orientation of the measure resulted merely in providing financial support for the projects of central state agencies for creating a new source of income, complementary to agriculture for the inhabitants, through the supplementary development of tourism.[1] Moreover, the lack of any bottom-up collective participation by local actors and the subsequent absence of the necessary structural support (promotion, advertisement) led initially to poor results and eventually to the com-plete failure of the projects.

Second, in the sector of power supply, despite the increase in demand over time and the significantly higher cost of electric power in compari-son with continental Greece, the implementation of the measure in the Northern Aegean islands and particularly in Lesbos suffered substantial delays and inefficiencies. In particular, the project for the creation of a power plant in Lesbos, which had been included in the initial plan of the IMP, experienced significant delays because of local clientelist reac-tions, which led to the wasting of financial resources. Thus, notwith-standing the existing range of unexploited yet renewable sources of power on the islands, the implementation of specific measures in the sector of electric power supply through conventional means was marked by a substantial differentiation between the Southern and Northern Aegean regions in degree of effectiveness and efficiency. This differentiation should be attributed to specific features of the institu-tional infrastructure in the Northern Aegean and particularly in Lesbos.

Third, in the sub-programmes focusing on the upgrading of both basic and tourist infrastructures, as well as on the level of human capital, a differentiation in the orientation of the funds and in the levels of effectiveness and efficiency between the Aegean islands regions has been identified, which is closely linked to critical deficiencies in the local institutional infrastructure and, at a second stage, to pressures from well-established local clientelistic networks. In particular, beyond the differentiation in the sector of transport linkages (ports, airports), which were identified in chapter six, the comparative failure of the Northern Aegean region in the measures of the infrastructural sub-programmes II and III, involving projects of tourist infrastructure (marines) and projects aimed at improving the general development infrastructure (e.g. Lesbos shell-fish production plant), has been attributed either to the incapacity of the local institutions, or to clientelist reactions of local actors (Ministry of National Economy, 1994a). Thus, the relatively good performance of the Northern Aegean in small-scale projects for the expansion and improvement of the road network of the islands is viewed as a consequence of the dominant role played by local clientelist networks in the planning and monitoring processes of the IMP.

Finally, in comparison with the Southern Aegean, the still high weight of agriculture in the use of ESF funds for training and the improvement of human capital[2] points to the maintenance of the agricultural orientation in the productive structure of the region.

In conclusion, the qualitative features of the local institutional infrastructure in the Northern Aegean islands (see chapter five) have become evident even in the planning and implementation processes of the IMP, despite its unified structure and the dominant role played by the central state in the management of the programme. These institutional weaknesses are further illustrated by the differentiation between the two regions in the qualitative features of the institutional actors involved in the implementation of the programme, as is demonstrated in the section 'Institution building, policy networks and adaptation' below.

The effectiveness gap in implementing the first CSF (MOP 1989–93)

The main feature of the effectiveness gap between the two Aegean islands regions in the implementation of the Multi-fund regional Operational Programmes (MOPs), as discussed in chapter six (Figure 6.4), is their differentiation in capacity for absorption of the allocated funds of the programme. Furthermore, the priority objectives put forward by the MOP for the Northern Aegean islands region correspond to the existing differentiation in the phase of the adaptation process in comparison with the Southern Aegean. Thus, they emphasize sectors that can facilitate the processes of structural and productive adjustment of the region. Hence, the main priorities of the programme are to improve the communications and energy infrastructures, to exploit raw materials and natural resources, to improve living conditions through upgrading the basic infrastructure and developing human resources (CEC, 1990a: 40–1). The specific measures financed by the ERDF to achieve the above objectives involve the improvement of transport and communication linkages, as well as water, sewerage, social and educational basic infrastructures, the exploitation of the cultural heritage and the provision of services to the SMEs. Additionally, the interventions financed by the ESF sub-programme in the region include vocational training measures in farming and spa-tourism, agricultural diversification, fisheries and geothermal energy. Finally, the EAGGF sub-programme is primarily focused on measures for the preservation and protection of natural resources and the environment, as well as the repair of damage caused by natural disasters.

Within this framework the distribution of financial resources in the MOP of the Northern Aegean region demonstrates a considerable orientation towards the sectors of social infrastructure, business support and agriculture-related measures. In particular, as Figure 7.1 reveals,[3] the sectors related to transport and communication physical infrastruc-

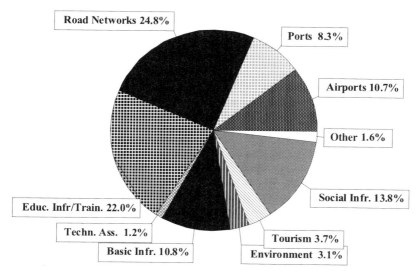

Figure 7.1   NAI MOP (1989–93): Distribution of Funds per Sector of Infrastructure
Source: adapted from Ministry of National Economy (1993b).

tures that are crucial for the islands, such as airports and ports, account for just 19 per cent of the programme, while the social and basic infrastructures, which correspond to sectors, such as health, security, housing and water and sewerage absorb 24.6 per cent of the allocated funds. Additionally, the high share of the road networks (24.80 per cent) deserves special reference. It is made up primarily of small-scale interventions that should be attributed to local clientelist pressures rather than to a demand rooted in real local needs.[4]

Finally, the major share of the funds allocated to the education and training sector (13.3 per cent) refers to the creation of educational infrastructure (school buildings) and only the remaining 8.7 per cent is earmarked for vocational training, from which a substantial amount goes to the agricultural sector.

The impact, however, of the problematic structural adjustment of the region on the management of EU funds becomes even more clear from analysis of the qualitative features of the absorption capacity per sub-programme. In particular, as Figure 7.2[5] demonstrates, the greater contributor by far to the funds allocated to the programme is the ERDF (78.99 per cent), whose primary orientation is structural interventions in the physical infrastructure (transport, communication). Conversely, the

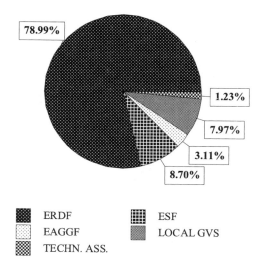

Figure 7.2   NAI MOP (1989–93): Structure per Sub-programme
Source: adapted from Ministry of National Economy (1993b).

Funds responsible for the creation of social infrastructure (ESF, EAGGF) represent a rather small part of the total funds of the programme.

On the other hand, by looking at the structure of the generally low (57 per cent) absorption rate of the region per subprogramme[6] (Figure 7.3), what emerges is the deficiencies of the structural adjustment of the region. In particular, the region demonstrates higher absorption rates (66 per cent and 67 per cent respectively) in the ESF and EAGGF sub-programmes, that is the lower-funded and social infrastructure-oriented sub-programmes. Conversely, it shows low rates of absorption (just 47 per cent) in the ERDF sub-programme, which provides financial assistance to physical infrastructure projects. Finally, the equally low level of absorption of the specific programme for projects undertaken by local governments (53 per cent) reflects the limited capacity for learning and adaptation of local governments in the region as a whole. Furthermore, this picture reflects the problematic implementation of a wide range of measures financed by the ERDF in basic infrastructure (promotion of the region's products, exploitation of the cultural heritage), while the only relatively successfully implemented measures are related to the activities of the mastic growers of Chios (see below) and the improvement of the tourist infrastructure of the island.

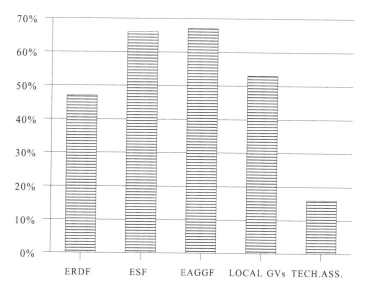

Figure 7.3   NAI MOP (1989–93): Absorption Rate per Sub-programme
Source: adapted from Ministry of National Economy (1993b).

Moreover, with regard to the contribution of the private sector to the Northern Aegean MOP, the following points should be emphasized. First, as shown in chapter six, even though primary (*ex ante*) data show a contribution of the private sector to the programme as high as 3.41 per cent, according to the ex-post (after implementation) data, it does not exceed 1.42 per cent (Ministry of National Economy, 1993a).

Second, this contribution is made up, almost exclusively, of the contributions of local governments to the projects of their specific sub-programme and to the measures of the EAGGF sub-programme for the processing of waste material from cattle farms. Finally, despite the relatively low level of private sector contribution to the Southern Aegean MOP (around 3 per cent, as in chapter six), it is well above the real rate of the Northern Aegean.

The impact, however, of local factors on the degrees of effectiveness and efficiency in the implementation and monitoring processes of the programme cannot be assessed without taking into account analysis at the prefectural level. Furthermore, whatever the differentiation in local needs and institutional capacity between Lesbos, Chios and Samos islands may be, it is expected to emerge from looking at inter-prefectural comparisons. Thus, as Figure 7.4 – which is based on ex-post data from the major structural interventions financed by the MOP[7] – reveals, the general trend in the distribution of EU financial resources per prefecture seems to follow the tradition established for the funds of the national Public Investment Programme, that is the percentage scheme of 40 per cent, 30 per cent, and 30 per cent for Lesbos, Chios and Samos respectively (see chapter five). This trend should be attributed to the dominant role of the Regional Secretariat in the allocation of EU resources through the mechanisms of the Public Investment Programme.

The Lesbos prefecture has the greater share in the two infrastructure-oriented categories of structural interventions, that is transport and communication linkages to combat the isolation of the islands and tourist development, which are mainly funded by the ERDF. Both categories, of tourist development and combating the isolation of the islands, involve a wide range of structural interventions from transport (airports, ports) linkages to water and sewerage infrastructure. However, the relatively balanced share with the Chios prefecture in the first category is attributed to the rather successful implementation of the specific National Programme of Community Interest (NPCI) for the Chios island, which was incorporated into the MOP in 1992 (see below).

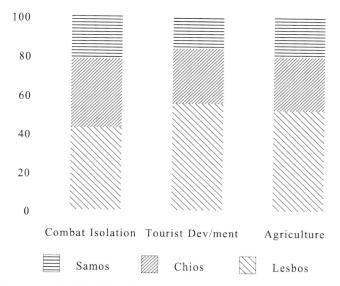

Figure 7.4 NAI MOP (1989–93): Share of the Prefectures in Sub-programmes
Source: adapted from Ministry of National Economy (1993b).

Nonetheless, in the third category of interventions in the agricultural sector, the case of the Lesbos prefecture deserves special reference. It provides evidence of the way in which the Common Agricultural Policy (CAP), based on the price subsidization mechanism, not only contradicts the goals of European regional policy, but also often provides counter motives for adaptation and adjustment, thus contributing to the widening, in the long-term, of the divergence gap among EU regions. In particular, the increased share of the Lesbos prefecture in the mainly EAGGF-funded and agricultural restructuring-oriented measures of the programme is distorted by the heavy subsidization of olive-oil production[8] through the CAP. The CAP subsidies have been one of the main reasons for the failure of the agricultural restructuring sub-programmes and measures of the IMP, the first CSF and most important of the LEADER Initiatives in Lesbos. Moreover, the heavily subsidized producers lack motivation to participate in local networks and development initiatives that focus on improving the adaptation capacity of the local economy by enhancing collective competitiveness.

Whereas the share of the Lesbos prefecture in almost all the categories of EU structural interventions is substantially increased, the absorption-rate data point in the opposite direction. In particular, as Figure 7.5 reveals, Lesbos demonstrates the lower absorption rate in the ERDF sub-programme over the whole programme period, which reflects the problematic implementation of specific measures of the sub-programme. The measures with major deficiencies in Lesbos are in the sectors of water and sewerage, educational infrastructure, airports and promotion of prefectural products. Although the factors that have affected these effectiveness and efficiency gaps in the management of the funds and implementation of the programme in Lesbos range widely from parochialist reactions closely linked to protection of individual interests to the institutional incapacity, what emerges from the qualitative analysis as the most important factor is the weakness of the local institutional infrastructure.

Conversely, Chios demonstrates, in comparative terms, a better performance, which partly reflects the rather successful implementation of basic social infrastructure measures and the measures of the specific National Programme of Community Interest (NPCI) for Chios,[9] which was mainly used to improve the production methods and promotion

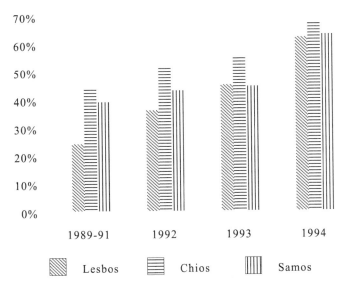

Figure 7.5   NAI MOP (1989–93): ERDF Sub-programme Absorption Rates
Source: adapted from Ministry of National Economy (1993b).

of mastic and mastic products. The successful implementation of the measures for market-research, promotion of new mastic products and training of mastic growers, in which the Mastic Growers' Association played the key role,[10] has contributed to the better overall performance of Chios in the ERDF sub-programme. However, the generally better quality of the local institutional infrastructure of Chios seems to be linked with the higher absorption rates in the sub-programme.

Finally, the comparatively satisfactory performance of Samos in the ERDF sub-programme is attributed to the rather successful implementation of the measure for creating tourist infrastructure (marinas) and the measure for improving the road network on Samos and Ikaria islands.

The existing differences in the capacity for learning and adaptation at local government level between the islands are illustrated by the absorption performance in the specific sub-programme for local governments (Figure 7.6). In particular, notwithstanding the incapacity of all local governments of the region to protect the environment, the Chios local authorities demonstrate a better performance in absorption rate during the whole period of the programme, when compared with

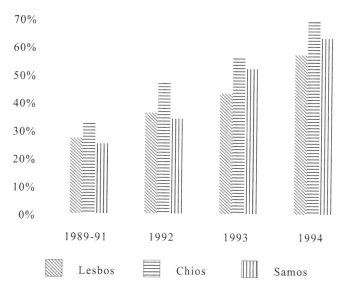

Figure 7.6   NAI MOP (1989–93): Local Government Sub-programme Absorption Rates
Source: adapted from Ministry of National Economy (1993b).

the worst performance of Lesbos and the medium performance of Samos. Thus Chios's local governments have proved particularly competent in comparison with their counterparts in other prefectures in most of the specific measures of the sub-programme, that is road networks, water and sewerage, tourist and socio-cultural infrastructures. Samos local governments' comparatively good performance, on the other hand, should be attributed to their competence in the specific measures of road networks and tourist infrastructure.

Nonetheless, their incapacity in the specific measure for protecting the environment contributed to its almost negligible rate of absorption. Finally, the institutional weakness of the Lesbos local governments is mainly illustrated by their failure in the specific measures of tourist and socio-cultural infrastructure and water and sewerage, while they proved incapable of carrying out the two major interventions in the protection of the environment (Ministry of National Economy, 1993a).

For the Community Initiatives, which do not constitute an integral part of the MOPs (see chapter six), despite the key role of the central state agencies (ministries, organizations of public sector utilities) in the planning and implementation processes, the evidence from the fieldwork research proved adequate for defining the most important Initiatives for the region and the specific actions financed by them. Thus, in contrast with the Southern Aegean region, only the VALOREN, INTERREG and LEADER Initiatives were identified as linked to the specific structural interventions in the region. In particular, the VALOREN Initiative financially supported the creation of Aeolic parks on Lesbos and Psara islands, the INTERREG financed part of the works for improveming the Mytilene port, whilst the LEADER Initiative supported measures for agricultural restructuring and development in the entire Lesbos prefecture. The real impact, however, of the Community Initiatives on the mobilization of local actors and the promotion of local partnerships, which is considered their crucial contribution as policy-making tools, will be considered in the following section.

The coincidence of the fieldwork research with the starting up of the implementation phase of the second CSF (1994–99), however, enables some preliminary comparative observations to be made, even though ex-ante evaluations were not possible. The following points deserve note. First, there is evidence in the second CSF (MOP) of a reorientation of the main development goals of the region towards the abandonment of the previous model based on the traditional sectors of each island (agriculture, maritime industry) and the adoption of tourism as the main developmental sector of the local economy supported by a small-scale agriculture. This shift is interpreted as an outcome of the dialogue, communication and learning processes initiated by the planning and monitoring procedures of the Structural Funds' programmes. Second, there is a significant improvement in the planning process characterized by an emphasis on the sectors of basic transport and communication infrastructure rather than on indirectly social policy-oriented measures. Finally, there is evidence of the strengthening of the role of local government institutions through the increased support in human and technical resources provided by the specific sub-programme for local governments (Regional Secretariat, 1994).

To sum up, this section has shown that the differentiation identified in chapter six between the Northern and Southern Aegean islands regions in absorption capacity and in the orientation of the funds is accompanied by considerable differences between the island-prefectures of the region. Thus, at the prefectural level the Lesbos prefecture, even though it has the greater share of allocated funds, demonstrates the worst performance in absorption in all the sub-programmes. Conversely, the Chios prefecture shows a comparatively high level of absorption rates, mainly because of the relatively successful implementation of the National Programme of Community Interest. Finally, Samos lies between the two in absorption performance. On the other hand, the Northern Aegean islands region, despite the highly subsidized national regional policy incentive scheme, does not show a high level of private investment in either the region or the contribution of the private sector to the Structural Funds programmes.

The third section assesses the impact of the weaknesses of the Northern Aegean islands' institutional infrastructure at regional and local levels, as identified in chapter five, on the adaptation process of the region within the European policy-making environment.

Institution-building, policy networks and adaptation

Chapter five, by drawing the institutional map of the region and assessing the structural characteristics of the local institutional networks of general exchange, examined the level of collective action and subsequently the capacity for learning and adaptation of the system of institutional interactions at regional and prefectural levels. This section evaluates the extent to which these qualitative features of the institutional infrastructure and, particularly, the capacity for collective action and learning, have affected the processes of institution-building and adaptation of the region to the new European environment.

Institution-building, policy networks and adaptation in the Northern Aegean Islands

The Europeanization of regional policy and the introduction of the programming approach with the first MOP (1989–93) have formed the most critical external constraint on both the institutional and policy adaptation of the Northern Aegean islands region. However, despite the presence of a relatively good administrative structure in terms of stability, continuity and hence efficiency of personnel at the regional level[11] (Regional Secretariat), the weaknesses of the local institutional infrastructure, as identified in chapter five, and the subsequent reliance on the central state for vital administrative and technical resources have proved to be key impediments to promoting the processes of adaptation and Europeanization. Thus, notwithstanding the significant improvement of the policy-making environment that has become favourable for institutional and policy adaptation, the region continues to lag behind the Southern Aegean islands in quality of network structure and hence in capacity for learning and adaptation.[12]

Within this framework, the Monitoring Committee for the implementation of the MOP, beyond its role as the institutionalized form of the linkages between supranational, national and subnational levels of governance, represents for the Northern Aegean region 'an unprecedented forum for dialogue and communication, focusing, almost exclusively, on the development *problematique* of the region'.[13]

As Table 7.1 demonstrates, this process of EU-induced institution-building is substantiated by the broadening of the regional council to include, beyond the prefects and the representatives of the local Associations of Municipalities, representatives of the most important interest group-organizations of each prefecture, such as the Chambers and the Lesbos Farmers' Association. Nevertheless, although the implementation and monitoring of the Structural Funds programmes brought about the creation of a series of new institutions in the region, it is not revealed at the regional level because of the lack of directly elected regional councils.[14] Conversely, as it will be shown, the creation of new institutions is particularly evident at the prefectural level.

The structure of the policy network at the regional level reflects the above features of the policy-making environment of the region. Thus, although the policy network shows an improved structure in comparison with the network of general exchange (Chapter 5), it continues to demonstrate the same general characteristics, that is low density and high centralization. In particular, even though the density of the policy network – which, to reiterate it, indicates the degree of network

Table 7.1   Northern Aegean Regional Partnership for Monitoring the MOP (1989–93)

A. President: Regional General Secretary	
B. Members:	
1. Prefects:	Lesbos, Chios, Samos
2. Local Ass. of Munic. & Communes:	Lesbos, Chios, Samos
3. Central Gov/ment (Ministries):	Agriculture, Interior, Employment, National Economy, Envoment & Public Works, Aegean
4. Interest Group Representatives:	Lesbos and Chios Chamb., Lesbos Farmers' Ass., Chios and Samos Trade Unions
5. Commission of the EC (DGs):	XVI, V, VI
6. Higher Education Institutions:	University of the Aegean

Source: Northern Aegean Regional Secretariat's document on the Monitoring Committee for the MOP.

cohesion – is improved in comparison with that of the general exchange network (0.277–0.237 out of 1 respectively), it remains extremely low, which reflects the small number of actors connected to each other within the network. Furthermore, as Table 7.2 with the centrality measures of both the general exchange and policy networks indicates, despite the improvement in the degree of centralization of the policy network, it remains highly centralized (79.22 per cent). What the low-density and high-centrality rates indicate is that, even within the EU policy environment, the network continues to demonstrate the same structural features, that is fragmentation at the prefectural level and centralization in the regional secretariat.

The following lessons are drawn from this comparative analysis. First, although the creation of the region has brought about a reform of the Greek administrative system, imposed, to a significant extent, by the Europeanization of regional policy, it shows a low degree of institutionalization within the local system of governance, even in the favourable environment of European regional policy. Second, despite the low capacity of the institutional infrastructure of the Northern Aegean in learning and adaptation, the European policy-making environment has functioned as an external impetus for the improvement of the main structural features of the local institutional network. Finally, the institution-building and adaptation processes are as slow as the learning process, especially under conditions of an unfavourable socio-cultural environment and a centralized state structure.

Table 7.2   NAI: Centrality Measures of General Exchange and Policy Networks

Organizations	General Exchange Network Centrality %	Policy Network Centrality %
1. Reg. Gen. Secretariat	100.00	100.00
2. Lesbos Pref. Council	40.91	40.91
3. Chios Pref. Council	36.36	36.36
4. Mytilene City Council	31.82	31.82
5. Samos Pref. Council	27.27	31.82
6. Lesbos Chamber	27.27	36.36
7. Chios Chamber	27.27	27.27
8. Chios City Council	27.27	31.82
9. University	22.73	27.27
10. Lesbos Farmers' Ass.	22.73	22.73
11. Samos City Council	22.73	18.18
12. Samos Chamber	22.73	27.27
13. Lesbos Ass. Munic. & Comm.	18.18	36.36
14. Chios Mastic Producers' Ass.	18.18	27.27
15. Samos Wine Makers' Ass.	18.18	18.18
16. Lesbos Training Centre	13.64	13.64
17. Chios Ass. Munic. & Comm.	13.64	13.64
18. Samos Ass. Munic. & Comm.	13.64	18.18
19. Aeoliki Dev. Agency	9.09	9.09
20. Mytilene Mun. Dev. Agency	9.09	18.18
21. Chios Mun. Dev. Agency	9.09	13.64
22. Chios Training Centre	9.09	9.09
23. Lesbos Local Dev. Agency	4.55	27.27
Total Network Centralization:	83.55	79.22

Source: Paraskevopoulos, C. J. (1998b).

The centrality measures of the individual actors within the policy network reflect the degree to which the role of any particular actor has been upgraded within the European regional policy environment. Thus, the upgraded role of the Lesbos Local Development Agency, the Mytilene Municipal Development Agency, the Aeoliki Development Agency and the Chios Municipal Development Agency in the policy network reflects their involvement in the implementation of specific programmes or initiatives (LEADER, IMP, VALOREN), which will become more clearly evident in analysis of the prefectural level. Additionally, the upgraded status of prominent private-interest or associational actors (Chambers, Local Associations of Municipalities and Communes, Chios Mastic Growers' Association) in the policy network should be attributed either to their participation in the Monitoring Committee or to their involvement in the implementation of specific programmes of the MOP at prefectural level. Finally, the relatively upgraded status of the University in the policy network corresponds to its participation in the Monitoring Committee, as well as to its involvement in implementation projects mainly through carrying out research studies.

The graph of the Figure 7.7 depicts the structure of the policy network in Northern Aegean. What the graph reveals is a structure of the network significantly similar to that of the general exchange network (chapter five). In particular, the Regional Secretariat, which remains the central actor within the network, is depicted at the centre of the graph, while the increased density of the network and the upgraded degree of centrality of particular actors is illustrated by the thicker structure of the actors at the prefectural level. Finally, what emerges from comparison with the policy network of the Southern Aegean (Chapter 6) is that, despite the common structural features of fragmentation and centralization, the policy network in the Southern Aegean demonstrates a better structure at the prefectural level.

Institution-building, policy networks and adaptation in Lesbos

As has been demonstrated in chapter five, the qualitative and quantitative features of Lesbos's institutional infrastructure reflect the lack of dialogue and communication among public and private actors and subsequently the lack of synergies at local level that would facilitate the learning and adaptation processes. This weakness of the local institutional network corresponds to and is affected by the lack of local

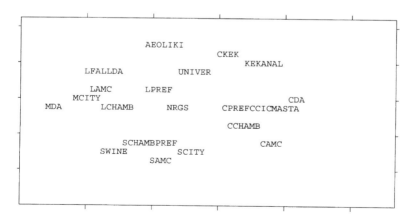

Figure 7.7   Policy Network in the NAI

leadership, almost since the 'golden age' at the start of the twentieth century. Therefore the incapacity for the formulation of an endogenously driven development strategy goes hand in hand with the lack of appropriate mechanisms for re-stabilizing the system of local interactions, which the learning process would require during periods of catching up with changes occurring in the external environment. Hence the dependence of the local system of governance either on central state agencies or on fragmented initiatives undertaken by specific actors (Chamber) for the necessary administrative, financial and technical resources should be seen as a logical consequence.

Nonetheless, even within this policy environment, the EU regional policy programmes act as an external constraint on both challenging the established relationships among the actors within the local institutional networks and promoting institution-building and adaptation. After the introduction of the programming approach with the CSFs and MOPs and the opening up of the process for bypassing the central state level and establishing direct supra-subnational linkages, there was a start-up of initiatives for enhancing the learning process within the local system of governance.[15]

This process, however, was marked by a tendency to create new institutions, since changes in the external conditions, such as the Europeanization of policy-making in this case, and the process of catching up entailed in learning, led to the redundancy of old institutions: hence the necessity for the creation of new ones.[16] Thus, the Chamber has been involved, along with the Farmers' Association and the Association of Municipalities, in the creation of the Local Development Agency for the management of specific Community Initiatives and, in particular, of the LEADER Initiative, so crucial for Lesbos's monocultural economy. Furthermore, the Mytilene Municipal Development Agency, created by the Mytilene City Council, operates as a municipal enterprise and has been involved in implementing projects which are part of the ERDF sub-programme of the MOP, such as the exploitation of geothermy in agriculture-related activities.[17] The Aeoliki development agency is another Municipal Development Agency, created during the implementation of the IMP by the Mytilene City Council. It was involved in the implementation of the VALOREN Initiative (which was managed by the state-owned electric power company) for building two wind-generators on the island. Finally, the Prefectural Council along with the local Association of Municipalities were involved in the creation of the Training Centre in an attempt to facilitate implementation of the ESF sub-programme of the MOP.[18]

This rather extended process of institution-building, however, did not significantly change the mainly regional secretariat and prefecture-dominated process of the implementation of the MOP in the prefecture, which is indicated by the density, centralization and structural equivalence measures of the policy network. Thus, although the density measure, which shows the degree of network cohesion, has been substantially improved in the policy network (0.564–0.418 of the general exchange), it is still inadequate for the adaptation process since it implies that only half the actors are connected with each other within the network.

Additionally, looking at the centrality measures (Table 7.3) similar structural characteristics to those from the density indicator emerge. In particular, even though the degree of centrality in the policy network is significantly lower when compared with the general exchange network (53.33 per cent–71.11 per cent respectively), the policy network retains its rather vertical structure, which indicates that power and resources are still unequally dispersed among the actors. Hence, what the density and centralization measures reveal is a structure of the policy network that is still unfavourable for shifting alliances, creating synergies and achieving collective action among public and private actors at the prefectural level, thus inhibiting the learning and adaptation processes within the network. Nonetheless, the significant improvement of both

Table 7.3   Lesbos Prefecture: Centrality Measures of General Exchange and Policy Networks

Organization	General Exchange Network Centrality % %	Policy Network Centrality %
1. Reg. Gen. Secretariat	100.00	100.00
2. Lesbos Pref. Council	70.00	70.00
3. Mytilene City Council	70.00	70.00
4. Lesbos Chamber	40.00	60.00
5. Lesbos Ass. Munic. & Comm.	40.00	80.00
6. University	30.00	40.00
7. Lesbos Farmers' Ass.	30.00	50.00
8. Lesbos Training Centre	30.00	30.00
9. Aeoliki Mun. Dev. Agency	20.00	20.00
10. Mytilene Mun. Dev. Agency	20.00	40.00
11. Lesbos Local Dev. Agency	10.00	60.00
Total Network Centralization	71.11	53.33

Source: Paraskevopoulos, C. J. (1998b).

the density and centralization measures in the policy network indicates that, even if the conditions for learning and adaptation are unfavourable (lack of social capital endowment and weak institutional infrastructure), the European regional policy challenges the resistance to change of the local institutional actors and initiates at least the starting up of the learning process.

From the centrality measures of the individual actors the following points deserve reference. First, the Regional Secretariat remains the central actor, even in the policy network. This dominance reflects the weakness of the local institutional network to provide varying leadership roles for endogenous institutional actors. Second, the upgraded status of the Association of Municipalities in the policy network reflects its crucial role primarily in monitoring and secondarily in the implementation processes of the MOP, and especially in the ESF sub-programme for vocational training and the specific sub-programme for local governments. What this upgraded status essentially brings about, however, is the traditional key role which the Association has as mediator between the first and second tiers of local government within the local system of governance. Furthermore, this status establishes expectations for other leadership roles in the local network, along with the Prefectural Council and the Mytilene City Council. Third, the strengthened position of the Local Development Agency (LLDA) points to the possibilities of its having a more important role within the local system of governance in the future, that might be favoured by successful learning and adaptation processes necessitated by the further Europeanization process. The LLDA would expect to gain a complementary role to that of the Association of Municipalities, providing local governments with technical and administrative assistance. Finally, the role of the University is further upgraded in the policy network, especially in comparison with the Southern Aegean. This corresponds to its joint involvement with the LLDA and the Mytilene Municipal Development Agency in the sub-programmes of the MOP.

The analysis of the structural equivalence, which categorizes actors according to their structural positions within the network, further strengthens the main structural features that derive from the centrality measures. In particular Figure 7.8 in comparison with the general exchange network (chapter five) reveals the following structural features of the policy network.[19] First, the Regional Secretariat (block one) remains the only leading institutional actor within the network. Second, the upgraded role of the LLDA (block two) places it among the leading institutional actors within the local system of governance,

	NRGS	LPREFC	MCITY	LLDA	LFARMA	LCHAMB	KEKANAL	LAMC	UNIVER	MDA	AEOLIKI
NRGS	1	1	1	1	1	1	1	1	1	1	1
LPREF	1	1	1		1	1	1	1	1		
MCITY	1	1	1			1		1	1	1	1
LLDA	1			1	1	1		1	1	1	
LFARMA	1	1		1	1	1		1			
LCHAMB	1	1	1	1	1	1		1			
KEKANAL	1	1					1	1			
LAMC	1	1	1	1	1	1	1	1	1		
UNIVER	1	1	1	1					1		
MDA	1		1	1						1	
AEOLIKI	1	1									1

Figure 7.8   Structural Equivalence of Policy Network Actors in Lesbos

along with the Prefecture Council, the Mytilene City and the Association of Municipalities. Third, the University and the other development agencies (Aeoliki and Mytilene), despite the relative improvement of their structural position in the policy network, remain at the margins of the local system of governance. Finally, although the structure of the policy network is better than that of the general exchange, it does not yet demonstrate the necessary structural features for crossing the public–private divide and thus facilitating collective action and the learning and adaptation processes.

The structural features arising from the structural equivalence are illustrated by the graph of the network (Figure 7.9), based on the multi-dimensional scaling technique. What the graph demonstrates is that, whilst the Regional Secretariat, depicted at the centre of the graph, remains the central actor of the network, the University, the Aeoliki and the Municipal Development Agencies are the most marginalized actors.

In conclusion, even within the process of European regional policy, the local system of governance of the Lesbos prefecture, despite the significant improvement of its structural characteristics, continues to

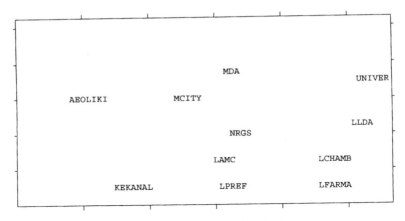

Figure 7.9   Policy Network in Lesbos

demonstrate weaknesses similar to the institutional network of general exchange. In particular, the creation of new institutions did not adequately improve the quality of the local institutional infrastructure, which is still characterized by a lack of capacity for local synergies, or overcome the public–private divide or achieve collective action among the actors. Hence, it seems to be still too weak for successful adaptation to the European environment.

Institution-building, policy networks and adaptation in Chios

Chapter five established that the Chios prefecture demonstrates a relatively better quality of institutional infrastructure than Lesbos, an indication of which is the voluntary merger of most of the communes of the island in five municipalities, that has improved the administrative and financial functions of local authorities. Additionally, the comparatively higher level of partnerships and synergies-creation among the actors have been facilitated by the presence of two active private-interest organizations, that is the Mastic Growers' Association and the Chamber, while the Chios City Council constitutes the most active public actor within the local institutional infrastructure.

However, within the framework of European regional policy a clearer differentiation in institutional capacity for learning and adaptation between Chios and the other Northern Aegean islands emerges. In particular, the programming approach to development initiated by the CSFs and MOPs enabled the active local actors and especially the

Chamber and the Mastic Growers' Association to be involved in sub-programmes and initiatives. In that respect the process of institution-building in the Chios prefecture did not lead to the creation of new institutions, but rather, opened up the game for the most capable local institutions to learn and adapt to changes in external conditions. The only new institution is the Municipal Development Agency, created by the City Council to focus mainly on the effective management of Community Initiatives. Conversely, the Training Centre has been created through an initiative of the Greek Centre for Productivity – a central state actor – and is mainly focused on the implementation of the ESF sub-programme in the prefecture.

Thus, while the implementation of the MOP was primarily run by the prefecture, the City Council, the Mastic Growers' Association and the Chamber were actively involved in the implementation of specific sub-programmes or initiatives. In particular, the Mastic Growers, arguably the most prominent private-interest actor of the prefecture, was involved in an INTERREG project undertaken at regional level, focusing on the development of cross-border cooperation with Turkey and Bulgaria. Furthermore, the Association was involved in one of the actually few intra-regional networks that developed around the LEADER I and II Initiatives. The first was based on an initiative taken by the City Council and the Municipal Development Agency, while the second, which refers to the second CSF, is based on joint action by the main local institutional actors. Finally, the most important involvement of the Mastic Growers' Association in European regional policy programmes was in the implementation of the National Programme of Community Interest (NPCI) for Chios.[20] As has already been pointed out in the previous section, the NPCI included specific measures for improved efficiency levels in the production of mastic, such as sectorial market research, promotion of mastic products and training in the production process.

The Chamber, on the other hand, beyond its participation in the Monitoring Committee for the implementation of the MOP, was actively involved in the local network for the LEADER Initiative, along with the Municipal Development Agency and the Mastic Association.[21]

Finally, the University was involved in the implementation of a project focusing on application of the telematique in the area of mastic production, but this venture was financed by STAR-TELEMATIQUE, the EU Initiative focused on promoting applications of telematique, which was run by a central state-agency (Ministry of Research and Development).[22]

The structure of the policy network in Chios reflects the above-mentioned features of the processes of institutional learning and adaptation in the prefecture. The density measure, which shows the degree of network cohesion, has significantly improved in the policy network, when compared with that of the general exchange (0.611–0.528). What the density measure indicates is that well over half the institutional actors are connected to each other within the network. Moreover, according to the centrality measures in Table 7.4, which reveal the dominant actors within the network, the degree of centralization in the policy network is significantly lower in comparison with that of the general exchange (50.00 per cent–60.71 per cent respectively). However, although the lower degree of centralization indicates a more horizontal structure of the policy network in comparison with the general exchange, this improvement should be mainly seen as the outcome of the upgraded status of the Mastic Growers' Association, the City Council and the Municipal Development Agency.

Thus, looking at the centralization measures for each individual actor in both the general exchange and policy networks, the following points should be underlined. First, the Regional Secretariat and secondarily the Prefecture Council are the most central actors within the network, which points to its domination by the hierarchical structure of the central state. Second, the City Council is the most central public

Table 7.4 Chios Prefecture: Centrality Measures of General Exchange and Policy Networks

Organization	General Exchange Network Centrality %	Policy Network Centrality %
1. Reg. Gen. Secretariat	100.0	100.0
2. Chios Pref. Council	87.5	87.5
3. Chios City Council	75.0	87.5
4. Chios Chamber	50.0	50.0
5. University	37.5	50.0
6. Chios Ass. Munic. & Comm.	37.5	37.5
7. Chios Mastic Producers' Ass.	37.5	75.0
8. Chios Mun. Dev. Agency	25.0	37.5
9. Chios Training Centre	25.0	25.0
Total Network Centralization	60.71	50.00

Source: Paraskevopoulos, C. J. (1998b).

actor, especially within the policy network, having outflanked the Association of Municipalities whose position can be characterized as marginal within the institutional structure of the prefecture given its formally key position within the local system of governance. Third, the Mastic Growers' Association constitutes the most important private-interest actor, but only within the policy network, which reflects its dynamic position within the local productive system, and may justify expectations for its role as the initiator of network development on intra-regional, interregional, or transregional bases. Conversely, the Chamber, which is the second most important private-interest institutional actor, demonstrates a stable but limited role within the local institutional infrastructure. Fourth, the upgraded role of the University, especially in the policy network, should be attributed to the location of one of its main departments (business administration) on the island and additionally to its involvement in MOP projects. Finally, the Municipal Development Agency demonstrates a considerable role within the policy network, while the role of the central state-run Training Centre is still rather marginal within the institutional structure of the prefecture.

The structural equivalence (Figure 7.10), which reveals common structural positions among the actors within the network, reflects the same structural features of the network as those that derive from analysis of the centrality measures. Thus the comparison between the structural equivalence of the policy network and the exchange network (chapter five) reveals the following structural features of the network. First, in both networks the block of the leading actors – which are connected with all the other actors of the other blocks – consists of public actors, namely the Regional Secretariat (NRGS), the Prefecture Council and the City Council. Second, in contrast to the network of general exchange, in the policy network there is evidence for a start-up of network-building among public and private actors, as illustrated especially in block four, which comprises both the private-interest organizations, that is the Chamber and the Mastic Growers (CMASTA). Third, the positions of the Association of Municipalities (CAMC) and the Training Centre (CKEK) remain marginal within both networks, while the participation of the Municipal Development Agency (CDA) in the MOP programmes (LEADER) and hence in public–private local networks has led to an improvement of its position within the policy network. Finally, despite the better structure of the policy network, it demonstrates weaknesses in the building of public–private synergies, which is considered a prerequisite for learning and adaptation.

	NRGS	CCITY	CPREF	UNIVER	CKEK	CAMC	CMASTA	CDA	CCHAMB
NRGS	1	1	1	1	1	1	1	1	1
CCITY	1	1	1	1		1	1	1	1
CPREF	1	1	1	1	1	1	1		1
UNIVER	1	1	1	1					
CKEK	1	1			1				
CAMC	1	1	1			1			
CMASTA	1	1	1				1	1	1
CDA	1	1					1	1	
CCHAMB	1	1	1				1		1

Figure 7.10   Structural Equivalence of Policy Network Actors in Chios

The graph of the network in Figure 7.11 depicts the main structural features of the policy network. This structure is, in many respects, similar to the structure of the general exchange network (chapter five). In particular, while the General Secretariat (NRGS) and the Prefecture Council (CPREF) are depicted as the central actors in both networks, the Training Centre (CKEK) and the Association of Municipalities (CAMC) are represented as marginal actors. Conversely, the position of the Mastic Growers' Association (CMASTA), the City Council (CCITY) and the Municipal Development Agency (CDA) is portrayed as significantly improved in the policy network when compared with the general exchange network.

Institution-building, policy networks and adaptation in Samos

As established in chapter five, the Samos prefecture demonstrates a weak institutional infrastructure, characterized by the lack of local initiatives and by major cooperation problems among the institutional actors, whose relationships are confined within the framework of the necessary exchanges imposed by the functions of the administrative hierarchy. This institutional structure of the prefecture corresponds to its isolation in transport, communication and administrative linkages from the other two prefectures of the Northern Aegean.

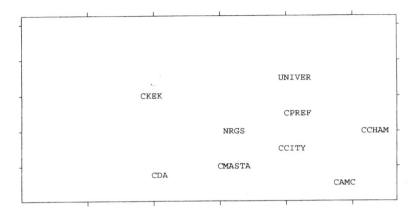

Figure 7.11   Policy Network in Chios

Within this policy environment the European structural policy pro-grammes, despite criticisms of unfair allocation of resources among the islands and the role of the central state in this process, are viewed as providing a unique opportunity for institutional and economic devel-opment.[23] However, the poor performance of the prefecture in institu-tion-building is illustrated by the lack of any new institutions and, even in the policy network, the relations between the institutional actors are determined by exchanges within the administrative hierar-chy. Additionally, beyond the formal participation of the Prefect and the Association of Municipalities in the Monitoring Committee of the MOP, the involvement of local institutional actors is extremely limited. In particular, given the lack of any development agency which could create networks around specific programmes or initiatives, only the City Council and the Association of Municipalities were involved in the INTERREG Initiative and in a local action group for the LEADER Initiative. Nonetheless, what best illustrates the capacity for learning and adaptation of the local institutional infrastructure is the complete failure of the proposal for participation in the LEADER I Initiative because of cooperation and coordination problems between the Association of Municipalities and the Wine Producers' Association.

The structural features of the policy network in Samos only partly reflect the incapacity of the institutional infrastructure for learning and adaptation, because of the limited number of actors and the presence of exchanges that derive from the fundamental administrative functions of each actor. Thus the density measure, which is an indicator of network cohesion, has been substantially improved in the policy network in comparison even with the comparatively high rate of the general exchange network (0.667–0.595 respectively). However, this rate does not correspond to the institutional capacity of the prefecture in learning and adaptation, given that its improvement refers to the (ex officio) participation of actors in administrative functions (such as the Monitoring Committee). Furthermore, the centrality measures (Table 7.5), which identify the central actors within the network, demonstrate in both general exchange and policy networks a relatively horizontal rather than vertical structure (53.33 per cent–46.67 per cent respectively). However, they do not reflect the real institutional capacity of the prefecture.

For the centrality measures of each individual actor in both general exchange and policy networks, the central role of the Regional Secretariat, the marginal role of the University and the relative involvement of the other actors deriving from the necessary administrative exchanges should be emphasized.

The main structural features that derive from analysis of the centrality measures are further strengthened by the structural equivalence, which identifies common structural positions among the actors within the network, according to the structure of their relationships. Thus the structural equivalence of the policy network (Figure 7.12) reflects the same structural features as the centrality measures, that is the centrality

Table 7.5   Samos Prefecture: Centrality Measures of General Exchange and Policy Networks

Organization	General Exchange Network Centrality %	Policy Network Centrality %
1. Reg. Gen. Secretariat	100.00	100.00
2. Samos Pref. Council	83.33	83.33
3. Samos City Council	83.33	66.67
4. Samos Chamber	50.00	66.67
5. Samos Ass. Munic. & Comm.	50.00	66.67
6. Samos Wine Producers' Ass.	50.00	66.67
7. University	16.67	16.67
Total Network Centralization	53.33	46.67

Source: Paraskevopoulos, C. J. (1998b).

of the Regional Secretariat (NRGS) and the marginal role of the University. All the other actors constitute a rather dense network, without, however, reflecting a real institutional capacity.

The graph of the network (Figure 7.13) represents the structure of the network, as described by the centrality and structural equivalence measures. What the comparison between the policy network and general exchange network reveals is that there are no important differences between the two networks. In particular, the Regional Secretariat and the University are depicted in both graphs as the most central and most marginal actors respectively. Additionally, the depiction of the other actors illustrates the looseness of the network with the small number of actors.

In conclusion, the Samos prefecture demonstrates a poor institutional infrastructure in the policy network which is characterized by a small number of institutional actors, linked mainly on the basis of the exchanges of the administrative system (e.g. Monitoring Committees). The structure of the policy network is similar to the general exchange network (see chapter five) despite the better density and centrality measures: hence, the dependence on the Regional Secretariat for leadership.

Conclusions

This chapter has shown that the differentiation identified in chapter six between the Southern and Northern Aegean islands in absorption capacity and the orientation of funds is accompanied by some differences among the island-prefectures of the Northern Aegean region. In particular, the Lesbos prefecture demonstrates the worst performance in absorption in all sub-programmes, while the evidence from the Chios prefecture is comparatively better because of the rather successful implementation of the National Programme of Community Interest (NPCI) for Chios. Finally, the Samos Prefecture lies between the two, even though its share in the MOP was relatively small. Furthermore, the Northern Aegean islands region, despite the highly subsidized national regional policy incentives scheme, shows neither a high level of private investment nor a considerable contribution of the private sector to the Structural Funds programmes. The problematic Europeanization of the region should be closely linked to the qualitative features of the institutional infrastructure at both regional and prefectural levels. As analysis of the processes of institution-building and adaptation in the region has shown, the institutional infrastructure at

	UNIVER	NRGS	SPREF	SCITY	SCHAMB	SAMC	SWINE
UNIVER	1	1					
NRGS	1	1	1	1	1	1	1
SPREF		1	1	1	1	1	1
SCITY		1	1	1	1	1	
SCHAMB		1	1	1	1		1
SAMC		1	1	1		1	1
SWINE		1	1		1	1	1

Figure 7.12   Structural Equivalence of Policy Network Actors in Samos

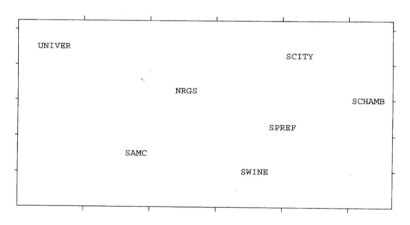

Figure 7.13   Policy Network in Samos

regional level is characterized by a combination of centralization of the network around the Regional Secretariat and fragmentation at the prefectural level. In that sense, it is similar to the general exchange network (chapter five). Additionally, at the prefectural level all the prefectures demonstrate a lack of local leadership and capacity for learning and adaptation of the local institutional infrastructure, despite the unquestionable improvement of policy networks in all islands. In particular, the following points should be emphasized for each island-prefecture. First, in Lesbos, despite the significant improvement of the structural characteristics in the policy network, it continues to demonstrate a lack of capacity for achieving local synergies and collective action among the actors. Second, Chios shows a comparatively better capacity for creating local synergies, learning and adaptation, while Samos demonstrates a poor institutional infrastructure in the number of institutional actors involved in joint projects.

The following lessons should be drawn from the case of the Northern Aegean. First, the structure of the system of intra-regional interactions plays a key role in facilitating the learning and adaptation processes. Second, even if the capacity of the local institutional infrastructure for learning and adaptation is poor, the Europeanization process constitutes an external shock for the local systems of governance that leads to the improvement of the local institutional infrastructure.

8
Conclusions: Social Capital, Institutional Learning and Adaptation within European Regional Policy. Implications for Integration Theory

Introduction

This book has shown that the concept of social capital, by facilitating the learning process within institutional networks at the regional and local levels, plays a crucial role in shaping intra-regional interactions among the actors and hence in determining the capacity for adaptation and adjustment by regional and local systems of governance within the European regional policy environment. Thus, the main hypothesis of this book, established in Chapter 2, is that the adaptation of local systems of governance to the European policy-making environment is dependent on:

a) the presence of dense, intra-regional, functional institutional networks at the local level that cross the public–private divide by achieving synergies between public and private resources and have a capacity for learning, whereby institutional relationships and policy outcomes adapt to changing conditions; and,

b) the presence of social capital endowments that, by resolving dilemmas of collective action and thus enabling actors to be actively involved in the provision of public goods and services that support the local productive system, facilitate the formation of the system of interactions and the learning process within institutional networks.

In addition, the capacity of the local institutional infrastructure for learning and adaptation is to a significant extent conditioned by:

c) the structure of the state and the functional and territorial distribution of power and resources through centre–periphery (intergovernmental) relations and the qualitative features of public administration; and,

d) the process of Europeanization of public policy, which challenges well-established institutional structures and creates conditions favourable for institution building, even if the pre-existing institutional capacity for learning is poor.

This final chapter evaluates the validity of the above theoretical framework, by drawing the most important conclusions that arise from the two cases, focusing on the main theoretical concepts of this book: social capital, learning and adaptation/Europeanization. It is divided into three sections. Section one examines the impact of the national (state structure) and international (Europeanization) factors upon the learning and adaptation capacity of the local institutional infrastructure. The second section, relying on the criteria for measuring learning and adaptation established in Chapter 2, assesses the learning and adaptation capacity of the institutional networks in the two regions and the role of social capital in this process. Finally, the last section discusses the emerging theoretical implications for regional integration in general and European regional policy in particular.

National structures, local institutional capacity and the European challenge

The capacity of local systems of governance for learning and adaptation to changing conditions brought about by the Europeanization of public policy-making is shaped by the way in which the system of interactions between subnational institutions, national structures and European environment is formulated. The national and supranational levels of governance provide the structural and functional parameters within which local governments act to achieve objectives corresponding to local needs. Thus, within this complicated policy environment local institutions have, theoretically, a variety of ways of performing their functions. Therefore, the structural external parameters for action may inhibit or facilitate the learning and adaptation capacities of local systems of governance. Based on our evidence from a centralized state structure and a weak civil society, we examine the impact that the structure of intergovernmental relations has had on local institutional capacity and the role of Europeanization in this process.

The structure of the state, in general, is considered a crucial component that affects the formation of the system of local institutional interactions (institutional networks) and the capacity for learning and adaptation of local systems of governance. Three interrelated factors are fundamental in this process: the power and resource-dependence relationships among tiers of government, the degree of centralization of the state and the presence of a directly elected regional government. This book, however, is based on the theoretical assumption that intergovernmental relations is a dynamic system which cannot be simply reduced to the constitutional structure of the state. Within this theoretical framework resource dependencies between central and subnational levels of government and between public and private actors shape the degree of boundedness for the subnational systems of governance and for any particular local actor. Thus, the system of interactions among the local actors through the recognition of their mutual dependence and hence their collectivity constitutes the most important factor for learning and adaptation and may additionally enable the local system of governance to exploit the channel of intergovernmental relations for the satisfaction of local needs irrespective of the degree of state centralization (Paraskevopoulos, 1998a; 1998b; Sabel, 1993b). The presence of a strong civil society and social capital endowments plays a key role in this process (Paraskevopoulos, 1998a). Within this dynamic system of intergovernmental and centre–periphery relations, intra-regional functional networks provide the locality with public goods and services and pursue endogenously driven policies that meet local needs, while, on the other hand, they can use intergovernmental networks to obtain access to additional resources and coordinating policies at the national level. Hence, while resource-interdependence is seen as the prerequisite for network-building, the presence of social capital and the strength of civil society at regional and local levels constitute the decisive factors enabling local actors to recognize their mutual dependence and collectivity, thus shaping the system of local interactions and facilitating the learning process within the networks.

The centralized and hierarchical structure of the state in Greece and the peculiarities of the system of intergovernmental and centre-periphery relations, characterized by the dominant role of the prefecture as a deconcentrated administrative unit of the central state at local level and by the lack of a directly elected regional government, did not inhibit the process of institution-building and network creation primarily in Dodecanese and secondarily in Cyclades since the 1960s. This process was a function beyond the boundaries of formal hierarchically structured intergovernmental networks. Chapter 4 provides evidence for this prompt formation of intra-regional interactions and network-building, which enabled local actors to avoid inter-local competition for resources from the central state and subsequently allowed, in comparative terms, for the collective moulding of policy priorities within the local system of governance. In particular, the Organization of Tourist Promotion and the Advisory Committee for Local Development in Dodecanese, as well as the informal tourist committees in Cyclades, constituted the nuclei for network-building and collective action at the local level. These networks provided the local productive system with vital public goods and services and facilitated the learning process and the prompt adjustment of the local system of governance and its policy outputs to the changing conditions of the external environment (shift towards tourism).

Conversely, in the prefectures of the Northern Aegean the poor institutional capacity and weak civil society (lack of social capital endowments) led the local system of governance to dependence on the hierarchical structure of intergovernmental relations for the necessary financial and administrative resources. Hence, its dependence on the central state is interpreted not merely as a consequence of the structure of centre–periphery relations, but mainly as a result of the weakness of the institutional infrastructure. Chapter 5 provides evidence for the way in which the lack of local networks and the weak civil society led to exogenously driven local systems of governance and subsequently to the problematic adjustment of these prefectures in terms of policy outcomes. Thus, the productive structures of the Northern Aegean islands remained crucially dependent on the traditional sectors of each island, that is the monoculture of the olive for Lesbos, the shipping-maritime industry for Chios and agriculture for Samos.

The gradual Europeanization of public policy in general and of regional policy in particular since the early 1980s brought about radical changes in the structure of the Greek state and the system of intergovernmental relations (Chapter 3). The creation of regions and regional councils – though without directly elected members – and the gradual move initially from the clientelist to a rather neo-corporatist pattern of regional-interest representation at the prefectural level with the 1982 reform of the prefectural councils, and later (1994) to the directly elected second tier of subnational government, constitute the most important reforms, attributed to pressures imposed by the European environment. Furthermore, the opening up of the system to bottom-up initiatives and the subsequent unclear distribution of functions among the tiers of government, coupled with the rationalization of local government finance introduced by the 'Central Autonomous Resources' scheme, opened up possibilities for dynamic flexibility in the system of intergovernmental relations. Finally, the ability of local governments to impose additional taxation for the completion of local-scale projects created an environment favourable for regions and localities who were institutionally capable of bottom-up initiatives in adapting their structures and policies.

The response of the two case study-regions to the intended and unintended consequences of Europeanization, however, was analogous to their pre-existing institutional capacity. The evidence provided in chapters six and seven supports the hypotheses, on the one hand, that regional differentiation in learning and adaptation capacities, though possible even within centralized states, usually reflects a pre-existing differentiation in institutional capacity, and on the other, that even if the pre-existing local institutional capacity is poor the challenge of Europeanization and involvement in EU programmes and initiatives constitutes a positive external shock for local systems of governance, which has brought about an improvement of the local institutional infrastructure. The cases demonstrate that the European dimension provides an alternative policy-making field for local governments that can counterbalance possible rigidities within the structures of the traditional nation-state.

Thus, the prefectures of the Southern Aegean were better able than their Northern Aegean counterparts to exploit the changes occurring in the system of intergovernmental and centre–periphery relations and to adapt their institutional structure and policy process to the new European environment. In particular, the pre-existing structure of local institutional networks in the Dodecanese and Cyclades prefectures was further improved by the strengthening of public–private synergies among the institutional actors. This process was substantiated by the intersection between the local sectoral networks already in place and the hierarchical intergovernmental networks between region, prefecture and city. The functional networks, emerging through the combination of public and private actors, provided an environment favourable for learning since they facilitated the exchange of information, ideas and knowledge about the new policy environment. Hence, despite the comparatively low level of the private-sector contribution to the Structural Funds programmes, because of the maintenance of past clientelistic practices operating around the national headquarters of regional policy, especially in the Dodecanese, a significant coordination of public and private resources took place. EU and public funds were used for the improvement of the physical infrastructure, while, even though the involvement of the private sector was in general low, it had a considerable presence in Community Initiative projects. These features are illustrated by the absorption rates, primarily of the Dodecanese and secondarily of the Cyclades prefectures, in all the sub-programmes and measures of the first CSF (Chapter 6). What both the significant improvement of the network-structure and the absorption rates in the Southern Aegean indicate is that, despite the centralized and hierarchical structure of the state and the system of intergovernmental relations, the pre-existing institutional capacity at the prefectural level led to a rather successful adaptation of the local economies and societies to the EU regional policy environment.

In a similar vein, in the prefectures of the Northern Aegean the learning capacity of the pre-existing institutional infrastructure played the most important role in the adaptation process. Although the qualitative features of both the network structure and the policy outputs have been substantially improved within the European regional policy environment, the three prefectures of the Northern Aegean lag behind the Southern Aegean and even most of the other Greek regions in adaptation capacity. In institutional infrastructure the lack of functional networks in the processes of general exchange, combining public and private actors within the European policy environment, was replaced by a process of institution-building which led to the creation of new institutions, especially in Lesbos, without, however, dramatically changing the structure of the networks. Thus, with the partial exception of the Chios prefecture which had shown some elements of qualitative change with the creation of public–private partnerships around the specific National Programme of Community Interest (NPCI), the structure of the policy networks in the prefectures of the Northern Aegean did not demonstrate the structural features necessary for crossing the public–private divide and thus facilitating collective action, learning and adaptation. Therefore, the predominance of the hierarchical structure of the system of intergovernmental relations, namely the Regional Secretariat, within the local system of governance reflects, to a significant extent, the weakness of local institutional

networks and should not be attributed exclusively to the state structure. The institutional weakness of the prefectures of the region is illustrated by the low level of effectiveness and efficiency of local systems
of governance in the management of EU funds. In particular, beyond
the low level of the private-sector contribution, the prefectures of the
region demonstrated one of the lowest rates of absorption capacity in
the country during the first CSF (MOP). Additionally, as the qualitative
analysis of the use of the funds shows, the bulk of EU funds was used
for social and small-scale physical infrastructure (road network, education) which only partly reflects local needs, given that its major part is
the outcome of clientelist pressures. Finally, the start-up of debate
among the main local actors of the Northern Aegean island-prefectures
on the necessity for adaptation of both the institutional structure and
policies (e.g. shift towards tourism) constitutes the most important
innovation brought about by the Europeanization of regional policy.
Hence, the improvement of the local institutional structure and the
establishment of learning procedures within the local system of governance in the Northern Aegean vindicate the hypothesis that the challenge of Europeanization, even in areas of poor institutional capacity,
acted as a positive external shock starting up institution-building and
the learning processes that eventually led to improvement of the local
institutional infrastructure.

To sum up, even though the state structure plays an important role
in determining the learning and adaptation capacity of local systems of
governance, this is crucially dependent on certain capacities for collective action at the local level which facilitate the formation of the
system of interactions among the actors. The presence of social capital
and a strong civil society is the most important factor in this process.
The Europeanization process, on the other hand, by providing an alternative to the nation-state policy-making field for local governments,
plays, especially within centralized states, a crucial role in changing the
rules of the game and thus enhancing the institution-building process
at the local level, which eventually leads to significant improvement of
the pre-existing institutional capacity.

Social capital, learning and adaptation: an agenda for Europe in the twenty-first century?

Institutional learning has been defined in Chapter 2 as a function
involving the changing of ideas, preferences or policy choices and the
improved capacity of institutional actors to design and implement

these new policies, all of which may affect the balance of power among the actors. This process is crucially influenced by the presence of social capital and the structure of the networks. This section evaluates the learning capacity of the institutional networks by using the criteria for measuring learning established in chapter two, and then examines the impact of social capital and type and structure of network on the learning process. Finally, it categorizes the case study-regions according to the measures of Europeanization also established in Chapter 2.

Measuring learning

Five criteria have been identified for measuring the learning capacity of local institutional infrastructure. First, the presence of fora for dialogue and communication among the actors is considered a prerequisite for the exchange of information, ideas and knowledge and hence for shaping the interactions among the actors. Second, the process of institution-building and adaptation of the network structure is the creation of new institutions or changes made to the existing institutional structure as a consequence of the learning process. The third criterion is the extent to which partnerships among public and private actors have been established to encourage the communication of new knowledge and information and hence the formulation of policy priorities. The fourth variable is the common understanding of the major issues facing the local system of governance, which is a precondition for dialogue among the actors. Finally, the adaptation of the policy output is the fifth criterion, which can reveal the way in which the institutional structure has responded to the requirements for policy change posed by changing conditions. Table 8.1 below presents a synopsis of the indicators of learning at the regional and prefectural levels.

The evidence for dialogue and communication is that the presence of multiple fora, some of which are not associated with European regional policy, is the main feature of the prefectures of the Southern Aegean. Thus, in the Dodecanese prefecture the Organization for the Promotion of Tourism, which focuses on the exchange of knowledge and information about policy for tourist development, had its origins in the 1960s and is an important component in the successful adaptation of the productive structure of the prefecture towards development of the tourist sector. Additionally, the advisory committee, comprising prominent public and private institutional actors of the prefecture, functioned as an advisory forum for dialogue and communication alongside the prefectural council until 1994, when the first elections for a directly elected council took place. Last, a series of conferences on

Table 8.1   Indicators of Learning Capacity in SAI and NAI

Criteria for Measuring Learning	Southern Aegean Region	Northern Aegean Region
Fora for Dialogue and Communication	A. Dodecanese pref.: 1. Tourist Promotion 2. Advisory Comm. 3. CSF Monit. Comm. 4. Tourism/Devel. 5. LEADER 6. VALOREN 7. HORIZON 8. INTERREG B. Cyclades pref.: 1. Tourist Committees 2. CSF Monit. Comm. 3. LEADER 4. ENVIREG 5. URBAN 6. PRISMA	A. Lesbos pref.: 1. CSF Monit. Comm. 2. LEADER 3. VALOREN B. Chios pref.: 1. CSF Monit. Comm. 2. NPCI 3. LEADER 4. STAR/TELEM. C. Samos pref.: 1. CSF Monit. Comm. 2. LEADER 3. INTERREG
Institution-Building (Network Creation)	A. Dodecanese pref.: 1. Org. Tourist Prom. 2. Cooperative Bank 3. DDA 4. KDA B. Cyclades pref.: 1. CYDA 2. ERMDA	A. Lesbos pref.: 1. LLDA 2. AEOLIKI 3. MMDA B. Chios pref.: 1. CDA 2. Chios Train. Centre C. Samos pref.: –
Crossing the Public–Private Divide (partnerships)	A. Dodecanese pref.: present B. Cyclades pref.: present	A. Lesbos pref.: almost absent B. Chios pref.: partly C. Samos pref.: absent
Problem Identification among the Local Actors	A. Dodecanese pref.: partly present B. Cyclades pref.: partly present	A. Lesbos pref.: starting up B. Chios pref.: starting up C. Samos pref.: starting up
Policy Adaptation	A. Dodecanese pref.: partly B. Cyclades pref.: partly	A. Lesbos pref.: starting up B. Chios pref.: starting up C. Samos pref.: starting up

the problems of tourist development, which had been organized mainly by the Chamber's initiatives since the early 1980s, are a good example of pioneering fora for the communication of primary knowledge and information, not all of which, however, are associated with European regional policy. Yet the Europeanization of regional policy, and the initiation of the Structural Funds programmes, contributed to the further improvement of dialogue and communication in the prefecture with new fora for dialogue required by the implementation of the partnership principle. In this category fall the Monitoring Committee for the CSF (MOP) and the fora created for the implementation of the Community Initiatives (LEADER, VALOREN, HORIZON, INTERREG).

The Cyclades prefecture demonstrates to a significant extent a similar environment for communication and dialogue. In particular, the tourist committees were primary fora for dialogue and policy advice to the prefecture bodies at the local/island level, which functioned until the first elections for the new prefectural councils took place (1994). In a similar vein to Dodecanese, the Monitoring Committee for the CSF, and the mobilization of local actors around specific Community Initiatives, contributed to the upgrading of the prefecture's capacity for dialogue and communication.

The prefectures of the Northern Aegean islands demonstrate a different picture. The existing fora for dialogue and communication are byproducts of the implementation of the Structural Funds programmes and Initiatives, given the lack of any pre-existing mechanisms for facilitating the communication of new information and the exchange of ideas. This weakness reflects the dependence of the local system of governance on the centralized structure of intergovernmental relations and hence the dominant role of the prefecture. Thus, the Monitoring Committee for the CSF and the Community Initiatives offer the only opportunities for dialogue in Lesbos and Samos, while the NPCI for Chios contributed substantially to the improvement of the island's capacity for dialogue and communication.

The evidence from the regions about the second variable of institution-building and network-creation reflects their differentiation in the capacity for dialogue. However, the strong tradition of the Dodecanese in local institutional capacity and institution-building, almost since its incorporation into the Greek state, led to its differentiation from all the other prefectures. Whereas in them the process of network-creation was closely linked to the Europeanization of regional policy, in the Dodecanese the EU programmes contributed to an improvement in the pre-existing network structure (Cooperative Bank, Organization for Tourist Promotion, etc.), and the new networks are well-connected within the institutional infrastructure. Thus the Europeanization of regional policy brought about the further improvement of existing Dodecanese networks rather than the creation of new institutions, which remained comparatively limited. This pattern contrasts with the Northern Aegean and particularly Lesbos, where the creation of new institutions and networks is a consequence of the redundancy of a major part of the old institutional infrastructure.

Under the third criterion, the presence of communication channels between public and private actors, the network structure of the Southern Aegean prefectures provides convincing evidence of public–private partnerships, which, on the one hand, are fora for dialogue, information exchange and the formulation of policy priorities, and on the other, are channels for linking the local system of governance with the central state through the structure of intergovernmental relations. Conversely the structure of the networks of the Northern Aegean island-prefectures reveals, with the exception of Chios, an absence of communication on a horizontal basis between public and private actors. In Chios the implementation of the NPCI has played an important role in enhancing partnerships between public and private actors. The leading actors in this process are the Mastic Growers' Association and Chamber.

For the fourth variable, the common understanding of the problems or challenges facing the localities, the evidence from the two regions proves they are similar in one respect: both face adaptation challenges of a different phase and scale. In particular, the major challenge for the prefectures of the Southern Aegean (Dodecanese and Cyclades), which are characterized by development of the mass tourist industry, is whether they will exploit the opportunities provided by European structural policy to adjust their policy priorities and reform their institutional structures to the new patterns of demand in leisure (small-scale tourism). The evidence shows that the local actors in both prefectures have to a significant extent a common understanding of the problems they face. The challenges facing the Northern Aegean islands, on the other hand, are to use Structural Funds money for building the necessary infrastructure and to adapt their institutional structure and policies towards development based on small-scale tourism, thus avoiding the paradigm of the mass tourist industry in which the Southern Aegean were trapped from the 1970s onwards. As the evidence from the Northern Aegean shows, this debate, which

involves the gradual shift from the traditional for each island's productive sectors, has just started in these islands.

Finally, the evidence on the crucial fifth criterion, policy adaptation,
corresponds to the level of problem identification for each prefecture.
Thus, the evidence for the presence of policy adaptation in Dodecanese
and Cyclades is illustrated by both the pursuit of innovative policies
and the orientation of the major part of EU funds. In particular, the
conclusions of the conferences organized by the Dodecanese Chamber,
which suggested changes in the priorities of tourist policy (conference
tourism, expansion of the tourist period to the winter underpinned by
small-scale units), were introduced into the policy priorities. This trend
has become evident by the policy for control of tourist development in
the islands of Rhodes and Kos and by the pursuit of small-scale tourist
development in the still underdeveloped islands of the prefecture.
Additionally, in Cyclades, where the problem of over-concentration is
less intense, the policy priorities adopted focus on expansion of the
tourist period, the promotion of qualitative tourism and avoidance of
concentration. The above policy priorities are reflected also in the orientation of EU funds and especially during the period of the second
CSF (1994–99) towards the creation of basic infrastructure on underdeveloped islands and of appropriate infrastructure for the promotion of
flexible forms of tourism (yachting). By contrast, the Northern Aegean
islands lag behind in policy adaptation, since they are currently in the
phase of early debate on the necessity for adaptation. Hence there is no
evidence of formulation of policy priorities and even less of policy
adaptation.

In conclusion, the evaluation of the case study-regions, according to
the criteria for measuring learning, indicates that in the Southern
Aegean islands prefectures an institutional structure and policy environment favourable for learning have facilitated the learning process
among the actors and hence the learning capacity of the local systems
of governance. Conversely, the lack of these features in the Northern
Aegean has led to an institutional environment poor in learning,
which shows some signs of improvement only within the framework
of the EU structural policy.

Social capital, networks and learning: evaluating Europeanization

This section tests the main hypothesis of this book, that the local
systems of governance better able to learn and adapt to changing conditions are those whose institutional structure is based on dense functional networks that combine public and private actors and have a

horizontal rather than a vertical structure. This process, however, is crucially determined by the presence of social capital and a strong civil society that facilitate communication, the sharing of new ideas and knowledge, and hence collective action among the actors, and the learning process within institutional networks. Therefore, social capital (trust, norms) and inter-organizational structure are to be assessed as the explanatory (independent-intervening) variables of the learning and adaptation capacity of the case-study regions.

Chapters four and five have shown that the institutional networks of general exchange in the Southern Aegean islands prefectures demonstrate substantially higher density rates in comparison with the equivalent networks of the prefectures of the Northern Aegean. In particular, in Dodecanese, which has the most dense network, the density rate is 0.727 out of 1, while in Cyclades, because of the low presence of the University of the Aegean, the density rate found was 0.545 out of 1. Conversely, the density rates of the networks in the prefectures of the Northern Aegean are significantly lower, 0.418 for Lesbos, 0.528 for Chios and 0.595 for Samos.

This differentiation in the density of the networks reflects differentiated levels of network cohesion among the prefectures. Primarily in Dodecanese and secondarily in Cyclades the comparatively high density rates reflect the presence of bonds of trust among the actors, which facilitate better communication of new ideas and knowledge and hence dialogue. Additionally, the dense networks correspond to the bringing together of public and private actors, thus achieving synergies and subsequently shared rules and a common understanding of the problems and challenges facing the local economy and society. By contrast, the low density rates in the networks of the prefectures of the Northern Aegean indicate a less shaped system of institutional interactions, which is characterized by the lack of channels for dialogue and communication among the actors and an absence of a common understanding of the problems that inhibit the learning process.

Variation in the degree of centralization among the prefectural networks, however, is more indicative than that of the density measures, given that centralization reveals the distribution of resources and power among the actors and subsequently the structure (hierarchical or horizontal) of the network. Thus, the centrality measures of the Dodecanese and Cyclades general exchange networks are significantly lower (33.33 per cent and 54.55 per cent respectively) than those of the Lesbos, Chios and Samos networks (71.11 per cent, 60.71 per cent and 53.33 per cent respectively).

This differentiation in centrality reflects the different structures of the networks. In the Dodecanese and Cyclades prefectures the structure of the networks is more horizontal than vertical. What this structure reveals is that the Dodecanese and Cyclades networks are based on cohesive functional networks that combine public and private actors and constitute key components for the formation of the local institutional interactions. Thus, despite the centralized structure of the state and subsequently the leading role of public actors (Regional Secretariat and Prefecture Councils), the core of the network structure consists of functional networks, comprising public and private actors well connected within the network structure. Additionally, actors in the functional networks may provide alternative solutions for leadership roles in the future, as the latest reforms lead to a less hierarchical structure of intergovernmental relations. The horizontal structure of institutional interactions in Cyclades and Dodecanese reflects the comparatively more balanced distribution of resources and power among the actors, which allows for horizontal exchange of valuable resources (knowledge, information) and enhances the learning and adaptation processes.

Conversely, the high centrality rates of the networks in the prefectures of the Northern Aegean indicate the lack of core functional networks that combine public and private actors and facilitate collective action and coordination of resources at the local level. Hence, the local systems of governance tend to have a vertical rather than a horizontal structure, which is overwhelmingly dependent on the central state through the system of intergovernmental relations. As identified in chapter two, the vertical-hierarchical structure of institutional networks inhibits the exchange of information, new ideas and knowledge and hence communication and dialogue among the actors. This weakness of the institutional infrastructure in the prefectures of the Northern Aegean has led to a policy-making environment characterized by the dominant role of the Regional Secretariat as the leading actor within the institutional structure of each prefecture and the lack of other leading actors to provide leadership from within the institutional structure. This vertical and hierarchical structure of the local systems of governance has been a major impediment to the learning and adaptation processes in the Northern Aegean islands, which is illustrated by the problematic adjustment of their economic structures to the changing economic environment in the 1960s and 1970s.

These characteristics of the institutional networks of general exchange played an important role in determining the adaptation capacity of the two regions to the European environment. Nonetheless, whereas in the Southern Aegean their pre-existing institutional capacity facilitated their comparatively successful adjustment to European regional policy, in the Northern Aegean the Europeanization of regional policy signalled the start-up of the process of institution-building, which led to a substantial improvement in local institutional capacity. Hence, improvement of the institutional structures in both regions is illustrated by the structural features (density, centralization, structural equivalence) of the policy networks.

Table 8.2 presents a synopsis of the territorial structure of institutional networks in the two regions per dominant actor. This table reveals the predominance of the prefectures of the Southern Aegean region in functional networks, the absence of intra-regional networks with the exception of the regional councils and the Monitoring Committees of the CSF, and weak interregional cooperation which is restricted to a sectoral network created by the Chambers. At the transnational level the dominant role of the Dodecanese Chamber, which has participated in numerous sectoral networks is clear. By contrast the participation of the Northern Aegean region in the EURISLES Initiative is characterized by the dominant role of local government agencies (Chios Association of Municipalities).

The differentiation in institutional capacity for learning and adaptation between the prefectures of the case-study regions, however, is linked to their categorization by degree of Europeanization. Thus, according to the criteria established in chapter two, the following points should be stressed. First, there is convincing evidence that the prefectures of the Southern Aegean, given the limitations of the Greek socio-political structure, may be easily categorized in the third stage of Europeanization, since they fulfil the criteria of management and communication of EU-related information among the actors, involvement in programmes and ability to gain access to more EU funding, as well as developing network structures which overcome the public–private divide among the actors. Additionally, the plan of the newly elected Dodecanese Prefecture Council along with other private and public actors of the prefecture for opening an office in Brussels is viewed as an indicator of its entering into the final stage of full Europeanization, characterized by the development of European-style initiatives at the local level and advisory channels towards the Commission through its participation in transEuropean networks. Second, the prefectures of the Northern Aegean are categorized in the second stage of Europeanization, given that they are involved in the

Table 8.2 Institutional Networks by Type in SAI and NAI Regions

Territory	Prefectural		Intra-regional		Interregional		Transregional	
Dominant Actor	*S. Aegean*	*N. Aegean*	*S. Aegean*	*N. Aegean*	*S. Aegean*	*N. Aegean*	*S. Aegean*	*N. Aegean*
Governmental		Lesbos Training Centre (Kekanal) Chios Train. Centre	Regional Council	Regional Council				Lesbos University/ Eurisles Chios CAMC/ Eurisles
Sectoral					Dodecanese and Cyclades Chambers Aegean Isls Chambers' Association	Lesbos Chios Samos Chambers Aegean Isls Chambers' Association	Dodecanese Chamber/ 1. Economic Obs/tory 2. Ecomost 3. Mercure 4. Tacis 5. Euroform	
Functional	Dodecanese Tourist Promotion, Cooperative Bank, DDA KDA, CYDA, ERMDA	LLDA	CSF (MOP) Monitoring Committee	CSF (MOP) Monitoring Committee				

management of information and mobilized around EU Structural Funds programmes, but they display a poor performance in the development of public– private networks. Finally, the evidence from the two regions should be interpreted in relative terms, given the still centralized state structure and the general weakness of local governments in Greece.

The explanatory variable for the diversified degree of learning and adaptation to the European environment among the Aegean islands regions is variation in the strength of civil society, and the presence of social capital endowments. Despite the difficulties for identifying clear-cut differences in the level of social capital among the regions, chapters four and five provide evidence based on qualitative research on the differentiation of the two regions in the strength of their civil society. Thus, beyond the clear superiority of the Southern Aegean in participation in all the categories of voluntarist organizations, the analysis of the data has revealed crucial qualitative differences in participation in the two regions. In particular the presence of numerous networks of civic engagement focusing on the provision of crucial public services (health care) in Dodecanese and Cyclades in comparison with the rather culture-oriented voluntarist organizations in the Northern Aegean islands has been illustrated by the involvement of the Dodecanese Association of persons with special needs in the implementation of the HORIZON I Initiative. Furthermore, the involvement of voluntarist organizations (Lyceums of women) in EU programmes had already become evident, even during the implementation phase of the Aegean IMP. This evidence seems consistent with the strong tradition in institution-building primarily in Dodecanese and secondarily in Cyclades since the 1960s. Thus, although the evidence demonstrates similarities between the two regions over 'law and order', a strong civil society and important voluntarist organizations are intrinsic elements of the local systems of governance in both prefectures of the Southern Aegean and they have eased the processes of general exchange and policy network-building.

Implications for policy and integration theory

The theoretical framework of this book initiated the idea that social capital and institutional (inter-organizational) networks are conceptual tools fundamental to understanding how the learning and adaptation processes of local systems of governance in the European regional policy environment were assisted. This final section draws together the main theoretical implications of this research for integration theory in general and European regional policy in particular.

Since both concepts, social capital and networks, have been used for explaining the adaptation process in industrial districts and areas of industrial decline, their introduction into the European policy-making process is linked to similar needs for adaptation and adjustment existing within the European environment. The increasing importance of the network paradigm across a wide variety of public-policy areas as a form of governance distinct from the models of market and hierarchy is related to its capacity for explaining the complex system of exchanges and interdependencies among the actors on a horizontal basis.

Subsequently, the use of the network metaphor in European regional policy implies the need for overcoming the traditional in the *problematique* of regional development state/market dichotomy and the respective theoretical implications for policy design, implementation and outcomes. By mapping institutional structures and hence actors' interdependencies, institutional networks challenge the main ontological assumption about actors' independence, upon which the market model is based. On the other hand, networks question the effectiveness and efficiency of hierarchically structured and top-down state intervention in achieving adaptation and positive economic outcomes at the regional level. Thus, the view of local systems of governance as systems of interactions emphasizes the role of the networks as appropriate conceptual tools for harnessing these interactions and the subsequent processes of resource exchange and interdependence among institutional actors at the local level. It is within this institutional environment that synergies among public and private actors are achieved and the public–private divide is overcome. In that sense, institutional networks constitute an organizational form of collective governance within which the pursuit of individual interests is seen as a function of collective rather than of autonomous, individual actions.

Within such a policy environment still dominated by rationality-based actors' preferences through the processes of exchange and interdependence, however, the concept of social capital emerges as a set of norms, internalized by individual actors, that introduces the notion of social structure into the rational-choice paradigm, thus bridging the gap between rational or purposive action and social structure, and facilitating collective action among the actors within the networks. Social capital is the prime conceptual tool for learning and adaptation processes for two main reasons. First, given that the learning process is crucially affected by the uncertainty and volatility that characterize modern institutional settings and depends on information exchange, communication and dialogue, social capital, by facilitating collective action among actors within networks, plays the most important role in enhancing learning and hence adaptation functions. Second, since the functions of institutional learning and adaptation usually undermine the stability of relations among actors, the forms of social capital (trust, norms) play a key role in re-stabilizing relations among the involved actors and thus the further development of the network structure.

Under these considerations, social capital and networks constitute key components of the main theoretical argument of this book: that learning, adaptation and hence convergence and socio-economic cohesion within the EU are socially and institutionally embedded processes which cannot be understood either by the old leftist tradition of state intervention or by the new-right orthodoxy which emphasizes governance by a self-regulating economy. This 'embeddedness thesis', which implies the overcoming of the notion of methodological individualism for utility maximization and hence neo-liberal predominance, constitutes the cornerstone of the notion of collective competitiveness (Paraskevopoulos, 1998a,b). Collective competitiveness, in turn, is the prerequisite for successful learning, adaptation and Europeanization of subnational governments across Europe. Within this framework the lesson drawn for European regional policy is that the main criterion for the evaluation of the success or failure of the Structural Funds programmes should be the degree of synergies and networks creation at regional and local levels through enhancement of the partnership principle.

From the evidence of European structural policy arise important implications for contemporary integration theory. First, 'traditional' theories of regional integration are, to varying degrees, incapable of explaining the complexities in the current state of the art of the integration process in Europe. In particular, even though neofunctionalism's emphasis on the role of supranational institutions and the 'top-down' process of transformation of loyalties and identities implicitly acknowledges a role for learning on a top-down basis, it is incapable of capturing the dynamics of the system within which the multiplicity of interests has been raised as its main feature. On the other hand, although intergovernmentalism's emphasis on the bargains between member-state governments adequately describes the formalities of the decision-making process in the EU, it overlooks the bottom-up dynamics of the system within which, at least after the completion of the SEA, the role of the nation-states has, to a significant extent, been replaced by the role of the market and civil society (Paraskevopoulos, 1998c).

Second, for the contemporary debate among the neo-institutionalist approaches to the integration process the evidence from structural policy underlines the limitations of the rational-choice new-institutionalism and the assumptions of methodological individualism upon which it is based. The attempt to introduce rationality-based actors' preferences as the only explanatory variable for the selection of specific formal institutional arrangements at the EU level neglects the role played by historical institutional evolution and the norms of institutional behaviour in determining actors' preferences and explaining institutional change within the EU. In a similar vein historical institutionalism's pure path-dependence logic and the deterministic interpretation of history, though involving a substantial amount of evolution that the learning process would imply, are incapable of capturing the bottom-up dynamics within the system.

Third, the notion of learning initiated by this book, by challenging the traditional domination of Western culture by the rationality-based models of market and hierarchy, introduces civic engagement and strong civil society as intrinsic elements of Western culture as alternatives to both the markets and hierarchies. In that respect this book emphasizes the role of social capital (norms) in the formulation of actors' preferences (Paraskevopoulos, 1998c). Additionally, in a parallel way to the constructivist approach (Checkel, 1997; 1998), it opens up the debate on the impact of the 'learning and socialization processes' (J. Checkel, 1998: 9) on integration in Europe through modes of interaction, construction of collective identities and thus the formulation of actors' preferences.

Finally, the challenge this book offers to the methodological individualism-based and rational choice-oriented approaches to European integration is consistent with the emerging literature in the field of international relations, which stresses the role of communication and knowledge in the processes of institution-building in the modern world set within the framework of 'epistemic communities' (P. Haas, 1992).

Notes

1 Social capital, institutional networks and learning

1. The Fordist paradigm is characterized by standardized mass production, which is based on the process of the division of labour. As for the institutional structures of the economy, economies of scale are internal (for the firms) and are obtained through fixed capital and labour productivity increases. Standardized products are obtained, using special-purpose machinery and predominately unskilled or semiskilled workers with fragmented and standardized tasks (division between conception and execution), while the prevailing form of the market is oligopolistic and the management of the economy organized at the national level. The crucial micro-regulatory problem for mass production is balancing supply with demand in individual markets, while the Keynesian welfare state emerged as the dominant form of macro-regulation during the post-war period, focusing on linking purchasing power to productivity growth (Piore and Sabel, 1984; Hirst and Zeitlin, 1992).

2. Extensive operationalization of the *growth-pole* theory took place in southern European countries from the early 1950s to the early 1980s. In Italy, through the activities of the Casa per il Mezzogiorno and the Agency for the South, public intervention started in the 1950s and ended in the 1970s with poor results in reducing disparities between North and South (Mezzogiorno) (Camagni, 1991). In Greece, in the two early programmes of economic and social development instigated after the restoration of democracy (1976–80 and 1978–82), the main goal was strengthening rival cities to Athens with the objectives of restraining the attraction of the Capital and forming dynamic centres in the periphery (see chapter three). For a discussion of Perroux, see Holland, 1976.

3. *Flexible specialization* is a new technological paradigm challenging the accepted model of industrial organization (mass production) in a classic Kuhnian style. It is based on flexible automation. Differentiated products with small batches of production are obtained using flexible, general-purpose machinery and skilled adaptable workers, with a close integration of mental and manual tasks. Thus, reduction of customization costs is achieved through economies of scope (Piore and Sabel, 1984).

4. A. Giddens's conceptualization of regionalization as a process concerning time and space and of 'regions' as 'contexts of interactions', thus combining structure and actors within the framework of structuration theory, is relevant to this point (1984: 110–32).

5. This distinction draws upon Hadjimichalis's analysis of regionalization and regionalism. The former is defined as a process designed 'from above' (by the state, local authorities or capital) aimed to facilitate the changing needs of profitable accumulation, while the latter means the reaction of local social groups, whose interests are threatened by such a regionalization. This

238

conflict provides evidence of the 'social logic of the place' (Hadjimichalis, 1987: 286–7).

6. M. Piore and C. Sabel adopted the notion of 'technological trajectory', as it has been defined by the French regulation school (Aglietta, 1979; Lipietz, 1987; Boyer, 1988, 1990), and distinguished two specific trajectories: mass production and flexible specialization. M.Piore referred to this definition as follows: 'it is that set of forces which propels the economy through history, causing it to outgrow any particular regulatory framework and enter into crisis' (Piore, 1992: 158).

7. The notion of *'synergistic effects'* implies the achievement of greater output through the cooperation–coordination of the participant actors and the available resources, than that which would be produced by the independent function of actors–partners (Cappellin, 1992: 7).

8. For the importance of non-economic factors for the endogenous development approach, see Piore and Sabel (1984); Hirst and Zeitlin (1992); Lorenz (1992); Sabel (1994a,b); Leonardi (1995a,b); Storper (1995); Garofoli (1992); Cappellin (1992).

9. The use of the term 'institution' in this book refers interchangeably to both institutions and organizations (institutional networks).

10. The evolutionary models in economics have emerged as a combination of socio-biology and economics through which parallels between the underlying features of genetic survival and evolutionary development among animals and similar patterns of behaviour among human beings are explored (North, 1990, ch. 3).

11. 'Knowledge' means primarily tacit knowledge, which is learned only by experience, rather than the standardized and codified variety, that is easily transferable. This variety of knowledge can be diffused only through personal exchange and mobility.

12. 'The tragedy of the commons' was the title of Garrett Hardin's famous article in *Science* (1968). The equally famous paradigm, which was used to illustrate the tragedy, refers to a herder who receives a direct benefit from his own animals but suffers delayed costs from the deterioration of the commons when his and others' cattle overgraze. Here is the tragedy: unlimited grazing destroys the common resource upon which the livelihood of all depends. For an extensive overview see Elinor Ostrom (1990: 2–4).

13. The 'Folk Theorem', one version of this strategy, holds that 'always defect' is not a unique equilibrium in the repeat-play prisoner's dilemma (Axelrod, 1984).

14. The *substantivist* school is identified especially with Karl Polanyi's (1944) idea of 'moral economy'. It stresses the importance of culture, social and institutional structure of the society as a whole in understanding the texture of economic relations. The *formalist* school, on the other hand, is strictly linked to the assumptions of neoclassical economic theory that denies any impact of social structure and social relations on economic behaviour. For an overview, see M. Granovetter (1993: 3–10).

15. Adrienne Windhoff-Heritier's notion of institution as 'restriction and opportunity' shows the compatibility between new institutionalism and rational-choice approach and hence it may be seen as the foundation of

rational-choice institutionalism (1991: 41). See also J. Coleman (1988: 97) and K. Dowding (1994a).

16. The term 'transaction costs' refers to the underestimated in the neoclassical economic theory 'information costs'. As D. North has pointed out, 'the costliness of information is the key to the costs of transacting, which consist of the costs of measuring the valuable attributes of what is being exchanged and the costs of protecting rights and policing and enforcing agreements' (1990: 27), that is costs associated with banking, insurance, finance, trade, lawyers and accountants.

17. In parallel with Granovetter, R. Burt has distinguished between 'atomistic' and 'normative' approaches, emphasizing the *structural* approach to action (Burt, 1982, 1993).

18. Though Coleman is considered the scholar who introduced and analysed the term, he credits *Glenn C. Loury* with introducing the concept into economics to identify the social resources useful for the development of human capital. See J. Coleman, (1990: 300–1).

19. S. Singleton and Michael Taylor defined *community* as: 'a set of people (a) with some shared beliefs, including normative beliefs and preferences, beyond those constituting their collective action problem, (b) with a more or less stable set of members, (c) who expect to continue interacting with one another for some time to come, and (d) whose relations are direct (unmediated by third parties) and multiplex' (1992: 315).

20. On the state-driven process of synergies and collective action, see: Peter Evans (1996 a,b), Jonathan Fox (1996), Patrick Heller (1996), Fellmeth Aaron X. (1996) and Elinor Ostrom (1996).

21. These terms refer to the process of 'learning to cooperate', which is the outcome of a project for the revitalization of Pennsylvania through the reorientation of economic development policies. The basic principle governing the new development strategy was a shift in consensus from the view that individual actors know their interests and government's role is to remove the obstacles to realizing them, to the view that it is only by recognizing their mutual dependence that actors can define their distinct interests, and that government's role is to encourage the recognition of their collectivity and the definition of their particularity (Sabel, 1993b: 120–40).

22. E. C. Banfield (1958) provides empirical evidence for the vicious circles resulting from the destruction of social capital, which provide an *exegesis* of the backwardness of Mezzogiorno. See also, M.Olson (1982).

23. This definition tries to embody Windhoff-Heritier's (1993), Cooke's (1996) and Kenis and Schneider's (1991) emphasis on joint involvement of public and private actors, Knoke and Kuklinski's (1982) main focus on linkages, and Aldrich and Whetten's (1981) approach to the bounded and holistic character of networks.

24. Mitchell J. Clyde (1969) 'The concept and use of social networks', pp. 1–50, in J. C. Mitchell (ed.), *Social Networks in Urban Situations* (Manchester England: Manchester University Press).

25. According to Dowding, however, there are cases where collective performance is achieved without the exercise of power, but based on the similarity of actors' preferences. The actors who benefit from the thus-achieved collective action are merely *lucky* (1996: 52–4).

26. J. C. Harsanyi (1969), 'Measurement of Social Power, Opportunity Costs, and the Theory of Two-person Bargaining Games', in P. Bell et al. (eds) (1969) *Political Power: A Reader* (London: Macmillan), pp. 226–38.
27. Functioning within neo-corporatist systems local actors usually constitute the grassroots organizational members of a hierarchically structured, vertical network dominated by an 'umbrella-peak association', which leaves little space for autonomous action – even in terms of interest intermediation – to local actors (Dunleavy, 1991).

2 Social learning and adaptation within European regional policy

1. The preamble of the Treaty of Rome (1957) contained a broad commitment to regional development by stressing the goal of 'reducing the differences existing between the various regions and the backwardness of the less favoured regions'. The goal was restated in Article 2, through which the member-states agreed to 'promote throughout the Community a harmonious development of economic activities, a continuous and balanced expansion'.
2. The non-quota section was focused primarily on regions affected by industrial decline, that is regions dependent on iron and steel, ship-building and textiles and clothing.
3. Regulation 1787 constitutes codification of the modified initial Commission proposal, which suggested the adoption of the integrated programme approach and a system for almost complete regionalization of quotas (Nanetti, 1990).
4. In Article 130c, in particular, by identifying the ERDF as the principal instrument for regional policy, cohesion is defined as the task to 'redress the principal regional imbalances in the Community through participating in the development and structural adjustment of regions whose development is lagging behind and in the conversion of declining industrial regions'.
5. The reform was carried out through five Council Regulations which became effective on 1 January 1989. These are: the Framework Regulation (2052/88) and four implementation Regulations (4253/88, 4254/88, 4255/88 and 4256/88) (Nanetti, 1990).
6. These are: Objective 1, the less developed regions whose GDP is below 75 per cent of the Community average; Objective 2, regions of industrial decline; Objective 3, regions with severe long-term unemployment; Objective 4, the employment of young people: Objective 5a, adjustment of agricultural structures; and Objective 5b, development of rural areas.
7. Later, in the light of the next enlargement towards the European Economic Area (EEA) countries, a new Objective (6) was created to cover the ultraperipheral regions of the Nordic countries.
8. Objective 1 regions constituted the main beneficiaries within the three regional objectives, given that 65 per cent of the total of resources of the three Funds has been targeted at these regions.
9. Under the 1988 reforms, 10 per cent of the funds was allocated to Community Initiatives, while the remaining 90 per cent was focused on financing measures of the CSFs (CEC, 1991).
10. The Initiatives of the first CSF were: coal areas (RECHAR); environmental protection (ENVIREG); improvement of research and development capacity

(STRIDE); transborder cooperation (INTERREG); ultra-peripheral zones (REGIS); natural gas (REGEN); small and medium-sized enterprises (PRISMA); telecommunications (TELEMATIQUE); rural development (LEADER); new transnational employment opportunities (EUROFORM); equal opportunities for men and women (NOW); and integration of handicapped people (HORIZON) (CEC, 1991).

11. The Initiatives of the second CSFs (1994–99) were: cross-border cooperation and energy networks (INTERREG II [incorporating REGEN]); rural development (LEADER II); remote regions REGIS II; human resources (EMPLOI [incorporating NOW, HORIZON and YOUTHSTART]); training (ADAPT); restructuring of coal areas (RECHAR); steel areas (RESIDER); textiles and clothing areas (RETEX); defence dependent areas (KONVER); Portuguese textile industry (TEXTILE); small and medium-sized enterprises (SMEs); depressed urban areas (URBAN); and fishing industry (PESCA) (CEC, 1994b).

12. This is the 'comitology' procedure famous within European policy-making jargon. It implies the involvement of numerous and multi-targeted (advisory, management, regulatory) committees in the process of decision-making in the EU and, in particular, during the so-called 'communication between Council and Commission' procedures. Those committees are considered purely intergovernmental instruments for checking the Commission's room for manoeuvre and thus falsify the supranational character of decision-making (Pollack, 1996: 445).

13. The overall evaluation of the IMPs was conducted in a project (1990) directed by Dr Robert Leonardi at the European University Institute and financed by the Commission of the European Communities (grant no. 88–88001).

14. Although decentralization policies have been pursued in almost all EU countries, the intensity of the devolution process varies. Thus, with regard to the constitutional structure, Loughlin (1996) distinguishes among *federal* states (Germany, Austria, Belgium), *unitary regionalized* states (France, Spain, Italy, Portugal), *unitary decentralized* states (Sweden, Finland, Denmark, Netherlands) and *unitary centralized* states (UK, Greece, Ireland).

15. This term (Marks *et al.*, 1996b: 355; Pollack, 1995: 362) means the way in which the outcomes of intergovernmental bargains, in particular the 1988 reforms of the Structural Funds, can, as perfectly as neofunctionalist theory would have predicted, lead to mobilization of the dynamics of the system, which in this case seems to have led to 'multi-level governance'. For analysis of the significance of unintended consequences of action for evolution and change in social systems, see A. Giddens, 1984, pp. 281–354.

16. As P. Taylor puts it: 'in terms of the current range of integration theories the dynamics which strengthen the community level are identified most clearly within *neofunctionalism*, whereas the pressures which tend to encapsulate the segments, in the form of the states, are identified best within *consociationalism*' (1991: 125). By concentrating, however, on cultural differentiation and hence on the role of the nation-state in the interest intermediation function within the EU, consociationalism underestimates the corporatist and the pluralist aspects within the system. However, the latter seem to be dominant after the completion of the SEM. On consociationalism and its theoretical cousin, the *confederal consociation* approach, which

combines elements of polity construction (*confederation*) with aspects of cultural differentiation (*segmented demos*) within integration theory, see D. N. Chryssochoou et al., 1999.

17. Institutions constitute a crucial component of this equation, a synopsis of which is:

   Actors' Preferences × *Institutions* = *Policy Outcomes*

18. In particular, Richardson (1996: 17–34) attempts to introduce the notion of 'epistemic communities', originally conceptualized in the field of international relations (Haas, 1992), within EU policy-making. Given that the concept of 'epistemic communities' emphasizes the uncertainty of international actors and thus points to the role of knowledge and information flows in facilitating cooperative relations, it is familiar with the concepts of social capital and institutional networks as components of the learning approach to regional integration in Europe. See also Checkel (1998) and Kohler-Koch (1996: 370–1).

19. However, as research by R. Bennett and G. Krebs (1994) on the LEDA Initiative shows, although EU-financed programmes and most importantly the Community Initiatives represent a start-up for network creation in Europe's less-favoured regions, by enhancing partnership, they cannot ensure the continuity of the newly created forms of interactions, which are primarily influenced by the local social and cultural context and secondarily by the structure of the state.

20. Existing evidence, however, on regional differentiation in institutional capacity that is disassociated with the state structure and the degree of mobilization at European level, points to the role played by other crucial factors affecting institutional capacity, such as culture and territorial identity (Jeffery, 1997; Keating, 1996; Marks *et al.*, 1996a).

21. As Putnam, Leonardi and Nanetti (1993: 174) put it: 'A vertical network, no matter how dense and how important to its participants, cannot sustain social trust and cooperation. Vertical flows of information are often less reliable than horizontal flows, in part because the subordinate husbands information as a hedge against exploitation. More important, sanctions that support norms of reciprocity against the threat of opportunism are less likely to be imposed upwards and less likely to be acceded to, if imposed.'

22. Andrew H. Van de Ven (1975) 'Design for Evaluating Inter-Agency Networks Among Texas Early Childhood Organizations', Working paper, College of Business, Kent State University, p. 12.

23. Around thirty-five interviews were conducted in each region. The choice of actors in each case was based on: 1) positional identification, and 2) reputational identification. According to the first, the selection of actors was linked to their position within a particular policy domain and within the region, whereas, according to the second, actors' selection was based on information collected during the interview process or on preliminary information. Respondents were asked with whom they had regular interactions to exchange resources (information) and with whom they had interactions within the framework of the EU Funds' programmes and initiatives. Because of the inherent difficulty in small, closed communities of identifying the presence or absence of linkages – given that the lack of regular meetings does not necessarily mean absence of linkage – a further two questions were

added: with whom did they undertake joint general activities? and with whom did they jointly participate in EU programmes or initiatives?

24. Density measurement is the degree of connectedness of the entire network whereby 0 indicates no connections between any actor and 1 means that all actors are linked to one another. Because density demonstrates the strength of ties, it can be used as a partial measurement for thickness. However, thickness has qualitative features, which were explored during the interviews. While density measures the degree of network cohesion, centralization is seen as the extent to which this cohesion is organized around specific actors: those with the greatest number of linkages (Scott, 1994). Centrality measurements reveal actors' involvement in network relations and demonstrate the structure – horizontal or vertical – of the networks and also constitute an indicator of the distribution of power among the actors. Finally, structural equivalence reveals the network structure by categorizing the actors in their relational linkages and according to their common structural positions (Scott, 1994). The research used the CONCOR technique of structural equivalence because it 'produces a classification of network actors into discrete, mutually exclusive and exhaustive categories' (Knoke and Kuklinski, 1982: 73) based on the nature of their inter-organizational relations.

25. The 'VOLMED' research project is financed by the EU Commission (DG V) and focuses on registering the voluntary organizations in Mediterranean countries. The research for Greece has been undertaken by the Panteion University of Social Sciences (Dept. of Social Statistics); coordinator: associate professor Olga Stasinopoulou.

3   Greece

1. The numbers of municipalities and communes derive from the most recent administrative charter, based on the 1991 population census.

2. This system of power distribution within the empire evolved from the diversified patterns of landownership. Thus, in contrast with the feudal lords of western Europe, who had clear ownership rights over the land (feuds), the main feature of the *timar* system of landholding in the Ottoman empire was that all land belonged to the sultan, while the timar holders had a non-hereditary right over part of the production. The peasants, on the other hand, had a hereditary right over their land, subject to cultivating it regularly. Consequently, the distribution of power among the sultan and the leading social classes (aristocracy) led to a highly centralized structure, which did not allow for high rates of mobility of people and exchange of goods and ideas, that was the main underpinning factor for the crucial role of the cities as loci of political, economic and social functions leading eventually to the emergence of capitalism in western Europe. Furthermore, this system of power-distribution inhibited the regionalization process within the empire and the emergence of regions as integrated units of productive specialization and socio-political governance, which was the most important territorial feature in western Europe. Conversely, the Ottoman system of governance was favourable for the early development of clientelistic networks at the local level (Mouzelis, 1978).

3. This historical debate is mainly dominated by the need to establish the argument favouring the continuity of Hellenism under Ottoman rule, on

which is founded the *Hellenic-Christian* ideological movement that accompanied the creation of the modern Greek state. In that sense, the emergence and expansion of the communes have been interpreted either as the continuation of the communes in Byzantium or as a renewed version of the Greek cities of Roman times (for an overview, see Kontogiorgis, 1982: 31–3).

4. The term refers to the ideological and political movement that, based on the Greek diaspora of the West, constituted the leading force of the independence struggle.

5. Capodistrias's endeavour to create a centralized state structure, an intrinsic element of which was the organization of the centre–periphery relations around the concept of the prefecture, has been interpreted as the first, failed, attempt to promote the 'modernization from above' process, which, being against the interests of the local clientelist networks *(prouchontism)*, eventually led to his assassination (Filias, 1974; Mouzelis, 1978).

6. It should be noted, that a major reform with the code name 'Capodistrias' focused on the creation of viable local government units by the compulsory mergers of communes into new demoi is currently under implementation in Greece.

7. The term means the combination of political clientelism and elements of corporatist interest representation, involving hierarchically structured umbrella organizations, most of which get preferential treatment by the central state (Tsoukalas, 1986: 92–5).

8. The expediency control of the Prefect, however, remained in policy areas, such as the sale of municipal or community land and buildings, budgeting and the names given to municipal roads.

9. The regions are: Eastern Macedonia and Thrace, Central Macedonia, Western Macedonia, Thessaly, Hepirus, Ionian Islands, Western Greece, Sterea Ellada, Peloponnese, Attica, Northern Aegean Islands, Southern Aegean Islands and Crete.

10. Although this reform is based substantially on the provisions of the 1986 legal framework (law 1622), the fact that elections for the new prefectural councils were not held until eight years later led to a further reformulation of the legal framework (laws 2218, 2240, 2273/94 and 2284, 2297, 2307/95).

11. With the exception of the hard-core functions of the central state (defence, foreign affairs, law and order, economic policy, statistics and administrative control of the first tier of local government by the Ministry of the Interior), all other functions of the state at the prefectural level have been transferred to the new nomarchal councils.

12. It is worth noting that the sum of the regular and extraordinary grants rose dramatically from about 40 per cent of local government revenue in 1974 to about 65 per cent in 1984 (Tatsos, 1988: 33–9).

13. According to this scheme, the central transfers are made up of 20 per cent of both personal and corporate income tax, 20 per cent of the tax on immovable property, 50 per cent of road tax and 3 per cent of the tax on the transfer of immovable property.

14. It should be noted that, given the high political costs implicit in the significance of immovable property for Greeks (the country has one of the highest rates of privately owned houses in Europe), and administration

problems (lack of real estate registry, evaluation difficulties), the revenue from tax on immovable property has always been insignificant, either for the central state, or for local governments, when compared to other sources of taxation (Tatsos, 1989: 35–7).

15. The same electoral system applies to elections for the second tier of local government (new nomarchal councils) after the 1994 reform.

16. As Tsoukalas argues, the bureaucratic organization in Greece does not correspond to organizational functions, but rather it is used, almost exclusively, for clientelistic political purposes, thus serving as a form of 'political division of labour' (1986: 121). Historically, this tendency goes back to the formulation of the patronage system of politics, when the enormous expansion of employment in the state bureaucracy had reached a rate disproportionate to the size of both population and resources. As has been calculated, by 1880 the ratio of civil servants to every 10,000 of the population was ten times higher in Greece than in the UK (Dertilis, 1976, 'Social change and military intervention in politics: Greece, 1881–1928', unpublished Ph.D thesis, University of Sheffield.; cited in Mouzelis, 1978: 17). After the last restoration of democracy, the revival of clientelism became evident from the 74 per cent increase in the number of civil servants in the period 1974–80 (Flogaitis, 1987: 247).

17. The term has been borrowed from similar accounts of the Italian public administration identified by S. Cassese (1983), *Il Sistema Administrativo Italiano* (Bologna: Il Mulino).

18. Athanasopoulos, D. (1983) *The Greek Administration* (Athens: Papazisis – in Greek).

19. Until 1994 administrative control was executed through the prefectural directions of the Ministry of the Interior.

20. It should be noted that higher education graduates represent only 9.9 per cent of municipal personnel, while the majority (90.1 per cent) are high school and secondary school graduates (Ministry of the Interior, 1996).

21. In the right wing of the political spectrum the pre-dictatorship, right-wing party of National Radical Union was replaced by a new party, the New Democracy (ND), that won the 1974 and 1977 elections and remained in power until 1981. In the centre and left wing, on the other hand, the legalization of the Communist left – that after the 1968 split was divided into the pro-Soviet Communist Party of Greece (KKE) and the Communist Party of the Interior (KKEes) – allowed for its first appearance in the formal political arena in the post-war period, while the emergence of the Panhellenic Socialist Movement (PASOK), which absorbed the pre-dictatorship, centre-wing party, the Centre Union, and gradually became the dominant party of the centre-left, led to a significant shift of the whole political spectrum towards the left. Since the late 1980s and early 1990s, however, the foundation – from the Communist Party of the Interior and other small left-wing parties – of the Coalition of the Left has redefined the boundaries of the centre-left wing of the political spectrum, which currently consists mainly of PASOK, the Communist party and the Coalition of the Left.

22. Of particular importance in this process was the reluctant attitude of PASOK towards EC membership until the late 1980s and general confrontation

with the US over policies in sensitive foreign affairs problems, such as the Cyprus issue.

23. The specification of the main goals of the programme was decided by the National Council for Spatial Planning and Environment (23 March 1979).

24. Despite several reforms, the main features of this framework, aimed at strengthening the attractiveness of peripheral regions for investment, have remained the same up to today.

25. The A and B zones of assistance comprise developed areas, such as the prefectures of Attica, Salonika, Corinth, Corfu (only for tourist enterprises), the city of Rhodes and so on, the C zone consists of areas of medium level of development, while in D zone of high assistance level contains the border areas, among which are the prefectures of Lesbos, Chios, Samos and Dodecanese (with the exception of the city of Rhodes). It must be noted that, as far as the tourist sector is concerned, the Cyclades prefecture (with the exception of Mykonos in B zone) belongs to the C zone.

26. The Regional Incentive Expenditure increased as a percentage of the national Gross Domestic Product (GDP) from 0.07 per cent in 1980 to 0.35 per cent in 1985 and to 0.49 per cent in 1990, and per head of the population of the assisted regions (ECU 1990 prices) from 7.13 in 1980 to 36.28 in 1985 and to 52.47 in 1990. Similar trends have been observed in Italy in the same period (CEC, 1994a: 135–42).

27. The financial control function of the Ministry of National Economy, implicitly based on the additionality principle, has resulted in the incorporation of EU financial resources into the state budget, through which indirect financial support for the Public Investment Programme is provided. However, this process is also commonly used for financing the national balance of payments deficit (Andrikopoulou, 1992: 201).

28. The case of the Crete IMP, in which development of tourist-related infrastructures (e.g. airports), despite the will of public and private actors representing tourism interests, was underfunded for the benefit of subsidized private hotel investment (Papageorgiou and Verney, 1993: 145).

29. The regional monitoring committees of the IMPs were chaired by regional secretaries and their members included sub-programme managers, local interest group representatives and officials from at least two directorate-generals of the EC Commission. However, because of the lack of pre-existing network experience and administrative dysfunctions, their role was marginal.

30. The private sector was involved in 10 per cent of individual interventions by the IMPs in comparison with around 46 per cent in France and 28 per cent in Italy (Bianchi, 1993).

31. The notion of 'cultural dualism', which in the Greek case has a cross-sectional nature in the sense that it is not exclusively identified with any specific institution or structure but rather cuts across every institution in Greek society, is used by Diamandouros within the conceptual framework of the 'critical juncture', that is as a determinant of the developmental trajectory useful in 'path-dependent analysis' and 'chaos theory' (Diamandouros, 1994: 6–7).

32. C. Moscof (1972), *The National and Social Consciousness in Greece: 1830–1909* (in Greek), p. 83 ff, Salonika.

33. The Ambelakia cooperative (an association of villages in Thessaly specializing in the production and export of high quality yarn) employed 40,000–50,000 people and had an accumulated capital of 20 million French francs, at the peak of its expansion – end of the eighteenth to the beginning of the nineteenth century (V. Kremmidas, 1976, *Introduction to the History of Modern Greek Society 1700–1821*, p. 143 (Athens: Exantas – in Greek; cited in Mouzelis, 1978: 10).
34. The most distinctive features of this culture are: the preponderant role assigned to the state vis-à-vis civil society; the underestimation of the role of institutions; the central role of the family in combination with clientelistic practices; and finally, a conspirational approach towards the Western world, combined with an overestimation of the importance of Greece in international affairs (Diamandouros, 1994: 15).
35. These are equivalent to a sort of ill-defined, complex norm of 'civic responsibility and contractual honesty' (Tsoukalas, 1995: 197), which, however, being considered as irrational reciprocities, are problematically treated within the rational analytic framework.

4   Institutional capacity and policy environment in SAI

1. National Statistical Service of Greece (NSSG): Population censuses 1961, 1971, 1981, 1991.
2. Interview with the President of the Rhodes Hotel Owners' Association (Rhodes, October 1996).
3. Ministry of the Interior: National Elections results 1974–96.
4. Ministry of the Interior: Prefectural Elections results, 1994.
5. NSSG, National Accounts (elaboration of primary data).
6. The weakness of the Greek periphery in medical personnel corresponds to the generally poor social infrastructure (Athanasiou, *et al.*, 1995: 51).
7. The *Location Quotient* is one of the main indicators used in regional analysis for the identification of regional specialization and for interregional comparisons of the economic structure of each region. It is based on indirect reference to the national data and its value (varying from lower than, equal to or higher than 1) shows the degree to which (lower, equal or higher respectively) a specific productive sector is developed in a specific region in comparison with the country as a whole.
8. EUROSTAT (1995) 'EC Tourism in the 1990s' – DG XXIII.
9. NSSG (1991): *Tourism Statistics*.
10. NSSG (1994): *National Accounts*: Section of *Regional Accounts*.
11. Compare this with the outcome of the Northern Aegean Islands sectoral analysis (chapter 5).
12. This special tariff regime, initially involving tariff reductions to a wide range of goods imported into the prefecture, has been gradually restricted to a small amount of goods such as china, textiles, umbrellas and cosmetics (Getimis, 1989: 137).
13. Southern Aegean Islands: development plan 1988–92.
14. NSSG (1998): *Firms and Employment Census per Sector of Production*.
15. The selection of actors is based on the criteria of their role within the local system of governance and productive structure of region or prefecture. Therefore, local branches of corporate-umbrella organizations (such as trade

unions) or central state agencies, which function as conveyors of central-state policy choices (such as the Ministry of the Aegean or the Tourist Training High School of Rhodes, run by the Greek Tourist Organization), have not been included in the matrix.

16. Interview with the president of the Hotel Owners' Association (Rhodes).
17. It should be noted that Greece and Albania are the only countries in Europe without a national land registry system.
18. The Organization for Tourist Promotion, whose origin should be traced back to an initiative undertaken by the Hotel Owners' Association in the 1960s, constitutes a unique forum (for Greece) for dialogue, communication and subsequent learning at the local level, which has facilitated local productive and economic systems in the adaptation process (Rhodes Hotel Owners' Association, 1991, anniversary edition).
19. Interview with the president of the Cyclades Chamber (Syros, November 1996).
20. In the particular case of Syros island, pursuit of the goal of sustainable development should not overlook the island's strong tradition in shipbuilding, given that the Syros shipyard still represents an important parameter of its economic structure and accounts for a considerable share of local employment.
21. Although the dislocation of the University departments among the Aegean islands cannot fully explain its extremely marginal role within the Cyclades institutional networks, the creation of a School for Fine Arts in Syros is planned. Additionally, there has been considerable University involvement in local networks during the implementation of the second CSF (1994–99).
22. The collection of the data has been facilitated by the 'VOLMED' research project, which is financed by the EU Commission (DG V) and focuses on the registration of voluntary organizations in the Mediterranean countries. The fieldwork research for Greece, which is now being carried out, has been undertaken by the Panteion University of Social Sciences and coordinated by the assistant professor, Dr Stasinopoulou.
23. Although voluntary associations membership is based on registration data, they demonstrate age-long trends in percentage of population since the membership is influenced by demographic and population trends. (Interview with the director for cultural policy of the Dodecanese prefecture).
24. More specifically, the answers for 'agree completely' and 'more or less agree' categories amounted to around 90 per cent of respondents to the statement: 'the citizens of the region usually obey the law only if it does not contravene their personal interests'. Conversely, the same answers accounted for more than 95 per cent of respondents to the statement: 'in this region usually people trust each other'.
25. Compare this with the Mytilene experience (chapter five), which demonstrates a significantly different picture.
26. Interview with the president of the organization (Syros, October 1996).
27. Interview with the president of the organization, a member of the Rhodes city council (Rhodes, November 1996).
28. Interview with the mayor of Ermoupolis (Ermoupolis October, 1996).
29. Interview with the president of the Kos women's society (Kos, November 1996).

5 Institutional capacity and policy environment in NAI

1. NSSG: *Population Censuses*, 1961, 1971, 1981, 1991.
2. Interview with the EU Commission (DG XVI) responsible for Structural Funds programmes on the Aegean Islands (Brussels, June 1996).
3. Interview with the president of the Local Association of Municipalities and Communes, Mytilene (October 1996).
4. Ministry of the Interior: National Elections results (1974–96).
5. In Greece, after the 1968 split which was crucially influenced by the Czechoslovakia invasion, there have been two Communist parties: the reformist and Euro-communist party (Communist Party of the Interior) that has more or less followed the trajectory of the Italian PCI and currently participates in the Coalition of the Left, and the hard-core, more powerful party (Communist Party of Greece), which was well-disposed towards the ex-Soviet Union.
6. Interview with the president of the Local Association of Municipalities and Communes (Mytilene, October 1996).
7. Ministry of the Interior: National Elections results (1974–96).
8. Ibid.
9. Ministry of the Interior: Prefectural Elections results, 1994.
10. NSSG, National Accounts: section of regional accounts (adapted from primary data).
11. NSSG: National Accounts: Section of Regional Accounts, 1994 (adapted from primary data).
12. Ibid.
13. Theodori-Markoyiannaki *et al.* (1986) and NSSG, 1991 census.
14. NSSG: National Accounts. Section of Regional Accounts, 1994 (adapted from primary data).
15. Ibid.
16. Interviews with the presidents of the Local Association of Municipalities and Communes and the Local Development Agency respectively (Lesbos, October 1996).
17. Interview with the president of the Chamber (Mytilene, October 1996).
18. Interview with the secretary of the Farmers' Association (Mytilene, October 1996).
19. The vast majority of the respondents (98 per cent), who, though they do not constitute a sample, represent the most prominent local organizations, stated the current situation regarding the prefecture and agricultural restructuring to be not at all satisfactory (Interviews, Nos 1–23, Lesbos Prefecture, October 1996).
20. Interviews with the secretary of the Research Committee of the University (Athens, November 1996) and the dean of the social anthropology department (Mytilene, October 1996).
21. The merger was a bottom-up initiative undertaken by the District Council of the northern part of the island before the compulsory merger, which is currently being imposed by the Ministry of the Interior in Greece, and has significantly improved the administrative and financial function of local authorities (interview with the local representative of the Coalition of the Left party; Chios, October 1996).
22. Interview with the president of the Chamber (Chios, October 1996).

23. Interview with the executive director of the Mastic Growers' Association (Chios, October 1996).
24. The percentage system of distribution of Public Investment Programme financial resources (40 per cent for Lesbos and 30 per cent for Chios and Samos) is viewed as a crucial factor that contributes to the deterioration and rivaling in relations among the island-prefectures (interview with the mayor of Samos city, Samos, November 1996).
25. Interview with the president of the Local Association of Municipalities (Samos, November 1996).
26. Interview with the mayor of Samos City Council (Samos, November 1996).
27. In particular, those respondents who answered 'absolutely agree' and 'more or less agree', (who, however, did not represent a full sample,) to the statement: 'the citizens of this region usually obey the law (traffic code, building regulations) only if it does not contravene their personal interests' reached 98 per cent in all the prefectures of the Northern Aegean. Compare this with the, in many respects, similar outcome of the Southern Aegean (chapter four).
28. Interviews, Nos 11, 4, 8, 6, 12 (Lesbos, Samos, October–November 1996).
29. Among others, the Agiassos Library, the Lesbos and Aeolic Studies Societies and the Mytilene Progressive Society 'Theophilos' deserve special reference.
30. However, given the distinction between active and non-active members there should be little doubt about the extent to which those data correspond to a really active voluntarism.
31. Of particular importance are the cases of the University dean and the president of the Association of Municipalities, who expressed serious doubts about the presence of social trust on the island in answer to the question 'in this region usually people trust each other'.
32. Interviews, Nos 4, 8, 10, 12 (Lesbos, October 1996).
33. Interview with the dean of the University – social anthropology department – (Lesbos, October 1996).

6 Policy networks and adaptation in SAI

1. The Leros-project was focused on the development of Leros island, whose economy was almost exclusively dependent on the asylum for the mentally ill located there. The goal achieved by the successful implementation of the programme was twofold: first, by facing the development challenges of the island in an integrated manner; and second, by bringing about a revolutionary reform 'for Greece' of the psychiatric system.
2. This distribution represents budget data of the (1989–93) MOPs for the Southern and Northern Aegean island regions (DGXVI, 1992), which may vary significantly from the ex-post (after implementation) data. However, in this particular case, they reflect the real outcome of the implementation process.
3. This trend in the Southern Aegean is identifiable in most of the other Greek regions as well, such as Western Macedonia, Central Macedonia and Eastern Macedonia and Thrace (DGXVI, 1992).
4. The data are taken from the final report of the programme manager for the Southern Aegean MOP (1989–93) (Aigaio Ltd, Syros, February, 1995).
5. Elaboration of primary data derived from the evaluation reports for both

MOPs (Ministry of National Economy, 1993a; 1993b).

6. For instance, the private sector's involvement in the Northern Aegean MOP has been substantially lower (1.42 per cent) than the 3.41 per cent indicated in the table (Ministry of National Economy, 1993b), while in the case of other regions such as Eastern Mecedonia/Thrace the high rate of private sector contribution to the MOP is related to the use of MOP funds for support of private investments through the national regional policy incentives scheme (DGXVI, 1992).

7. Although there have been valid proposals for reforming this categorization of the islands (such as for the inclusion of Mykonos in group III, the most developed islands, and of Syros in group II, the islands of medium level of development), it formed the basis for the planning and evaluation procedures of the first CSF (Ministry of National Economy, 1993a).

8. In particular, whilst, according to the evaluation report for the MOP, the absorption rates for groups I and III range between 66.3 per cent (1993) and 102.6 per cent (1992) and 79.5 per cent (1993) and 102.4 per cent (1991) respectively, the rate for category II has not exceeded 79.6 per cent (1992) (Ministry of National Economy, 1993a).

9. The Community Initiatives which are managed by the central state (Ministry of National Economy and other ministries) constitute a sort of parallel to the CSF structural interventions, but they are not considered an integral part of the MOPs.

10. Interview with the president of the Rhodes Hotel Owners' Association conducted in Rhodes (October 1996).

11. Interview with the general secretary of the Southern Aegean islands region (Ermoupolis, Syros, November 1996).

12. Ibid.

13. In the Cyclades prefecture only recently (within the framework of the second CSF 1994–99) have local institutional actors started to seek the University's cooperation either for joint participation in projects or for preparation of project proposals (Interviews, Nos 42 and 44, Syros, November 1996).

14. In the Dodecanese, despite their limited role, the presence of the Society of Rhodes Women and the Leros Metropolis as implementation agents must be stressed.

15. Compare this with the evidence from the Northern Aegean island-prefectures (chapter seven).

16. Interview with the executive of the DDA (Rhodes, November 1996).

17. Interview with the president of the Chamber (Rhodes, November 1996).

18. Interview with the newly elected prefect of Dodecanese (Rhodes, November 1996).

19. Because of the extremely large extent of actor participation in specific programmes, measures or initiatives, the structural equivalence of actors in the policy network is based on identification of linkages and does not represent the extent of programme participation for each organization.

20. The Syros Lyceum of Greek Women and the Santorini Commune were amongst the few non-state organizations involved in the implementation of specific projects of the programme (Ministry of National Economy, 1994a).

21. The mayor of Mykonos is the president of both the local Association of Municipalities and the Cyclades Development Agency.
22. Interviews with the mayor of Ermoupolis and the president of the Chamber (Ermoupolis, October 1996).

7   Policy networks and adaptation in NAI

1. Although the implementation of the measure was managed by the Ministry of Agriculture, the most well-publicized projects were the women's agro-tourist cooperatives of Petra (Lesbos) and Mesta (Chios), in which the active involvement of Mrs Papandreou, the wife of the then prime minister, played the decisive role. The 84 agro-tourist units in the Northern Aegean islands were located as follows: 41 in Lesbos, 11 in Chios and 32 in Samos (Ministry of National Economy, 1994a).
2. The trainees in the agricultural sector of the Northern Aegean account for 17 per cent of the total trainees, while the percentage for the entire Aegean islands region is just 7.2 per cent (Ministry of National Economy, 1994a: 84).
3. It is based on data from the evaluation report of the MOP of the Northern Aegean (Ministry of National Economy, 1993b).
4. Compare these data with equivalent data for the Southern Aegean, where the airports and ports-related infrastructure represents 28 per cent of the funds, the road networks 14.9 per cent and the social services-related infrastructure not in excess of 16 per cent (see chapter six).
5. The data derive from the evaluation report and hence relate to the final structure of the programme as it was formulated after the successive reforms brought about by the Monitoring Committees (Ministry of National Economy, 1993b).
6. The data derive from the evaluation report and reflect the 1993 state of the implementation process of the programme (Ministry of National Economy, 1993b). It should be noted that non-absorbed funds of the first MOP were transferred to the second MOP (1994–99).
7. Because of the lack of appropriate (after implementation) data on the allocation of funds at the prefectural level per Fund/sub-programme (ERDF, ESF, EAGGF), Figure 7.4 draws on data per category of structural interventions (Ministry of National Economy, 1993b).
8. In particular, the production subsidies in Lesbos amounted to 4.33 per cent and 6.05 per cent of the 1993 and 1994 Gross Prefectural Product respectively, while the amounts seem to be similarly high during the following years, depending on the size of production (interviews with the responsible directors of the Ministry of Agriculture and the Lesbos Prefecture, Athens, Mytilene, October 1996).
9. The National Programme of Community Interest (NPCI) for Chios was an ERDF-financed (21 858 000 ecus) programme for the period 1 January 1988–31 December 1992 focusing on the sectors of basic infrastructure, manufacturing and tourism. After a decision taken by the Monitoring Committee in 1992, those funds unabsorbed by 31 December 1992 were transferred into the MOP and hence the implementation of the programme was carried out through the sub-programmes of the MOP.

10. Interview with the director of the Mastic Growers' Association (Chios, October 1996).
11. Interview with the person responsible in the DG XVI (EU Commission) for the Aegean islands' Structural Funds programmes (see chapter 5).
12. This trend had become evident even during the implementation of the IMP for the Aegean islands, when, whilst in the Southern Aegean there was a considerable presence of non-state local actors and voluntary organizations (see chapter 6), in the Northern Aegean the implementation was a state-driven process.
13. Minutes from the 14 December 1994 meeting of the Monitoring Committee (interview No 1 with the General Secretary of the region, Mytilene, October 1996).
14. Moreover, the only presence of the region in transnational networks is in the EURISLES programme, through a mini-network, comprising the Research Unit for islands' Development of the University and the Chios Association of Municipalities, which had undertaken the implementation of the programme in the Northern Aegean.
15. Interview with the president of the Chamber (Mytilene, October 1996).
16. This phenomenon, however, should be compared with what happened in the Southern Aegean and particularly in Dodecanese, where, because of the pre-existing qualitative features of the local institutions in learning and adaptation, the process of institution-building took the form of adjusting existing institutional structures to the new environment (see chapter six).
17. Interview with the responsible councilor of the Mytilene City Council (Mytilene, October 1996).
18. Interview with the prefect of Lesbos (Mytilene, October 1996).
19. As in the Southern Aegean region, because of the extremely extensive actors participation in specific programmes or initiatives, the structural equivalence in the policy network is based on linkages identification and does not represent the number of programmes for each organization.
20. Interview with the president of the Mastic Growers' Association (Chios, October 1996).
21. Interview with the president of the Chamber (Chios, October 1996).
22. Interviews with the secretary of the Research Committee of the University of the Aegean (Athens, November 1996).
23. Interviews with the mayor of Samos City Council and the prefect (Samos, November 1996).

Appendix

Descriptive graphs*

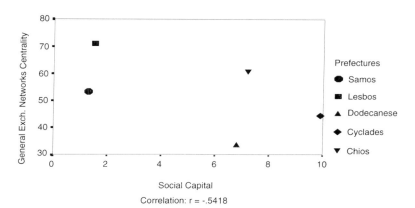

Graph A.1 Social Capital and Exchange Networks (education controlled)

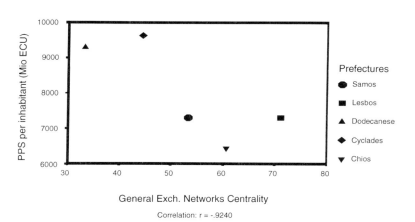

Graph A.2 Exchange Networks and Economic Performance (education controlled)

* These graphs derive from correlations among the variables. However, because of the small number of cases, they are statistically insignificant and hence they are presented as descriptive graphs.

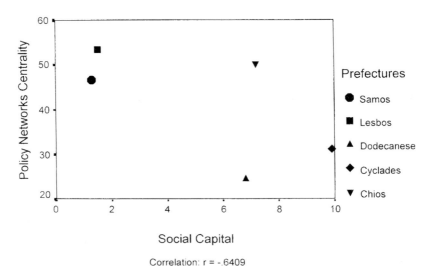

Graph A.3   Social Capital and Policy Networks (education controlled)

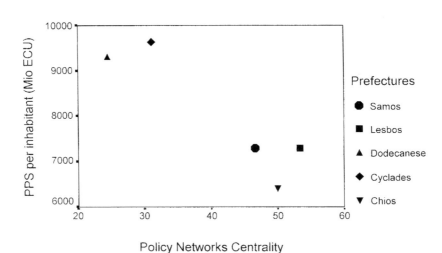

Graph A.4   Policy Networks and Economic Performance (education controlled)

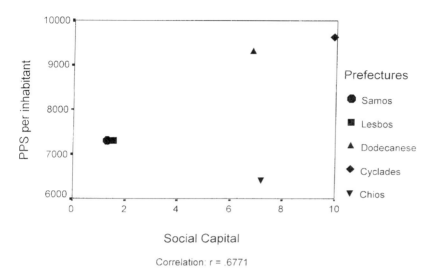

Graph A.5   Social Capital and Economic Performance (education controlled)

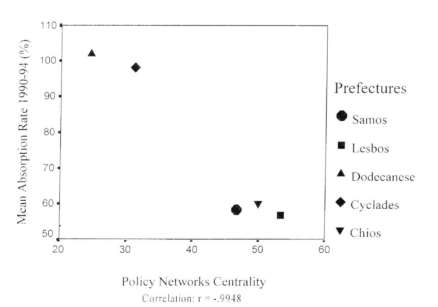

Graph A.6   Policy Networks and Absorption Capacity (education controlled)

Bibliography

Aglietta, M. (1979) *A Theory of Capitalist Regulation: the US Experience*, London: New Left Books.

Aldrich, Howard and D. A. Whetten (1981) 'Organization-sets, Action-sets, and Networks: Making the Most of Simplicity', in P. C. Nystrom and W. H. Starbuck (eds), *Handbook of Organizational Design: Vol. 1; Adapting Organizations to their Environments*, Oxford: Oxford University Press, pp. 385–408.

Amin, A. (1994) 'Post-Fordism: Models, Fantasies and Fantoms of Transition', in A. Amin (ed.), *Post-Fordism: A Reader*, Oxford: Blackwell.

Amin, A. and A. Malmberg (1994) 'Competing Structural and Institutional Influences on the Geography of Production in Europe', in A. Amin (ed.), *Post-Fordism: A Reader*, Oxford: Blackwell, pp. 227–48.

Amin, A. and N. Thrift (1994) 'Living in the Global', in A. Amin and N. Thrift (eds), *Globalisation, Institutions and Regional Development in Europe*, Oxford: Oxford University Press, pp. 1–22.

Amin, A. and J. Tomaney (1995a) 'The Regional Dilemma in a Neo-Liberal Europe', *European Urban and Regional Studies*, 2: 2, 171–88.

Amin, A. and J. Tomaney (1995b) 'A framework for Cohesion', in A. Amin and J. Tomaney (eds), *Behind the Myth of the European Union: Prospects for Cohesion*, London, Routledge.

Anderson, J. J. (1990) 'Skeptical Reflections on a Europe of Regions: Britain, Germany, and the ERDF', *Journal of Public Policy*, 10: 4, 417–47.

Anderson. J. J. (1995) 'The State of the (European) Union: From the Single Market to Maastricht, from Singular Events to General Theories', *World Politics*, Vol. 47, pp. 441–65.

Andrikopoulou, Eleni (1992) 'Whither Regional Policy? Local Development and the State in Greece', in M. Dunford and G. Kafkalas (eds), *Cities and Regions in the New Europe: The Global-local Interplay and Spatial Development Strategy*, London: Belhaven Press.

Andrikopoulou, E., P. Getimis and G. Kafkalas (1988) 'Spatial Regulation in Greece: from Central Administration to Corporatism?', in G. Kafousis, N. Konsolas, N. Petralias, M. Lambrinidis and T. Pakos (eds), *Festschrift for Sakis Karagiorgas*, Regional Development Institute (RDI), Athens (in Greek).

Apter, D. (1987) *Rethinking Development: Modernization, Dependency and Post-modern Politics*, London: Sage.

Armstrong, H. (1989) 'Community Regional Policy', in J. Lodge (ed.), *The European Community and the Challenge of the Future*, London: Pinter.

Athanasiou, L., P. Kavadias, D. Katichianou, P. Tonikidou (1995) *Interregional Analysis: Basic Data per Region and Prefecture*, Athens: KEPE Greek Centre of Economic Research – in Greek.

Athanasoponlos, D. (1983) *The Greek Administration*, Athens: Papazisis (in Greek).

Axelrod, Robert (1984) *The Evolution of Cooperation*, New York: Basic Books.

Axelrod, Robert (1997) *The Complexity of Cooperation: Agent-Based Models of Competition and Collaboration*, Princeton: Princeton University Press.

Banfield, Edward C. (1958) *The Moral Basis of a Backward Society*, Glencoe: The Free Press.

Barro, R. J. and X. Sala-i-Martin (1991) *Convergence Across States and Regions*, Brookings Papers on Economic Activity, no 1 April.

Bates, Robert H. (1988) 'Contra Contractarianism: Some Reflections on the New Institutionalism', *Politics and Society*, 16: 2–3, 387–401.

Benington, John and Janet Harvey (1994) 'Spheres or Tiers? The Significance of Transnational Local Authority Networks', *Local Government Policy Making*, 20: 5, 21–30.

Bennett, Robert J. and Guenter Krebs (1994a) 'Local Economic Development Partnerships: An Analysis of Policy Networks in EC-LEDA Local Employment Development Strategies', *Regional Studies*, 28: 2, 119–40.

Bennett, Robert J., Peter Wicks and Andrew McCoshan (1994b) *Local Empowerment and Business Services*, London: UCL Press.

Berkowitz, Stephen D. (1982) *An Introduction to Structural Analysis: The Network Approach to Social Research*, Toronto: Butterworths.

Bianchi, Giuliano (1993) 'The IMPs: A Missed Opportunity? An Appraisal of the Design and Implementation of the Integrated Mediterranean Programmes', in R. Leonardi (ed.), *The Regions and the European Community: The Regional Response to the Single Market in the Underdeveloped Areas*, London: Frank Cass, pp. 47–70.

Borgatti, S. P., M. G. Everett and L. C. Freeman (1992) *UCINET IV Version 1.00*, Columbia: Analytic Technologies.

Boyer, Robert (1988) 'Technical Change and the Theory of Regulation', in G. Dosi, C. Freeman, R. Nelson, G. Silverberg, and L. Soete (eds), *Technical Change and Economic Theory*, London: Pinter, pp. 67–94.

Boyer, Robert (1990) *New Directions in Management Practices and Work Organisation: General Principles and National Trajectories*, Paris: OECD.

Bulmer, Simon J. (1994) 'The Governance of the European Union: A New Institutionalist Approach', *Journal of Public Policy*, 13: 4, 351–80.

Bulmer, Simon J. (1998) 'New Institutionalism and the Governance of the Single European Market', *Journal of European Public Policy*, 53, 365–86.

Burt, Ronald S. (1982) *Toward a Structural Theory of Action: Network Models of Social Structure*, New York: Academic.

Burt, Ronald S. (1993) 'The Social Structure of Competition', in R. Swedberg (ed.), *Explorations in Economic Sociology*, New York: Russell Sage Foundation, pp. 65–103.

Camagni, R. (1991) 'Regional Deindustrialisation and Revitalisation Processes in Italy', in L. Rodwin and H. Sazanami (eds), *Industrial Change and Regional Economic Transformation: The Experience of Western Europe*, London: Harper Collins, pp. 137–67.

Campbell, J. K. (1964) *Honour, Family and Patronage: A Study of Institutions and Moral Values in a Greek Mountain Community*, London: Oxford University Press.

Cappellin, Riccardo (1992) 'Theories of Local Endogenous Development and International Co-operation', in M. Tykkylaeinen (ed.), *Development Issues and Strategies in the New Europe*, pp. 1–19, Aldershot: Avebury.

Cassese, S. (1983) *Il Sistema Administrativo Italiano*, Bologna: Il Mulino.

Checkel, Jeffrey T. (1997) 'International Norms and Domestic Politics: Bridging the Rationalist-Constructivist Divide', *European Journal of International Relations*, 3: 4, 473–95.

Checkel, Jeffrey T. (1998) *Social Construction, Institutional Analysis and the Study of European Integration*, paper presented at the 26th ECPR-Joint Sessions of Workshops, University of Warwick, 23–8 March.

Cheshire, Paul, R. Camagni, Jean-Paul de Gaudemar and R. Cuadrado Roura Juan (1991) '1957 to 1992: Moving Toward a Europe of Regions and Regional Policy', in Lloyd Rodwin and Hidehiko Sazanami (eds), *Industrial Change and Regional Economic Transformation: The Experience of Western Europe*, London: Harper Collins Academic, pp. 268–300.

Christofilopoulou, Paraskevi (1990) 'Decentralization in Post-Authoritarian Greece', unpub. Ph.D thesis, LSE.

Chryssochoou, D. N., M. J. Tsinisizelis, St. Stavridis and K. Ifantis (1999) *Theory and Reform in the European Union*, Manchester: Manchester University Press.

Clogg, Richard (1979) *A Short History of Modern Greece*, Cambridge: Cambridge University Press.

Coleman, James S. (1988) 'Social Capital in the Creation of Human Capital', *American Journal of Sociology*, 94, Supplement, 95–120.

Coleman, James S. (1990) *Foundations of Social Theory*, chs 8, 12, Cambridge MA: Belknap Press of Harvard University Press.

Cooke, Philip (1996) 'Policy Networks, Innovation Networks and Regional Policy: A Review of the Literature and an Example from South Wales', in H. Heinelt and Randall Smith (eds), *Policy Networks and European Structural Funds*, Aldershot: Avebury.

Croxford, G. J., M. Wise and B. S. Chalkley (1987) 'The Reform of the European Regional Development Fund: A Preliminary Assessment', *Journal of Common Market Studies*, 26: 1, 25–37.

Diamandouros, Nikiforos (1994) *Cultural Dualism and Political Change in Postauthoritarian Greece*, Estudio/Working Paper 1994/50, Madrid: Juan March Institute.

DiMaggio, Paul and Walter Powell (1991) 'Introduction', in Powell and DiMaggio (eds), *The New Institutionalism in Organizational Analysis*, Chicago: University of Chicago Press.

Dogan, Mattei and Dominique Pelassy, (1990) *How to Compare Nations: Strategies in Comparative Politics*, 2nd edition, New Jersey: Chatham House.

Dowding, Keith M. (1991) *Rational Choice and Political Power*, Aldershot: Edward Elgar.

Dowding, Keith M. (1994a) 'The Compatibility of Behaviouralism, Rational Choice and "New Institutionalism"', *Journal of Theoretical Politics*, 6: 1, 105–17.

Dowding, Keith M. (1994b) *Policy Networks*: Don't Stretch a Good Idea Too Far, paper presented to the Policy Communities/Policy Networks Workshop of the PSA Conference, University of Swansea, 29–31 March.

Dowding, Keith M. (1996) *Power*, Buckingham: Open University Press.

Dunford, M. and G. Kafkalas (1992) 'The Global-local Interplay, Corporate Geographies and Spatial Development Strategies in Europe', in M. Dunford and G. Kafkalas (eds), *Cities and Regions in the New Europe: The Global-local Interplay and Spatial Development Strategies* London: Belhaven Press.

Dunleavy, Patrick (1991) *Democracy, Bureaucracy and Public Choice: Economic Explanations in Political Science*, London: Harvester Wheatsheaf.

Evans, Peter (1996a) 'Introduction: Development Strategies across the Public-Private Divide', *World Development*, 24: 6, 1033–7.

Evans, Peter (1996b) 'Government Action, Social Capital and Development: Reviewing the Evidence on Synergy', *World Development*, 24: 6, 1119–32.

Fellmeth, Aaron Xavier (1996) 'Social Capital in the United States and Taiwan: Trust or Rule of Law?', *Development Policy Review*, 14, 151–71.

Filias, Vassilis (1974) *Society and Power in Greece: The Spurious Civil Class-Formation 1800–1864*, Athens: Makryonitis (in Greek).

Finas, K. (1981) *The Trade in Dodecanese*, Dodecanese Chamber: Rhodes (in Greek).

Finnemore, Martha (1996) 'Norms, Culture, and World Politics: Insights from Sociology's Institutionalism', *International Organization*, 50: 2, 325–47.

Flogaitis, S. (1987) *The Greek Administrative System*, Athens: Sakkoulas (in Greek).

Fox, Jonathan (1996) 'How Does Civil Society Thicken? The Political Construction of Social Capital in Rural Mexico', *World Development*, 24: 6, 1089–103.

Gambetta, Diego (1988) 'Can We Trust Trust?', in D. Gambetta (ed.), *Trust: Making and Breaking Cooperative Relations*, Oxford: Blackwell, pp. 213–38.

Garmise, Shari O. (1995a) 'Institutional Networks and Industrial Restructuring: Local Initiatives toward the Textile Industry in Nottingham and Prato', unpublished Ph.D thesis, LSE.

Garmise, Shari O. (1995b) 'Economic development strategies in Emilia-Romagna', in Martin Rhodes (ed.), *The Regions and the New Europe: Patterns in Core and Periphery Development*, Manchester: Manchester University Press.

Garofoli, Gioacchino (1992) 'Endogenous Development and Southern Europe: An Introduction', in G. Garofoli (ed.), *Endogenous Development and Southern Europe*, Aldershot: Avebury, pp. 1–13.

Garrett, Geoffrey and George Tsebelis (1996) 'An Institutional Critique of Intergovernmentalism', *International Organization*, 50: 2, pp. 269–99.

Getimis, P. (1989), 'Development Issues and Local Regulation: The Case of the Dodecanese prefecture', in K. Psychopedis and P. Getimis (eds), *Regulation of Local Problems*, Athens: Foundation for Mediterranean Studies (in Greek).

Giddens, Antony (1984) *The Constitution of Society*, Cambridge, Polity Press.

Goldberg, Ellis (1996) 'Thinking About How Democracy Works', *Politics and Society*, 24: 1, 7–18.

Goldsmith, Mike (1993) 'The Europeanization of Local Government', *Urban Studies*, 30: 4/5, 683–99.

Grabher, Gernot (1993) 'The Weakness of Strong Ties: The Lock-in of Regional Development in the Ruhr Area', in G. Grabher (ed.), *The Embedded Firm: On the Socioeconomics of Industrial Networks*, London: Routledge, pp. 255–77.

Granovetter, Mark (1973) 'The Strength of Weak Ties', *American Journal of Sociology*, 78: 6, 1360–80.

Granovetter, Mark (1985) 'Economic Action and Social Structure: The Problem of Embeddedness', *American Journal of Sociology*, 91: 3, 481–510.

Granovetter, Mark (1993) 'The Nature of Economic Relationships', in R. Swedberg (ed.), *Explorations in Economic Sociology*, New York: Russell Sage Foundation, pp. 3–41.

Green, Donald P. and Ian Shapiro (1994) *Pathologies of Rational Choice Theory: A Critique of Applications in Political Science*, New Haven: Yale University Press.

Grote, Juergen R. (1997) *'Interorganizational Networks and Social Capital Formation in the "South of the South"'*, Working Paper, RSC, No 97/38 Florence: EUI.

Haas, E. B. (1958) *The Uniting of Europe: Political, Social and Economic Forces 1950–1957*, London: Stevens and Sons.

Haas, Peter M. (1992) 'Introduction: Epistemic Communities and International Policy Coordination', *International Organization* Special Issue, 46: 1, 1–35.

Haas, Peter M. (1998) 'Compliance with EU Directives: Insights from International Relations and Comparative Politics', *Journal of European Public Policy*, 5: 1, 17–37.

Hadjimichalis, Costis (1987) *Uneven Development and Regionalism: State, Territory and Class in Southern Europe*, London: Croom Helm.

Hadjimichalis, Costis (1994) 'The Fringes of Europe and EU Integration: A View from the South', *European Urban and Regional Studies*, 1: 1, 19–29.

Hall, Peter A. (1993) 'Policy Paradigms, Social Learning and the State: The Case of Economic Policymaking in Britain', *Comparative Politics*, 25, 275–96.

Hall, Peter A. and Rosemary C. R. Taylor (1996) 'Political Science and the Three New Institutionalisms', *Political Studies*, 44, 936–57.

Hamilton, I. (1986) (ed.), *Industrialization in Developing and Peripheral Regions*, London: Croom Helm.

Harvie, Christopher (1994) *The Rise of Regional Europe*, London: Routledge.

Heller, Patrick (1996) 'Social Capital as a Product of Class Mobilization and State Intervention: Industrial Workers in Kerala, India', *World Development*, 24: 6, 1055–71.

Hirst, P., and J. Zeitlin (1992) 'Flexible Specialisation versus Post-Fordism: Theory, Evidence, and Policy Implications' in M. Storper and A. J. Scott (eds), *Pathways to Industrialisation and Regional Development*, London: Routledge, 70–115.

Hix, Simon (1998) 'The Study of the European Union II: The "New Governance" Agenda and its Rival', *Journal of European Public Policy*, 5: 1, 38–65.

Hix, Simon (1999) *The Political System of the European Union*, London: Macmillan.

Hoffmann, S. (1966) 'Obstinate or obsolete? The Fate of the Nation-State and the Case of Western Europe', *Daedalus*, 95, 862–915.

Holland, S. (1976) *Capital Against Regions*, London: Macmillan.

Holland, S. (1980) *Uncommon Market: Capital, Class and Power in the European Community*, New York: St. Martin's Press.

Hooghe, Liesbet and Michael Keating (1994) 'The Politics of European Union Regional Policy', *Journal of European Public Policy*, 1: 3, 367–93.

Hooghe, Liesbet (1995) 'Subnational Mobilization in the European Union', *West European Politics*, 18: 3, 175–98.

Hooghe, Liesbet (1996) 'Building a Europe with the Regions: The Changing Role of the European Commission', in L. Hooghe (ed.), *Cohesion Policy and European Integration: Building Multi-Level Governance*, Oxford: Oxford University Press, pp. 89–126.

Hooghe, Liesbet and Gary Marks (1997) *The Making of a Polity: The Struggle over European Integration*, paper presented at the 25th ECPR-Joint Sessions, University of Bern, February.

Inglehart, R. (1988) 'The Renaissance of Political Culture', *American Political Science Review*, Vol. 82, No 4, pp. 1203–30.

Ioakimidis, P. C. (1996) 'EU Cohesion Policy in Greece: The Tension Between Bureaucratic Centralism and Regionalism', in Liesbet Hooghe (ed.), *Cohesion Policy and European Integration: Building Multi-Level Governance*, Oxford: Oxford University Press, pp. 342–63.

Jeffery, Charlie (1995) 'Whither the Committee of the Regions? Reflections on the Committee's Opinion on the Revision of the Treaty on European Union', *Regional and Federal Studies*, 1: 2, 247–57.

Jeffery, Charlie (1997) *Sub-National Authorities and European Integration: Moving Beyond the Nation-State?*, paper presented at the Fifth Biennial International Conference, European Community Studies Association, 29 May–1 June 1997, Seattle, USA.

Jenkins-Smith, Hank C. and Paul A. Sabatier (1993) 'The Dynamics of Policy-Oriented Learning', in Paul A. Sabatier and Hank C. Jenkins-smith (eds), *Policy Change and Learning: An Advocacy Coalition Approach*, Boulder: Westview Press, pp. 41–56.

Jessop, Bob (1994) 'Post-Fordism and the State', in A. Amin (ed.), *Post-Fordism: A Reader*, Oxford: Blackwell, pp. 251–79.

John, Peter (1994) 'What is the European function?', *Local Government Policy Making*, 20: 5, 11–13.

Kardasis, V. A. (1987) *Syros: Crossroads of Eastern Mediterranean (1832–1857)*, Athens: Cultural Foundation of National Bank of Greece (in Greek).

Kassim, Hussein (1994) 'Policy Networks, Networks and European Union Policy Making: A Sceptical View', *West European Politics*, 17: 4, 15–27.

Kazakos, P. (1991), *Greece between Adjustment and Marginalization*, Athens: Diatton (in Greek).

Keating, Michael (1996) *The Invention of Regions: Political Restructuring and Territorial Government in the Western Europe*, paper presented at the ECPR Joint Sessions of Workshops, Oslo, 29 March to 3 April.

Kenis, Patrick and Volker Schneider (1991) 'Policy Networks and Policy Analysis: Scrutinizing a New Analytical Toolbox', in Bernd Marin and Renate Mayntz (eds), *Policy Networks: Empirical Evidence and Theoretical Considerations*, Colorado: Westview Press.

Keohane, Robert O. and Stanley Hoffmann (1991) 'Institutional Change in Europe in the 1980s' in Robert O. Keohane and Stanley Hoffmann (eds), *The New European Community: Decisionmaking and Institutional Change*, Oxford: Westview Press, pp. 1–39.

Klausen, K. and M. Goldsmith, (1997) 'Conclusion: Local Government and the European Union', in M. Goldsmith, K. Klausen (eds), *European Integration and Local Government*, Cheltenham: Edward Elgar

Knoke, David (1990) *Political Networks: The Structural Perspective*, Cambridge MA: Cambridge University Press.

Knoke, D. and J. H. Kuklinski (1982) *Network Analysis*, Beverly Hills: Sage Publications.

Kohler-Koch, Beate (1996) 'Catching up with Change: The Transformation of Governance in the European Union', *Journal of European Public Policy*, 3: 3, 359–80.

Konsolas, N. (1985), *Regional Economic Policy: (I) An Overview*, Athens: Papazisis (in Greek).

Konsolas, N. (1992) 'EEC Regional Policy and the Integrated Mediterranean Programmes', in Markku Tykkylainen (ed.), *Development Issues and Strategies in the New Europe*, Aldershot: Avebury.

Konsolas, N., A. Papadaskalopoulos, K. Ranos and E. Sidiropoulos (1993) *Regional Prospects in Greece: A GREMI-EEC Research Project-National Report*, Athens: Regional Development Institute – RDI.

Kontogiorgis, G. (1982), *Social Dynamics and Political Self-Government: The Greek Communes under Turkish Occupation*, Athens: Nea Synora (in Greek).

Kontogiorgis, G. (1985), *Political System and Politics*, Athens: Polytypo (in Greek).

Krugman, Paul R. and A. J. Venables (1990) 'Integration and the Competitiveness of Peripheral Industry', in C. Bliss and J. B. de Makedo (eds), *Unity with diversity in the European economy: the Community's Southern frontier*, Cambridge: Cambridge University Press, pp. 56–75.

Leonardi, Robert (1995a) *Convergence, Cohesion and Integration in the European Union*, London: Macmillan.

Leonardi, Robert (1995b) 'Regional Development in Italy: Social Capital and the Mezzogiorno', *Oxford Review of Economic Policy*, 11: 2, 165–79.

Leonardi, R. and S. Garmise, (1993) 'Sub-National Elites and the European Community', in R. Leonardi (ed.), *The Regions and the European Community: The Regional Response to the Single Market in the Underdeveloped Areas*, London: Frank Cass, pp. 247–74.

Levi, Margaret (1996) 'Social and Unsocial Capital: A Review Essay of Robert Putnam's *Making Democracy Work*', *Politics and Society*, 24: 1, 45–55.

Lindberg, L. N. and S. A. Scheingold (1970) *Europe's Would-Be Polity: Patterns of Change in the European Community*, Harvard: Harvard University Press.

Lindberg, L. N. and S. A. Scheingold (eds), (1971) *Regional Integration: Theory and Research*, Harvard: Harvard University Press.

Lipietz, Alain (1987) *Mirages and Miracles: The Crises of Global Fordism*, Norfolk: Verso.

Logothetis, M. (1983), *The Economy of the Dodecanese in 1981–82*, Dodecanese Chamber: Rhodes (in Greek).

Lorenz, Edward H. (1992) 'Trust, Community and Cooperation: Toward a theory of Industrial Districts', in M. Storper and A. J. Scott (eds.), *Pathways to Industrialisation and Regional Development*, London: Routledge, pp. 195–204.

Loughlin, J. (1996) 'Representing Regions in Europe: The Committee of the Regions', *Regional and Federal Studies*, 6: 2, 147–65.

Lundvall, Bengt A. (ed.) (1992) *National Systems of Innovation: Towards a Theory of Innovation and Interactive Learning*, London: Pinter.

Lyberaki, Antigone (1993) 'Greece–EC Comparative Economic Performance: Convergence or Divergence?', in Harry J. Psomiades and Stavros B. Thomadakis (eds), *Greece, the New Europe, and the Changing International Order*, New York: Pella, pp. 179–216.

Lyrintzis, Christos (1993) 'PASOK in Power: From "Change" to Disenchantment', in Richard Clogg (ed.), *Greece, 1981–89: The Populist Decade*, London: Macmillan, pp. 26–46.

March, James and Johan Olsen (1989) *Rediscovering Institutions: The Organizational Basis of Politics*, New York: Free Press.

Marin, Bernd (1990) 'Introduction', in Bernd Marin (ed.), *Governance and Generalized Exchange: Self-organizing Policy Networks in Action*, Frankfurt: Campus Verlag, pp. 13–25.

Marin, Bernd and Renate Mayntz (1991) 'Introduction: Studying Policy Networks', in Marin and Mayntz (eds), *Policy Networks: empirical evidence and theoretical considerations*, Frankfurt: Campus Verlag.

Marks, G. (1992) 'Structural Policy in the European Community', in A. Sbragia (ed.), *Euro-politics, Institutions and Policy-making in the 'New' European Community*, Washington D. C.: The Brookings Institution, pp. 191–224.

Marks, G. (1993) 'Structural Policy and Multilevel Governance in the EC', in A. Cafruny and Glenda Rosenthal (eds), *The State of the European Community: The Maastricht debates and Beyond*, vol. 2 London: Longman, pp. 391–410.

Marks, Gary (1996) 'Exploring and Explaining Variation in EU Cohesion Policy', in Liesbet Hooghe (ed.), *Cohesion Policy and European Integration: Building Multi-Level Governance*, Oxford: Oxford University Press, pp. 367–422.

Marks, Gary, Francois Nielsen, Leonard Ray, and Jane Salk (1996a) 'Competencies, Cracks and Conflicts: Regional Mobilization in the European Union', in Gary Marks. Fritz W. Scharpf, Philippe Schmitter and Wolfgang Streeck (eds), *Governance in the European Union*, London: Sage Publications, pp. 40–63.

Marks, Gary, Liesbet Hooghe, and Kermit Blank (1996b) 'European Integration from the 1980s: State-Centric v. Multi-level Governance', *Journal of Common Market Studies*, 34: 3, 341–78.

Mavrogordatos, George (1988), *Between Pityokamptes and Prokroustes: Employers' Organizations in Contemporary Greece*, Athens: Odysseas (in Greek).

Mavrogordatos, George (1993), 'Civil Society under Populism', in Richard Clogg (ed.), *Greece, 1981–89: The Populist Decade*, London: Macmillan, pp. 47–64.

Mazey, Sonia and Jeremy Richardson (1993) 'Introduction: Transference of Power, Decision Rules, and Rules of the Game', in Sonia Mazey and Jeremy Richardson (eds), *Lobbying in the European Community* Oxford: Oxford University Press, pp. 3–26.

McKay, David (1999) 'The Political Sustainability of European Monetary Union', *British Journal of Political Science*, 29: 3, 463–85.

Metcalfe, Les (1981) 'Designing Precarious Partnerships', in P. C. Nystrom and W. H. Starbuck (eds), *Handbook of Organizational Design: Vol. 1; Adapting Organizations to their Environments*, Oxford: Oxford University Press, pp. 503–30.

Mitsos, Achilleas (1995) *The Community's Redistributive and Development Role in the Post-Maastricht era*, mimeo.

Moe, Terry M. (1990) 'Political Institutions: The Neglected Side of the Story', *Journal of Law, Economics, and Organization*, 6, Special Issue, 213–53.

Molle, W. and R. Cappellin (eds) (1988) *Regional Impact of Community Policies in Europe*, Avebury: Aldershot.

Moravcsik, A. (1991) 'Negotiating the Single European Act', in Robert O. Keohane and Stanley Hoffmann (eds), *The New European Community: Decisionmaking and Institutional Change*, Oxford: Westview Press, pp. 41–84.

Moravcsik, A. (1993) 'Preferences and Power in the European Community: A Liberal Intergovernmentalist Approach', *Journal of Common Market Studies*, 31: 4, 473–524.

Moravcsik, A. (1995) 'Liberal Intergovernmentalism and Integration: A Rejoinder', *Journal of Common Market Studies*, 33: 4, 611–28.

Morgan, Kevin (1992) 'Innovating by Networking: New Models of Corporate and Regional Development, in M. Dunford and G. Kafkalas (eds), *Cities and*

Regions in the New Europe: The Global-local Interplay and Spatial Development Strategies, London: Belhaven Press.

Mouzelis, Nicos P. (1978) *Modern Greece: Facets of Underdevelopment*, London: Macmillan.

Mouzelis, Nicos P. (1986) *Politics in the Semi-Periphery: Early Parliamentarism and Late Industrialisation in the Balkans and Latin America*, London: Macmillan.

Mouzelis, Nicos P. (1995) 'Greece in the Twenty-first Century: Institutions and Political Culture', in Dimitri Constas and Theofanis G. Stavrou (eds), *Greece Prepares for the Twenty-first Century*, Washington, DC: Johns Hopkins University Press and Woodrow Wilson Center Press, pp. 17–34.

Myrdal, Gunnar (1957) *Economic Theory and Under-developed Regions*, London: Duckworth.

Nanetti, Raffaela Y. (1990) *The Community's Structural Funds and the Search for a European Regional Policy*, paper presented at the annual meeting of the American Political Science Association, August 30–September 2, San Francisco.

Nanetti, Raffaella Y. (1996) 'EU Cohesion and Territorial Restructuring in the Member States', in Liesbet Hooghe (ed.), *Cohesion Policy and European Integration: Building Multi-Level Governance*, Oxford: Oxford University Press, pp. 59–88.

North, Douglass C. (1990) *Institutions, Institutional Change and Economic Performance*, Cambridge: Cambridge University Press.

Olson, Mancur (1971) *The Logic of Collective Action: Public Goods and the Theory of Groups*, Cambridge MA: Harvard University Press.

Olson, Mancur (1982) *The Rise and Decline of Nations: Economic Growth, Stagflation and Social Rigidities*, New Haven, Conn: Yale University Press.

Oppenheim, A. N. (1996) *Questionnaire Design, Interviewing and Attitude Measurement*, London: Pinter.

Ostrom, Elinor (1986) 'An agenda for the study of institutions', *Public Choice*, 48, pp. 3–25.

Ostrom, Elinor (1990) *Governing the Commons: The Evolution of Institutions for Collective Action*, Cambridge, MA: Cambridge University Press.

Ostrom, Elinor (1992) 'Community and the Endogenous Solution of Commons Problems', *Journal of Theoretical Politics*, 4: 3, 343–51.

Ostrom, Elinor (1995a) 'Self-organization and Social Capital', *Industrial and Corporate Change*, 4: 1, 131–59.

Ostrom, Elinor (1995b) 'Constituting Social Capital and Collective Action', in Robert Keohane and Elinor Ostrom (eds), *Local Commons and Global Interdependence: Heterogeneity and Cooperation in Two Domains*, London: Sage Publications, pp. 125–60.

Ostrom, Elinor (1996) 'Crossing the Great Divide: Coproduction, Synergy and Development', *World Development*, 24: 6, 1073–87.

Ostrom, Elinor (1998) 'A Behavioral Approach to the Rational Choice Theory of Collective Action', *American Political Science Review*, 92: 1, 1–22.

Papageorgiou, Fouli and Susannah Verney (1993) 'Regional Planning and the Integrated Mediterranean Programmes in Greece', in R. Leonardi (ed.), *The Regions and the European Community: The Regional Response to the Single Market in the Underdeveloped Areas*, London: Frank Cass, pp. 139–61.

Paraskevopoulos, C. J. (1988) *Interregional Structure of the Manufacturing Branches in Greece (1963–84) and the Impact of the Institutional Framework of Regional Development*, M Phil. thesis, Athens: RDI (in Greek).

Paraskevopoulos, C. J. (1997) 'Social Capital and Learning Institutional Networks: Making Sense of Subsidiarity in European Regional Policy', *TOPOS Review of Urban and Regional Studies*, Summer, 3–29 (in Greek).

Paraskevopoulos, C. J. (1998a) 'Social Capital and the Public/Private Divide in Greek Regions', *West European Politics*, 21: 2, 154–77.

Paraskevopoulos, C. J. (1998b) 'Social Capital, Institutional Learning and European Regional Policy: Evidence from Greece', *Regional and Federal Studies*, 8: 3, 31–64.

Paraskevopoulos, C. J. (1998c) *Institutional Learning and Adaptation: Redefining the 'Limits' of the Integration Process in Europe with Evidence from Structural Policy*, paper presented to the 26th ECPR-Joint Sessions Workshop on 'Institutional Analyses of European Integration', University of Warwick, 23–8 March.

Parri, Leonardo (1989) 'Territorial Political Exchange in Federal and Unitary Countries', *West European Politics*, 12: 3, 197–215.

Perroux, F. (1955) 'Note sur la notion de Pole de Croissance', *Economie Appliquée*, 7.

Peters, Guy B. (1999) *Institutional Theory in Political Science: The 'New Institutionalism'*, London: Pinter.

Peterson, John (1995) 'Policy Networks and European Union Policy Making: A Reply to Kassim', *West European Politics*, 18: 2, 389–407.

Peterson, John (1995) 'Decision-making in the European Union: Towards a Framework for Analysis', *Journal of European Public Policy*, 2: 1, 69–93.

Petropoulos, John (1968) *Politics and Statecraft in the Kingdom of Greece 1833–1843*, Princeton: Princeton University Press.

Pierson, Paul (1996) 'The Path to European Integration: A Historical Institutionalist Analysis', *Comparative Political Studies*, 29: 2, 123–63.

Pierson, Paul (1997) *Increasing Returns, Path Dependence and the Study of Politics*, Jean Monnet Chair Papers, 44, Badia Fiesolana: European University Institute – The Robert Schuman Centre.

Piore, M. J. and C. Sabel (1984) *The Second Industrial Divide: Possibilities for Prosperity*, New York: Basic Books.

Piore, M. J. (1992) 'Technological Trajectories and the Classical Revival in Economics', in M. Storper and A. J. Scott (eds.) *Pathways to Industrialisation and Regional Development*, London: Routledge, pp. 157–70.

Polanyi, Karl (1944) *The Great Transformation: The Political and Economic Origins of Our Time*, Boston: Beacon Press.

Pollack, Mark A. (1995) 'Regional Actors in an Intergovernmental Play: The Making and Implementation of EC Structural Policy', in Carolyn Rhodes and Sonia Mazey (eds), *The State of European Union, Vol. 3: Building a European Polity?*, Boulder, Colo: Lynne Rienner Publishers, pp. 361–90.

Pollack, Mark A. (1996) 'The New Institutionalism and EC Governance; The Promise and Limits of Institutional Analysis', *Governance*, 9: 4, 429–58.

Pollack, Mark A. (1997) 'Delegation, Agency, and Agenda Setting in the European Community', *International Organization*, 51: 1, 99–134.

Powell, Walter, W. (1990) 'Neither Market nor Hierarchy: Network Forms of Organization', in *Research in Organizational Behaviour*, 12, 295–336.

Psychopedis, Kosmas and Panayotis Getimis (1989) *Regulation of Local Problems*, Athens: Foundation for Mediterranean Studies (in Greek).

Putnam, Robert D. (1995a) 'Bowling Alone: America's Declining Social Capital', *Journal of Democracy*, 6: 1, 65–78.

Putnam, Robert D. (1995b) 'Tuning In, Tuning Out: The Strange Disappearance of Social Capital in America', *Political Science and Politics*, 28: 4, 664–83.

Putnam, Robert D. with R. Leonardi and R. Y. Nanetti (1993) *Making Democracy Work: Civic Traditions in Modern Italy*, Princeton: Princeton University Press.

Rhodes, Martin (1995) 'Conclusion: The Viability of Regional Strategies' in Martin Rhodes (ed.), *The Regions and the New Europe: Patterns in Core and Periphery Development*, Manchester: Manchester University Press.

Rhodes, R. A. W. and David Marsh (1992) 'New Directions in the Study of Policy Networks', *European Journal of Political Research*, 21, 181–205.

Rhodes, R. A. W., Ian Bache and Stephen George (1996) 'Policy Networks and Policy-Making in the European Union: A Critical Appraisal', in Liesbet Hooghe (ed.) *Cohesion Policy and European Integration: Building Multi-Level Governance*, Oxford: Oxford University Press, pp. 367–87.

Richardson, Jeremy (1996) *Actor Based Models of National and EU Policy-Making*, discussion paper, No 103, Department of Government, University of Essex, April.

Robson, P. (1987) *The Economics of International Integration*, London: Allen and Unwin.

Rokkan, S. and D. W. Urwin (1983) *Economy, Territory, Identity: Politics of West European Peripheries*, London: Sage.

Rose, Richard (1990) 'Inheritance Before Choice in Public Policy', *Journal of Theoretical Politics*, 2: 3, 263–91.

Sabatier, Paul A. (1993) 'Policy Change over a Decade or More', in Paul A. Sabatier and Hank C. Jenkins-Smith (eds), *Policy Change and Learning: An Advocacy Coalition Approach*, Boulder: Westview Press, pp. 13–39.

Sabel, Charles F. (1993a) 'Constitutional Ordering in Historical Context', in Fritz Scharpf (ed.), *Games in Hierarchies and Networks: Analytical and Empirical Approaches to the Study of Governance Institutions*, Frankfurt/Main: Campus Verlag, pp. 65–123.

Sabel, Charles F. (1993b) 'Studied Trust: Building New Forms of Cooperation in a Volatile Economy', in R. Swedberg (ed.), *Explorations in Economic Sociology*, New York: Russell Sage Foundation, pp. 104–44.

Sabel, Charles F. (1994a) 'Flexible Specialisation and the Re-emergence of Regional Economies', in Ash Amin (ed.), *Post-Fordism: A Reader*, Oxford: Blackwell, pp. 101–56.

Sabel, Charles F. (1994b) 'Learning by Monitoring: The Institutions of Economic Development', in N. J. Smelser and Richard Swedberg (eds), *The Handbook of Economic Sociology*, Princeton: Princeton University Press.

Sabetti, Filippo (1996), 'Path Dependency and Civic Culture: Some Lessons From Italy About Interpreting Social Experiments', *Politics and Society*, 24: 1, 19–44.

Scharpf, Fritz W. (1989) 'Decision Rules, Decision Styles and Policy Choices', *Journal of Theoretical Politics*, 1: 2, 149–76.

Scharpf, Fritz W. (1991) 'Games Real Actors Could Play: The Challenge of Complexity', *Journal of Theoretical Politics*, 3: 3, 277–304.

Scharpf, Fritz W. (1993) 'Coordination in Hierarchies and Networks', in Fritz Scharpf (ed.), *Games in Hierarchies and Networks: Analytical and Empirical*

Approaches to the Study of Governance Institutions, Frankfurt/Main: Campus Verlag, pp. 125–65.

Scharpf, Fritz W. (1994) *Community and Autonomy: Multilevel Policy-Making in the European Union*, Working Paper, RSC, No 94/1, Florence: EUI.

Schmidt, Susanne K. (1996) 'Sterile Debates and Dubious Generalizations: European Integration Theory Tested by Telecommunications and Electricity', *Journal of Public Policy*, 16: 3, 233–71.

Schmitter, Philippe C. (1986) 'An Introduction to Southern European Transitions from Authoritarian Rule: Italy, Greece, Portugal, Spain, and Turkey', in Guillermo O'Donnell, Philippe C. Schmitter, and Laurence Whitehead (eds), *Transitions from Authoritarian Rule: Southern Europe*, London: The Johns Hopkins University Press.

Schmitter, Philippe C. (1991) *The European Community as an Emergent and Novel Form of Political Domination*, Working paper 26, Centre for Advanced Study in the Social Sciences, Madrid: Juan March Institute.

Schmitter, Philippe C. (1995) 'Organized Interests and Democratic Consolidation in Southern Europe', in Richard Gunther, P. Nikiforos Diamandouros and Hans-Jurgen Puhle (eds), *The Politics of Democratic Consolidation: Southern Europe in Comparative Perspective*, London: The Johns Hopkins University Press.

Schmitter, Philippe C. (1996) *Is It Really Possible to Democratize the Euro-Polity?*, paper presented at the 24th ECPR Joint Sessions of Workshops, Oslo, 29 March to 3 April.

Schneider, Gerald and Lars-Erik Cederman (1994) 'The Change of Tide in Political Cooperation: A Limited Information Model of European Integration', *International Organization*, 48: 4, 633–62.

Scott, John (1994) *Social Network Analysis: A Handbook*, London: Sage.

Scott, A., J. Peterson and D. Millar (1994) 'Subsidiarity: A "Europe of the Regions" v. the British Constitution?', *Journal of Common Market Studies*, 32: 1, 47–67.

Shepsle, Kenneth A. (1989) 'Studying Institutions: Some Lessons from the Rational Choice Approach', *Journal of Theoretical Politics*, 1: 2, 131–47.

Singleton, Sara and Michael Taylor (1992) 'Common Property, Collective Action and Community', *Journal of Theoretical Politics*, 4: 3, 309–24.

Siphnaeou, Evridiki (1996), *Lesbos: Economic and Social History* (1840–1912), Athens: Trochalia (in Greek).

Stokowski, Patricia A. (1994) *Leisure in Society: A Network Structural Perspective*, London: Mansell Publishing Limited.

Storper, Michael (1995) 'The Resurgence of Regional Economies, Ten Years Later: The Region as a Nexus of Untraded Interdependencies', *European Urban and Regional Studies*, 2: 3, 191–221.

Streeck, Wolfgang and P. C. Schmitter (1991) 'From National Corporatism to Transnational Pluralism: Organised Interests in the Single European Market', *Politics and Society*, 19: 2, 133–64.

Tarrow, Sidney (1974) *Partisanship and Political Exchange in French and Italian Politics: A Contribution to the Typology of Party Systems*, Sage Professional Papers in Contemporary Political Sociology, Series No 06-004, London: Sage.

Tarrow, Sidney (1977) *Between Center and Periphery: Grassroots Politicians in Italy and France*, New Haven: Yale University Press.

Tarrow, Sidney (1996) 'Making Social Science Work Across Space and Time: A Critical Reflection on Robert Putnam's *Making Democracy Work*', *American Political Science Review*, 90: 2, 389–97.

Tatsos, N. (1987), *Decentralization of Taxation: The Tax System of Local Government in Greece*, Athens: Greek Agency for Local Development and Self-Government – EETAA (in Greek).

Tatsos, N. (1988), *State Grants to Local Government*, Athens: EETAA (in Greek).

Tatsos, N. (1989), *The Taxation of Immovable Property as a Means of Financing Local Government*, Athens: EETAA (in Greek).

Taylor, Paul (1991) 'The European Community and the state: assumptions, theories and propositions' *Review of International Studies*, 17: 109–25.

Taylor, Paul (1993) *International Organisation in the Modern World: the Regional and the Global process*, sec. 2, London: Pinter.

Teague, Paul (1995) 'Europe of the Regions and the Future of National Systems of Industrial Relations', in A. Amin and J. Tomaney (eds), *Behind the Myth of the European Union: Prospects for Cohesion*, London: Routledge.

Thelen, Kathleen and Sven Steinmo (1992) 'Historical Institutionalism in Comparative Politics', in Sven Steinmo, Kathleen Thelen and Frank Longstreth (eds), *Structuring Politics: Historical Institutionalism in Comparative Analysis*, Cambridge: Cambridge University Press, pp. 1–32.

Theodori-Markoyiannaki, E. (1986) *Basic Data per Prefecture and Region*, Athens: KEPE (in Greek).

Tsoukalas, Constantine (1986), *State, Society and Labour in Postwar Greece*, Athens: Themelio (in Greek).

Tsoukalas, Constantine (1995) 'Free Riders in Wonderland; or Of Greeks in Greece, in Dimitri Constas and Theofanis G. Stavrou (eds), *Greece Prepares for the Twenty-first Century*, Washington, DC: Johns Hopkins University Press and Woodrow Wilson Center Press, pp. 191–219.

Tsoukalis, Loukas (1993) *The New European Economy: The Politics and Economics of Integration*, Oxford: Oxford University Press.

Tsoukalis, Loukas (1998) *The European Agenda: Issues of Globalization, Equity and Legitimacy*, Jean Monnet Chair Papers, 49, Badia Fiesolana: European University Institute – The Robert Schuman Centre.

Verney, Susannah and Fouli Papageorgiou (1993) 'Prefecture Councils in Greece: Decentralization in the European Community Context', in R. Leonardi (ed.), *The Regions and the European Community: The Regional Response to the Single Market in the Underdeveloped Areas*, London: Frank Cass, pp. 109–38.

Watts, Ronald L. (1981) 'Federalism, Regionalism, and Political Integration', in D. M. Cameron (ed.), *Regionalism and Supranationalism: Challenges and Alternatives to the Nation – State in Canada and Europe*, Montreal: Institute for Research on Public Policy, pp. 3–19.

Whiteley, Paul, F. (1997) *Economic Growth and Social Capital*, paper presented at the 25th ECPR-Joint Sessions of Workshops, University of Bern, Switzerland, 28 February to 4 March, 1997.

Williamson, O. E. (1975) *Markets and Hierarchies: Analysis and Antitrust Implications*, New York: Free Press.

Williamson, Oliver E. (1995) 'Hierarchies, Markets and Power in the Economy: An Economic Perspective', *Industrial and Corporate Change*, 4: 1, 21–49.

Windhoff-Heritier, Adrienne (1991) 'Institutions, Interests and Political Choice', in Roland M. Czada and Adrienne Windhoff-Heritier (eds), *Political Choice:*

Institutions, Rules, and the Limits of Rationality, Frankfurt: Campus Verlag and Westview Press, pp. 27–52.

Windhoff-Heritier, Adrienne (1993) 'Policy Network Analysis: A Tool for Comparative Political Research', in Hans Keman (ed.), *Comparative politics: New directions in theory and method*, Amsterdam: VU University Press, pp. 143–60.

Yin, Robert K. (1994) *Case Study Research: Design and Methods*, Second Edition, London: Sage. (First edition 1939).

Official documents (European Union)

Commission of the European Communities (CEC) (1987) *Third Periodic Report on the Social and Economic Situation of the Regions of the Community*, Luxembourg: Office for Official Publications of the European Communities.

CEC (1990a) *Community Support Framework 1989–93 for the Development and Structural Adjustment of the Regions whose Development is Lagging Behind (Objective 1) GREECE*, Luxembourg: Office for Official Publications of the European Communities.

CEC (1990b) *European Regional Development Fund. Fourteenth Annual Report (1988)*. Luxembourg: Office for Official Publications of the European Communities.

CEC (1991) *Guide to the Community Initiatives*, Luxembourg: Office for Official Publications of the European Communities.

CEC (1992a) *The Community's Structural Interventions: Statistical Bulletin/No2*, Brussels: Directorate-General for the Coordination of Structural Policies – DG XXII, April.

CEC (1992b) *The Community's Structural Interventions: Statistical Bulletin/No4*, Brussels: Directorate-General for the Coordination of Structural Policies – DG XXII, December.

CEC (1992c) *Reform of the Structural Funds: A Tool to Promote Economic and Social Cohesion*, Luxembourg: Office for Official Publications of the European Communities.

CEC (1992d) *Commission's Decision on the Approval of the 1989–93 MOP for Northern Aegean Region*, Brussels.

CEC (1993) *Community Structural Funds 1994–99: Regulations and Commentary*, Luxembourg: Office for Official Publications of the European Communities.

CEC (1994a) *Competitiveness and Cohesion: Trends in the Regions. Fifth Periodic Report on the Social and Economic Situation and Development of the Regions in the Community*, Luxembourg: Office for Official Publications of the European Communities.

CEC (1994b) *Guide to the Community Initiatives 1994–99*, Luxembourg: Office for Official Publications of the European Communities.

CEC (1995) *Evaluation of the Community Support Frameworks for the Objective 1 Regions in the Period 1989–1993: Synthesis Report*, prepared by Price Waterhouse.

CEC (1997) *Agenda 2000. For a Stronger and Wider Union*, Supplement 5/97, Luxembourg: Office for Official Publications of the European Communities.

DG XVI (1992) *Action Plan for the Improvement of Inter-fund Synergy in Regional Multi-fund Operational Programmes and IMPs in Greece*, Athens: Urban and Regional Development and Policy – URDP.

EUROSTAT (1993) *TOURISM 1991, Annual Statistics*, Luxembourg: Office for Official Publications of the European Communities.

EUROSTAT (1995) *EC Tourism in the 1990s* – DG XXIII.

EUROSTAT (various years), REGIO *codebook and data bank*, Luxembourg: Office for Official Publications of the European Communities.

EUROSTAT (various years) *Regional Statistical Yearbook*, Luxembourg: Office for Official Publications of the European Communities.

Treaties Establishing the European Communities (1987), Luxembourg: Office for Official Publications of the European Communities.

The Unseen Treaty: Treaty on European Unity, (1992) Maastricht.

Official documents (Greece)

AIGAIO Ltd. (1995) *Final Report of the Project Manager of the Southern Aegean MOP 1989–93*, Ermoupolis, Syros (in Greek).

HELMICO S. A. & Tsekouras Ltd (1994), *Ex-ante Evaluation of the Southern Aegean Regional Operational Programme (ROP) 1994–99*, Athens (in Greek).

Ministry of the Aegean (1996), *Special Measures Programme for the Aegean Islands*, Athens (in Greek).

Ministry of the Interior, Public Administration and Decentralization (various years), *National and Prefectural Elections' Results*, Athens (in Greek).

Ministry of the Interior, Public Administration and Decentralization, (1996), *Statistical Bulletin of Public Sector Personnel; Census of 31 December 1994*, Athens (in Greek).

Ministry of National Economy (1992), *Modification of the Monitoring Committee for the First Northern Aegean MOP 1989–93*, Athens (in Greek).

Ministry of National Economy (1993a), *Evaluation of the Southern Aegean Islands Regional Operational Programme 1989–1993*, Athens: Tsekouras Ltd (in Greek).

Ministry of National Economy (1993b), *Evaluation of Northern Aegean Islands Regional Operational Programme (ROP) 1989–1993*, Athens and Mytilene: Ecotechnica (in Greek).

Ministry of National Economy (1994a), *Evaluation of the Integrated Mediterranean Programme – IMP – for the Aegean*, Athens: S.P.E.E.D Ltd (in Greek).

Ministry of National Economy (1994b), *Community Support Framework (CSF) 1994–99. Southern Aegean MOP: Ex-ante Evaluation*, Athens: S.P.E.E.D Ltd (in Greek).

Ministry of National Economy (1995), *Modification of the Monitoring Committee for the 2nd MOP for the Northern Aegean*, Athens (in Greek).

National Statistical Service of Greece (NSSG) (various years), *Population, Firms and Employment Censuses*, Athens (in Greek).

National Statistical Service of Greece (NSSG) (various years), *Tourism Statistics*, Athens (in Greek).

National Statistical Service of Greece (NSSG) (various years), *National-Regional Accounts*, Athens (in Greek).

Northern Aegean Regional Secretariat (1994) *Minutes of the First Meeting of the Monitoring Committee for the 1994–99 MOP*, Mytilene (in Greek).

Rhodes Hotel Owners' Association 1991, *40 Years: 1950–1990*, Rhodes (in Greek).

Index

absorption   161–2
  NAI   192–3, 195–8
  SAI   164–5, 167–9
adaptation   54–5, 58–9, 218–19
  economic structure, boundedness
      and: NAI   130–6; SAI   99–108
  institution-building, policy
      networks and: NAI   199–215;
      SAI   171–86
  social capital, learning and
      224–34
  state structures, local institutional
      capacity and   219–24
additionality   38, 39
adjacency matrices   62
administrative capacity   79–83
Aeoliki Development Agency   202,
  204, 207
agriculture
  NAI   99, 131, 132–4, 158, 190
  SAI   99, 105, 106–7
airports   158, 161
Ambelakia cooperative   91
Amin, A.   4, 23, 26
Anderson, J.J.   56, 57
Andrikopoulou, E.   69, 86, 87
Armstrong, H.   32
Association of Persons with Special
  Needs   123
Associations of Municipalities   71,
  79
  Chios   146, 211, 212
  Cyclades   119, 183
  Dodecanese   114, 178
  Lesbos   139–42, 206
  Samos   148, 214
Athanasiou, L.   131
Axelrod, R.   13, 18, 52

backwash effects   2
balanced reciprocity   18
Banfield, E.C.   24
Barro, R.J.   47

Bates, R.H.   11, 14, 14–15
Benington, J.   42
Bennett, R.J.   53
Berkowitz, S.D.   22
Bianchi, G.   44
binary comparison methodology
  59–63
Borgatti, S.P.   62
boundedness
  NAI   130–6
  SAI   99–108
Britain   33
Bulmer, S.   51
bureaucracy, quality of   79–83

Campbell, J.K.   92
capitalism, Greek   91–2
Cappellin, R.   1, 5, 6
Cederman, L.-E.   51
Central Association of Municipalities
  and Communes (CAMC)   71, 79
Central Autonomous Resources of
  Local Government   77
centrality   62, 230–1
  NAI   137–8, 200–3; Chios   145–6,
      210–11, 228; Lesbos   141–2,
      205–6; Samos   149, 214
  SAI   109–10, 173–4; Cyclades
      118–19, 183–4; Dodecanese
      113–14, 177–9
centralized states   57–8
centre-periphery relations   76–9
centre-periphery theories   3
Centre Union   98
Centres of Intensive Development
  Programmes   85
chambers of commerce
  Chios   144–5, 208–9, 211
  Cyclades   117–18, 183
  Dodecanese   111, 114, 176–7, 229
  Lesbos   139, 142
  Samos   149
change, stability and   26–9

Checkel, J.T.   49, 237
Cheshire, P.   32, 33, 34
Chios   155, 215, 217, 221, 230
   economic structure   134–5, 136
   implementation of CSF   196–7,
      197–8, 199
   institution-building, policy
      networks and adaptation
      208–12, 213
   institutions and institutional
      networks 144–8
   learning capacity   226, 227, 228
   local factors and political climate
      126–30
   NPCI   194, 196–7, 209, 223, 227,
      228
   social capital and civil society
      152, 153
Chios City Council   144, 146, 208–9,
   210–11, 212
Chios Municipal Development
   Agency 146, 202, 209, 211, 212
Christofilopoulou, P.   66, 68, 80,
   82
city councils   *see under individual
   names*
civic engagement   234, 237
   SAI   121–4
   social capital and   16–21
civil society   220, 234, 237
   and the cultural schism   90–3
   NAI   150–4
   SAI   121–4
   social capital and building   16–21
clientelism   64–83
   from local clientelism to state
      clientelism   65–9
   state clientelist corporatism
      69–76
Coalition of the Left   98, 129, 130
cohesion   38
Cohesion Fund   38–9, 40, 46
Coleman, J.S.   14, 16–17, 18
collective action   10–11
   rational actors and dilemmas of
      11–13
collective competitiveness   236
commerce   134–5
Committee of Regions (CoR)   38–9

Common Agricultural Policy (CAP)
   33, 195
common understanding of problems
   62–3, 225, 226, 228–9
communes   65–7, 79–80
communication and dialogue   9–10,
   62, 225–7
Communist Party of Greece (KKE)
   82, 128, 129, 130, 152–4
Community Initiatives (CIs)   38,
   39–40, 170, 198, 227
Community Interest Programmes
   (CIPs)   35, 38
Community Support Frameworks
   (CSFs)   37, 87, 89–90, 156,
      188
   planning and implementing:
      NAI   160–2, 190–9; SAI
      159–71
   private sector contribution   43–4,
      162–3, 194
comparative case study methodology
   59–63
conditionality   39
constructability   19
core-dominance hypothesis   45–6
corporatism, clientelist   69–76
council tax   106
Croxford, G.J.   33
cultural voluntary organizations
   123–4
cultural schism   90–3
cumulative causation theory   2
Cyclades   61, 125, 221, 222–3
   civil society   123–4, 234
   CSF   165–71
   economic structure   106–7
   institution-building, policy
      networks and adaptation
      181–6
   institutions and institutional
      networks   116–21, 230–1
   learning capacity   226, 227,
      229
   local characteristics and political
      climate   95–9
Cyclades Development Agency
   (CYDA)   109, 118, 182, 183–4,
      185

defence sector 132, 133
density 23–4, 27–8, 62, 173, 200–1,
    230
  Chios 145, 210
  Cyclades 118, 183
  Dodecanese 113, 177
  Lesbos 141, 205
  Samos 149, 214
  and the socialization function
    51–6
development axes 84
dialogue and communication 9–10,
    62, 225–7
Diamandouros, N. 90
distribution of functions 72–5
Dodecanese 61, 125, 232
  civil society 123–4, 234
  CSF 165–70
  economic structure 104–6
  institution-building, policy
    networks and adaptation
    175–81
  institutions and institutional
    networks 110–16
  learning capacity 225–7, 227–8,
    229
  local characteristics and political
    climate 95–9
  social capital, networks and
    learning 230–1
  state structure and local
    institutional capacity 221,
    222–3
Dodecanese Cooperative Bank
    112
Dodecanese Development Agency
    (DDA) 109, 114, 115, 173, 176,
    179, 221
Dogan, M. 60
domestic preference formation
    function 49–50
dominant actors 22–3
double convergence 3
Dowding, K. 22, 24, 25, 28
Dunford, M. 4

East Asia 19
economic and monetary union (EMU)
    32, 38, 40

economic structure
  NAI 130–6
  SAI 99–108
education 96, 127, 192
effectiveness gap 160–2, 190–9
elections 79–80
electric power supply 189
embeddedness 15, 236
employment
  NAI 133–4, 135
  SAI 99, 102–3, 104, 105
endogenous development 5–8
Ermoupolis City Council 118, 119,
    185
Ermoupolis Development Agency
    (ERMDA) 117, 182, 183–4,
    185
European Agricultural Guidance and
    Guarantee Fund (EAGGF) 33,
    35, 37
  MOP sub-programme 159, 167,
    191, 192–3
European Investment Bank (EIB)
    33
European Regional Development
    Fund (ERDF) 33–5, 36–7, 46
  MOP sub-programme 159, 166,
    168, 191, 192–3, 196–7
European regional policy 31–63,
    234–7
  emergence on the policy-making
    agenda 33–7
  and Europeanization of local
    systems of governance
    31–44
  methodology for study of social
    capital, institutional learning
    and 58–63
  NAI policy networks and
    adaptation 188–217
  SAI policy networks and adaptation
    156–87
  social capital, institutional
    networks and learning
    48–56
  state structure and local learning
    capacity 56–8
  and 'traditional' integration theory
    44–8

European Social Fund (ESF)   33, 35, 37
  MOP sub-programme   159, 166, 191, 192–3
Europeanization
  evaluating   229–34
  local systems of governance 31–44
  state structures, local institutional capacity and   219–24
  subnational governments   41–4
Evans, P.   19
exchange   24–6, 27–8
  general exchange networks 222–3, 230–2; NAI   136–50; SAI   108–21

financial Europeanization   42
Financial Instrument for Fisheries Guidance (FIFG)   40
financial resources   76–9
Finas, K.   105
Finnemore, M.   52
flexible specialization   3
Flogaitis, S.   80
fora for dialogue and communication 62, 225–7
Four Motors of Europe project   46
full Europeanization   43
functional networks   22–3, 53, 231, 232, 233
  intra-regional   23, 38–9
functions, distribution of   72–5

Gambetta, D.   12, 13, 20
game theory   11–13
Garmise, S.O.   4, 28, 33, 43, 45
  institutional networks and learning 8, 9
  types of network   22–3
Garofoli, G.   6, 7
Garrett, G.   51
GDP
  NAI   130–1, 132
  per capita GDP index   101, 131
  SAI   99–101, 103–4
general exchange networks   222–3, 230–2
  NAI   136–50
  SAI   108–21

generalized reciprocity   18
Germany   19–20, 47
Getimis, P.   97, 104, 106, 113, 122
  distribution of functions   74
  Public Investment Programme 78
  regional policy   86
global-local interplay   4
globalization   1–5
Goldsmith, M.   10, 41, 42, 59–60
governance   1–30
  globalization and local response 1–5
  re-conceptualizing regional governance   5–8
  social capital, institutional networks and learning debate 8–29; institutional networks and learning   21–9; new institutionalism   13–16; rational actors and dilemmas of collective action   11–13; social capital and civil society 16–21
governmental networks   22–3, 233
Grabher, G.   20, 24
Granovetter, M.   15, 24
graphs of network structure   62
  NAI   138–9, 203; Chios   147, 148, 212, 213; Lesbos   143, 144, 207, 208; Samos   150, 151, 215, 216
  SAI   110, 174–5; Cyclades   120–1, 185–6; Dodecanese   116, 179–80,181
Greece   59, 64–94
  civil society and cultural schism 90–3
  regional policy   84–90
  state structure and intergovernmental relations 64–83, 221–2; local clientelism and state clientelism   65–9; local government finance and centre-periphery relations 76–9; state clientelist corporatism   69–76; subnational political elites and quality of bureaucracy   79–83
growth-poles approach   2, 85

Haas, P.M. 25, 237
Hall, P.A. 8, 9, 14, 16
handicrafts 91–2
Harsanyi, J.C. 25
Harvey, J. 42
Harvie, C. 5
health-care organizations 123
historical new institutionalism
    15–16
Hix, S. 50
Holland, S. 2
hollowing out of the state 4
Hooghe, L. 41, 47
horizontal networks 57, 231
hotel owners' associations 111–12,
    118

incentives 86–7
Industrial Areas Network 85
industrial sector 99, 105, 132, 134–5
information 25
infrastructure
    NAI 189–90, 191–2
    SAI 158, 161, 166, 170
Inglehart, R. 90
institution-building 62, 225, 226,
    227–8
    NAI 199–215
    SAI 171–86
institutional capacity, local 219–24
institutional lock-in 24
institutional networks 8–29, 218,
    234–7
    evaluating Europeanization
        229–34
    and learning 21–9
    methodology of study 58–63
    NAI 136–50
    power and exchange 24–6
    SAI 108–21
    social capital, learning and in EU
        regional policy 48–56
    stability and change 26–9
institutional thickness *see* density;
    thickness
integrated approach to development
    35
Integrated Mediterranean
    Programmes (IMPs) 35–6, 43–4,
    46, 87, 89–90

Aegean Islands 156–9; NAI
    158–9, 188–90; SAI 158–9,
    175–6, 181–2
integration theory 44–56, 234–7
    'socializing' rational-choice new
        institutionalism in 48–56
    'traditional' 44–8
intergovernmental relations 57
    and state structure in Greece
        64–83
intergovernmentalism 45–8
INTERREG Initiative 198, 209
interregional networks 22, 23, 232,
    233
intra-regional functional networks
    23, 28–9
intra-regional networks 22, 23, 232,
    233
Ireland 33

Jeffery, C. 56, 59
Jenkins-Smith, H.C. 62, 63
Jessop, B. 4
John, P. 42

Kafkalas, G. 4
Kardasis, V.A. 98
Kazakos, P. 93
Keating, M. 47
Kenis, P. 25
Klausen, K. 10, 59–60
Knoke, D. 21, 22, 62
knowledge 25
Konsolas, N. 85, 89, 131
Kontogiorgis, G. 66
Kos 106, 163
Kos City Council 112
Kos Development Agency 176
Kos Hotel Owners' Association
    111–12
Kos women's society 124
Kuklinski, J.H. 21, 62

landed gentry 91
law, obedience to 122
LEADER Initiative 198, 204, 209
leadership 53–4
learning 8–29, 29–30, 218–19,
    237
    institutional networks and 21–9

learning *(continued)*
  local learning capacity *see* local
    learning capacity
  methodology for study 58–63
  social capital, adaptation and
    224–34;
  evaluating Europeanization
    229–34
  social capital, institutional
    networks and in EU regional
    policy 48–56
Leonardi, R. 4, 6, 16, 45, 53, 89
  institutional infrastructure 7
  types of network 22
Leros-project 158
Lesbos 154–5, 215, 217, 221, 223,
    230
  CSF 194, 195–6, 198, 199
  economic structure 132–3, 134
  institution-building, policy
    networks and adaptation
    203–8
  institutions and institutional
    networks 139–44
  learning capacity 226, 227, 228
  local factors and political climate
    126–30
  power plant project 189
  social capital and civil society
    152, 153–4
Lesbos Farmers' Association
    (LFARMA) 140, 142
Lesbos Local Development Agency
    202, 204, 206–7
Local Associations of Municipalities
    and Communities (LAMC) 79
  see also Associations of
    Municipalities
local clientelism 65–9
local government 7
  Europeanization 41–4
  finance 76–9
  functions 73
  political elites 79–83
Local Government sub-programme
    167, 169, 170, 197–8
local institutional capacity 219–24
local learning capacity 56–8, 219–24
  measuring 62–3, 225–9

NAI 136–50
SAI 108–21
local networking 42
local response to globalization 1–5
logic of collective action 12
Logothetis, M. 106
Lundvall, B.A. 9
Lyberaki, A. 59, 90
Lyceum of Greek Women 124

Maastricht Treaty 38
Marin, B. 26, 27
Marks, G. 45, 47, 48
Marsh, D. 26, 27
Mastic Growers' Association 144–6,
    208–9, 211, 212, 228
Mayntz, R. 26
Mazey, S. 41
McKay, D. 40
Metcalfe, L. 24–5
minimal Europeanization 42
Ministry of National Economy 86,
    87, 88, 89
miscellaneous services 103, 133
Molle, W. 1
Monitoring Committee for CSF
    (MOP) implementation 71
  NAI 200, 227
  SAI 172, 182, 227
moral resources 20
Moravcsik, A. 49
Morgan, K. 47
Mouzelis, N.P. 67, 83, 90, 91, 93
Multi-fund regional Operational
    Programmes (MOPs)
  NAI 190–9
  SAI 159–71, 176, 182
Municipal Code 1980 68–9
municipal enterprises 69
Municipal Urban Centres 85
municipalities 65, 79–80
Mykonos 107
Mykonos City Council 118, 119,
    183
Myrdal, G. 2
Mytilene 127
Mytilene City Council 141
Mytilene Municipal Development
    Agency 202–7

Nanetti, R.Y.   33, 34, 35, 36, 37
National Centre for Planning and
    Economic Research (KEPE)   85
national government   73
National Programmes of Community
    Interest (NPCI)   35
  NPCI for Chios   194, 196–7, 209,
      223, 227, 228
national structure   *see* state structure
Naxos Development Agency   182
negotiation   26
network analysis   61–2
New Democracy   68, 82, 98, 129
new institutionalism   13–16, 236–7
  integration theory   48–56
  rational-choice new
      institutionalism   14–15, 50–1,
      237
nomarchal local authorities   76,
    78–9
norms   18
North, D.C.   12–13, 14
Northern Aegean Islands (NAI)
    60–1, 126–55, 188–217
  economic structure, boundedness
      and adaptation   130–6
  effectiveness gap in implementing
      CSF   160–2, 190–9
  institution-building, policy
      networks and adaptation
      199–215
  learning capacity   225–9
  local factors and political climate
      126–30
  local institutional networks and
      their learning capacity
      136–50
  planning and implementing the
      IMP   188–90
  social capital and civil society
      150–4
  social capital, networks and
      learning   230–4
  state structure and local
      institutional capacity   221–4

olive oil   128, 132–3
Olson, M.   12
Oppenheim, A.N.   62

Organization for Tourist Promotion
    112, 221, 225
Orthodox Church   90–1
Ostrom, E.   12, 18
Ottoman Greece   65–6

Panhellenic Socialist Movement
    (PASOK)   69, 82–3, 98, 129, 130
Papageorgiou, F.   70, 87, 89, 157
Paraskevopoulos, C.J.   20, 45, 85, 92,
    220, 237
  collective competitiveness   236
Parri, L.   26
participatory decision making   70
partnership principle   35, 37–8
Pelassy, D.   60
Peripheral Public Investment
    Programme   78
Perroux, F.   2
Phanariotes   91
planning, economic   85–6, 87–9
policy adaptation   225, 226, 229
policy networks   223
  NAI   199–215
  SAI   171–86
political climate
  NAI   126–30
  SAI   95–9
political elites, subnational   79–83
Pollack, M.A.   50–1
population
  NAI   126–7
  SAI   95–6
power   24–6
  distribution among actors *see*
      centrality
power supply sector   189
prefects   67, 68, 70
prefectural councils   69–70, 76
  Chios   146, 147, 210, 211, 212
  Cyclades   117, 119
  Dodecanese   114, 115, 178, 180
  functions   73
  Lesbos   141
Prefectural Local Authorities   70
prefectural networks   232, 233
prefectures   65, 67, 78
  share in sub-programmes   165–6,
      194, 195

prisoner's dilemma   11–12, 13
private sector
   contribution to CSFs   43–4, 162–3,
      194
   public–private partnerships   63,
      222–3, 225, 226, 228
production   3–4
Psychopedis, K.   74, 78, 86
public administration bureaucracy,
      quality of   79–83
public goods   12, 17
Public Investment Programme   78,
      86, 87–8, 112–13, 194
public–private partnerships   63,
      222–3, 225, 226, 228
Putnam, R.D.   12, 16, 17, 18

rational actors   11–13
rational-choice new institutionalism
      14–15, 50–1, 237
reciprocity   18
refugees   128
regional development
   paradigm shift   5–8
   theories   1–5
Regional Development Agencies
      (RDA)   84–5
Regional Development Plans (RDPs)
      87
regional GDP   103–4, 131, 132
regional government   7, 71
   Europeanization   41–4
   functions   73
   re-conceptualization   5–8
Regional Operational Programmes
      (ROPs)   89–90
regional policy   1–5
   European   *see* European regional
      policy
   in Greece   84–90
Regional Secretariat   71
   NAI   127–8, 138–9, 203, 231;
      Chios   146, 147, 210, 211,
      212; Lesbos   141, 142, 143,
      206; Samos   148, 149, 150,
      214, 215
   SAI   109, 174; Cyclades   117,
      119, 120; Dodecanese   115,
      178, 180

regionalism   5
regionalization   5
Rhodes, M.   8, 9
Rhodes, R.A.W.   26, 27
Rhodes   106, 163
Rhodes City Council   112, 114
Rhodes Hotel Owners' Association
      111–12
Richardson, J.   41, 49
Rome, Treaty of   33
rotating credit associations   17–18

Sabatier, P.A.   26, 62, 63
Sabel, C.F.   2, 3, 9–10, 17, 20, 52
Sala-i-Martin, X.   47
Samos   155, 217, 221, 230
   CSF   194, 197, 198, 199
   economic structure   133–4, 135
   institution-building, policy
      networks and adaptation
      212–15, 216
   institutions and institutional
      networks   147–50, 151
   learning capacity   226, 227
   local factors and political climate
      126–30
   social capital and civil society
      152–3, 154
Scharpf, F.W.   11
Schmitter, P.C.   47, 48, 92
Schneider, G.   51
Schneider, V.   25
Scott, A.   48
Scott, J.   113
sectoral networks   22–3, 232, 233
sectors, economic
   NAI   131–6
   SAI   99, 102–6
services   99, 102–6, 131, 133, 134–5
Shepsle, K.A.   14, 15
shipbuilding   91–2
'side payment' approach   45–7
Single European Act (SEA)   37
Single European Market (SEM)   37,
      45–6
Siphnaeou, E.   128, 152
social capital   8–29, 218, 220,
      234–7
   building civil society   16–21

institutional networks and learning
in EU regional policy   48–56
learning and adaptation   224–34
methodology for study   58–63
NAI   150–4, 230–4
SAI   121–4, 230–4
Social Network Analysis (SNA)   62
socialization function   51–6
sociological new institutionalism
15–16
Southern Aegean Islands (SAI)   60–1,
95–125, 156–87
economic structure, boundedness
and adaptation   99–108
groups of islands by level of
development   164–5
from IMP to MOPs   156–9
institution-building, policy
networks and adaptation
172–85
learning capacity   226, 227–9
local characteristics and political
climate   95–9
local institutional networks and
their learning capacity
108–21
planning and implementing CSF
159–71
social capital and civic culture
121–4
social capital, networks and
learning   230–4
state structure and local
institutional capacity   221–4
space   6
spread effects   2
stability, change and   26–9
STAR-TELEMATIQUE   209
state   2
hollowing out of   4
state-society synergies   19–20
structure   *see* state structure
state clientelist corporatism   69–76
state clientelist patronage   65–9
state structure
Greece   64–83
local institutional capacity and
Europeanization   219–24
and local learning capacity   56–8

Stokowski, P.A.   3, 21, 106, 170
Storper, M.   10, 18, 53
Streeck, W.   47, 48
strength/weakness of linkages   24
structural equivalence   62
NAI: Chios   146–7, 211–12; Lesbos
142–3, 206–7; Samos   150,
151, 214–15, 216
SAI: Cyclades   119–20, 184–5;
Dodecanese   114–15, 179, 180
Structural Funds   31–2, 33–7, 40, 42
1988 reform   32, 37–8
see also under individual funds
structure-induced equilibrium   14
studied trust   20
subnational governments
distribution of functions   72–5
Europeanization of   41–4
political elites   79–83
see also communes;
intergovernmental relations;
local government;
municipalities; prefectures;
regional government
subsidiarity   44
synergistic relationships   19–20
Syros   107, 117, 123
Systems of Agricultural or
Agro-Industrial Urban Centres
85

Tarrow, S.   81
Tatsos, N.   77
taxation   77, 84, 106
Taylor, R.C.R.   14, 16
territorial scope   22, 23
territory   6
thickness, institutional   23–4, 27–8
and the socialization function
51–6
see also density
third-party enforcement   12–13
Thrift, N.   4, 23, 26
tourism   21
NAI   133, 135, 194
SAI   103–7, 158, 163, 170
tourist agents' associations   112,
114, 118
tragedy of the commons   11

Training Centres
  Chios   146, 147, 209, 211, 212
  Cyclades   118, 119, 184, 185
  Lesbos   204–5
transport and communication
  134–5, 158, 170, 194
transregional networks   22, 23, 233
  Dodecanese   177, 178
Treaty on European Union (TEU)   38
trust   17–18, 122, 153
  studied trust   20
Tsebelis, G.   51
Tsoukalas, C.   92
Tsoukalis, L.   2, 32, 36, 40

unemployment   99, 100, 130
University of the Aegean   110
  NAI   138, 203; Chios   145–6, 147,
    209, 211; Lesbos   140–2, 206,
    207; Samos   148–9, 150, 214,
    215
  SAI   174; Cyclades   118, 184;
    Dodecanese   114, 115, 179

VALOREN Initiative   198, 204
Van de Ven, A.H.   57
Venizelos, E.K.   67
Verney, S.   70, 87, 89, 157
vertical networks   57–8, 231
vocational training   166, 191
voluntary organizations   62, 234
  NAI   150–4
  SAI   121–4
  see also social capital

Watts, R.   5
weakness/strength of linkages   24
welfare   101–2, 131
'westernizers'   90–1
Windhoff-Heritier, A.   60
Wine Producers' Association   148,
  213
women's organizations   124

Yin, R.K.   59, 60